Frontiers of the 21st Century:
Argumentation, Debate and the Struggle
for a Civil Society

Frontiers of the 21st Century:
Argumentation, Debate and the Struggle for a Civil Society

Proceedings of the 2004 and 2005 International Debate Education
Association Conference in Turkey and Estonia

Edited by Alfred C. Snider

International Debate Education Association
New York • Amsterdam • Brussels

Published by
International Debate Education Association
400 West 59th Street
New York, NY 10019

Library of Congress Cataloging-in-Publication Data

Frontiers of the 21st century: argumentation, debate and the struggle for a civil society
edited by Alfred Snider.
    p. cm.
 Papers from the 2004 and 2005 IDEA conferences.
 ISBN-13: 978-1-932716-31-3
 1. Debates and debating--Congresses. I. Snider, Alfred.
 PN4181.F73 2008
 808.53--dc22 2007043377

Printed in the United States

 IDEBATE® Press

CONTENTS

MESSAGES FROM THE FRONTIER: AN INTRODUCTION

The 20th century was certainly an eventful one. Two world wars, the beginning of the nuclear age, the breakup of vast colonial empires followed by the emergence of democratic nations as well as authoritarian regimes, the rise and collapse of fascism and communism, the spread of a global market, the powerful effects of "people power" near the end of the century ending authoritarian regimes in nations such as the Philippines and Chile, the establishment of two global governance institutions (one that failed), the rise of electronic media, the deterioration of the environment, the technological revolution in everyday life, and much more. I have been lucky enough to live through the last half of that eventful century. What a long, strange trip it has been.

We now stand on the frontier of the 21st century. It is a place we have barely entered; we are just inside its borders. No one knows what this century will bring, what events will shape it, or how it will be remembered. Nevertheless, we are obliged to make predictions and engage in conjecture about what our journey will be like. Despite the uncertainties and unknowns, the 21st century will be affected by our actions and efforts, both individually and collectively.

For these and other reasons I find this volume very interesting. It contains papers from some amazing individuals who are, in many ways, likely candidates to have an impact on how the 21st century will turn out. This may sound presumptuous, but I believe it to be true.

A look back at the 20th century can tell us a little about some of the problems we will face. The, problems that began to present themselves in the last half of the previous century will have to be addressed, and new crises will probably occur even more rapidly and unexpectedly. Democratic regimes may well be in the ascendancy, but the struggle to establish lasting democratic systems has only begun. Democracy, if it is seen merely as a form of government, may well fail. To succeed as a system, it requires the meaningful contributions and participation of an informed and reasoning citizenry. Elections centered on colorful posters and vacuous media advertisements and covered by a press that treats them like horse races will result in governments chosen by popular appeal, not by issues and policy proposals. Such contests are not likely to adequately address either the problems that we inherit from the 20th century or the new problems we will confront in the 21st century.

This volume documents some of the voices that can make a difference. As a group, they represent commitment to forging a 21st century citizenry, one that learns, thinks, and speaks with a concerned and critical voice. They are not concerned so much with changing politicians as with changing the citizens who select them through a bottom-up approach that can test the proposition that if the people lead, the leaders will follow.

Several points are evident in examining these articles and conference papers. First, they are similar in some very basic ways. All of them hold that logic and reason applied to issues and ideas through a process of debate can make a difference in how those who participate view their world and their role in it. The comfortable mask of apathy can be willingly shed through a process of argumentation and debate that can be as easily applied to the future of our forests and oceans as to where we go to dinner. These are people who view the human race as a thinking and reasoning species that can, with some guidance, apply these skills to the issues of the day.

Second, their authors have very different backgrounds and histories. They are not only from many different parts of the world, in a stunning display of global diversity, but they are also from many different walks of life. There are youth workers, teachers, professors, community activists, business people, NGO representatives, science policy experts, students, educational consultants, and others. They come from Canada, Germany, Hong Kong, Macedonia, Romania, Russia, Slovenia, and the United States. The debates and arguments they discuss can be found in public life, student essays, debate competitions, and many other areas. They have different presentational modes, some writing as scholars, others as personal diarists. They represent a broad section of current human society.

Third, they represent an emerging force for the 21st century. They are a new group that began to manifest themselves in the 1990s as a result of two forces. In many nations that have a tradition of argument and debate, the communities there began to look to other nations in the hope of broadening the discussions and the networks. As communism crumbled, they found new partners and stakeholders in an idea of global "multilogue." At about this time, the Open Society Institute, through a network of Soros Foundations in various post-Communist countries, began to advance the idea of promoting democracy and civil society through discussion and debate. A network of debate clubs, organizations, and teams began to take shape and then engaged with the established argument and debate communities, resulting in both learning and developing. The result was a new global community and the creation of the International Debate Education Association, which sponsored the two conferences that are documented here. This "emerging" continues and will probably extend into the 21st century in exciting ways that I cannot yet predict.

Given this emerging similarity and diversity, the contents of the volume offer a wide array of perspectives and practices that many different disciplines and interests may find useful.

The first section offers some different approaches to understanding the ancient field of argumentation in a modern context. J. Anthony Blair offers an application of argumentation ideas to the everyday needs of critical thinking. Vadim Golubev takes the basic tenets of argument and applies them to the rhetoric of Vladimir Putin in dealing with the issue of terrorism in Russia, disclosing some interesting gaps in logic and application of rhetorical principles. Steven Woods and Jianglong Wang offer a comparative analysis as well, discussing how cultural settings can influence the willingness and even the ability to engage in a debate, and noting that participants must first "agree to disagree" before a productive debate can take place. Benjamin Sovacool takes the traditional concept of "topoi" from classical rhetoric and observes how they operate today in contemporary American academic debate competitions, finding that they are indeed alive and well. Keith West examines some of the most controversial concepts in current debating practice, the ideas of fiat and micropolitical argument.

The second section of this volume deals with new and innovative ways to train young people in the arts and skills of debating. Sam Greenland discusses the system that has been introduced in Hong Kong to train debaters at age levels well below those previously thought appropriate. Kate Shuster then introduces and documents one of the most dynamic educational programs in the world today, the middle school debating program, in which thousands of students who were previously thought of as too young for debating have shown themselves to be active, able, and extremely skilled.

The third section of this volume relates the skills of argumentation and debating directly to the challenge of active citizenship. Korry Harvey and Steven Woods document their efforts to take competitive debate activities and mold them to serve community needs through the extremely successful "Let's Talk" program, which brings different advocates, citizens, and debaters together to address current issues of concern to the local community they operate within. Candace Williams documents the existence of a civic skepticism that doubts that individuals can have a productive role in social organization and change, and how efforts can be undertaken to convert this skepticism into civic virtue. Joseph Zompetti discusses the central role that public debate can and does have for creating civil societies on a broader level. Michael Hoppmann shares an innovative and new debate form developed in Germany that he believes better represents the debating that students are likely to encounter as active citizens. Boyan Maricic discusses the important role that public debate projects have played in Macedonia as a part of its youth empowerment project. Finally, Danielle Stevens documents an extremely interesting program to bring about civic virtue through debate to a population that we would not usually associate with such activities—the inmates of a prison—with some surprising results and experiences.

The following section of this volume contains a number of extremely useful presentations about using debate as an active method to teach traditional subjects as well as assist students in mapping out their own educational journeys. Mackay Miller talks about his experience in using debate to provide youth with a method to guide their own education instead of relying on professional authorities to do that for them. Liana Miholič and Martina Domajnko discuss their years of groundbreaking work in using debating techniques in the classroom to improve the teaching of fairly traditional subjects. Frank Duffin documents an experience in Rhode Island that used debate widely in various classrooms to teach a variety of subjects with some generally impressive results.

Next is a section that features what one would expect from a group of people promoting argumentation and debate, an analysis of the questions surrounding some possible dangers involved in debate training. Aaron Fishbone addresses the issue of whether debate training merely promotes more effective demagoguery, and he has some productive suggestions for resolving this potential problem. Liza-Marie Curteneau also addresses this issue and frames it as a debate between pro and con presentations on the dangers of debate training. She then offers guidelines for dealing with this constant challenge.

The final section of this volume involves some important issues that must be addressed, since they involve the often extraordinary commitment teachers make to debating activities. Jack Rogers and Arthur Rennels deal with the very real challenge that debate professionals confront in balancing their demanding commitment to this field with their commitment and obligations to their partners and families. They investigate the issues of professional forensics retention and the attrition of motivation among debate professionals as revealed by their research.

I would be remiss if I did not thank Noel Selegzi of the International Debate Education Association for the many opportunities he has given me to work with such an exciting group of people as are represented here. I also want to thank Martin Greenwald for his support and assistance in this effort and Eleanora von Dehsen for her excellent assistance in this project.

The two years that are represented by these conferences in Turkey and Estonia were exciting and revealing for me, as I know they were for the participants and attendees. My experiences tell me that this is only the beginning, and that while we stand on the frontier of the 21st century, I am optimistic about what lies ahead as we continue to struggle for a world of far more civil societies.

Alfred Snider

November 2007

Chapter 1
Argumentation

Argument Evaluation and Fallacies for Critical Thinking

J. Anthony Blair

PREFACE

Let me say what an honor and pleasure it is to be at the IDEA Conference in Tallinn. Tallinn is an interesting and attractive city. And I value the opportunity to talk with, and learn from, you who are working in debate education, with the goals of teaching skills in reasoning and argumentation and an understanding for their role in civil society. This, too, has been the objective of my teaching for 35 years.

INTRODUCTION

When Charles Hamblin was about to publish his 1970 book on fallacies, one of his friends said he hoped that the title Hamblin planned to use—*Fallacies*—was not an accurate description of the contents of the book. Part of my title today is "Fallacies for Critical Thinking." I hope it is not an accurate description of the contents of my talk. I don't want to propose some fallacies for us to commit when we are thinking critically. I want to talk, instead, about a method of argument evaluation that involves identifying fallacies, and to suggest that this is a tool that can be used in thinking critically—and that can be used in teaching our students to think more critically.

All of you are involved in teaching, coaching, judging or participating in debating and debates. Debate is a type of argumentation, if we take argumentation in general to be a kind of attempt to resolve or otherwise manage a disagreement by trying to convince another party using reasons or arguments.

Argumentation is typically a kind of verbal communication. (It is "typically" but not "necessarily" verbal, since there can be visual arguments, and perhaps arguments can be communicated in yet other ways.) It is a use of symbols to try to accomplish certain communicative goals or objectives. In the process, people present arguments to others in order to try to persuade them to modify their views—that is, their beliefs, attitudes or evaluations, or to change their intentions about what to do—or else we use arguments in order to try to persuade observers or members of a wider audience to modify the content of, or degree of commitment to, their opinions or other attitudes or intentions (as is the case with arguments ostensibly between political opponents aimed at influencing the voting public).

Each type of argumentation can be identified and described by the rules that govern its operations. These rules specify things like who may speak, for how long, and so on (in general, what their rights and obligations are in the activity, what count as legal moves or turns, what kinds of move are prohibited, and so on). These rules are designed with a view to achieving the objectives of the particular activity of argumentation in the best way. Each system of debate is thus specified by its rules. Among the rules of deba tes of all kinds are rules requiring that arguments be presented at various points; and usually even the specific goal of such arguments at each point in the debate is specified.

Now this argumentation—the arguments, the uses they are put to, and the ways they are managed—can be evaluated from at least the following three points of view. The argumentation can be assessed for its legality (for how well the moves follow the procedures specified for the activity), the arguments can be assessed for their effectiveness (for how well they succeed in achieving their goals of influencing their target audience), and the arguments can also be assessed for their cogency (for how solidly they actually prove their point). In other words, the arguments used in debates can be assessed for their procedural propriety, for success as communications, and for their substantive merits. To put this point in yet another way, the arguments of the debate can be assessed from a pragmatic point of view, from a rhetorical point of view, and from a logical point of view. A well-argued debate will satisfy all three kinds of norms: pragmatic, rhetorical, and logical.

Now, in terms of these distinctions I can be clearer about what I want to talk about today. I want to talk about just the *logical* evaluation of the arguments used in debates (and other kinds of argumentation), and in particular I want to present to you one approach to the logical evaluation of arguments.

The ARS Approach

In a textbook that my colleague at the University of Windsor, Ralph Johnson, and I wrote, called *Logical Self-Defense* (reissued by IDEBATE Press in 2006), we proposed a different set of criteria for a logically good argument from those typically found in the logic texts of the day. One of those typical criteria was "soundness"—the property that the premises be true and the argument be deductively "valid" in the technical sense that the premises deductively imply the conclusion (i.e., if the premises were true, the conclusion could not possibly be false). A more sophisticated criterion was that the argument must either be sound in this sense or else that it have true premises and be inductively strong.

We proposed that an argument is logically good if and only if it meets the criteria we called *acceptability, relevance,* and *sufficiency.* That is, first, its premises must be acceptable to (and worthy of acceptance by) the audience. Second, in combination, they must bear on or be relevant to the conclusion. And, third, taken together they must provide sufficient support for the conclusion. We labeled these the ARS criteria, for short.

One benefit of this formulation is that arguments that meet the old textbook criteria of soundness or of inductive strength are also recognized by the ARS criteria as logically cogent. That is, deductively valid arguments with true premises, and also deductively invalid but inductively strong arguments with true premises, both count on ARS grounds as logically good arguments. An added benefit is that arguments that are invalid and not inductively strong in any standard way, but that are nonetheless cogent also count as logically good arguments. Beyond that, the ARS conditions work well for the practical tasks of interpreting and assessing arguments as they occur in everyday discourse, and they seem to students to be quite intuitive and so are easy to for them to learn.

Besides introducing the ARS approach, we also wanted our textbook to teach students how to identify the informal fallacies. It was and still is our view that by learning how to identify informal fallacies in actual arguments and how to make a case for an accusation of fallacy, students pick up all sorts of useful skills in dealing with arguments. They have to learn how to interpret texts, how to relate them to their contexts and purposes, how to identify and describe the arguments in the texts, how to read them critically—that is, evaluate them—and how to formulate cogent arguments to support their critical judgments.

In order to give the informal fallacies a bit of theoretical coherence, we proposed that a fallacy be defined as a violation of any one of the three ARS criteria: acceptability, relevance, or sufficiency. A logically good argument, then, is one that is free of fallacies. We found it possible to classify the standard fallacies as failures of acceptability, failures of relevance, or failures of sufficiency.

What might be idiosyncratic about our concept of fallacy is that according to it an argument can contain a fallacy but not be destroyed by it. A fallacy in our sense is not necessarily fatal to the argument containing it. If an argument fails to provide good enough grounds to establish its conclusion, it contains a fallacy, but perhaps more evidence or additional or different kinds of reasons can be found. In that case, the argument should not be dismissed or abandoned, but repaired. For instance, if a premise as it stands is irrelevant, there is a fallacy. (E.g., "The accused is left-handed, so he is guilty.") But perhaps there is an unexpressed assumption which, when made explicit and added to the challenged premise, makes the pair relevant and gives support to the conclusion. (E.g., "The accused is left-handed, and the experts assure us that the murderer must have been left-handed, so the accused is guilty.") In the latter case, the argument has merit; its reasoning just needed to be made more explicit. As well, fallaciousness in our sense comes in degrees: some instances of a fallacy can do more damage than others.

The implications that a fallacy does not necessarily destroy its argument and that fallacies come in degrees might seem counter-intuitive, but they have the following virtue. They require the student who has identified a fallacy in an argument to go further and think how badly the argument has been harmed and whether it can be repaired (and if so, how). Thus, fallacy analysis is not a device for dismissing arguments. Instead, it is a way to lead the student more deeply into the appreciation of arguments.

Teaching fallacies in this way as an evaluative tool has another virtue. It provides bite-sized chunks of material that students can quite easily assimilate. The students do not have to spend several weeks or months mastering a complicated theory of argument before starting to engage in argument interpretation and assessment. And as they learn and work with each new fallacy, their general interpretation and assessment skills keep improving.

Of course, it is one thing to understand a fallacy theoretically, and quite another to be able to recognize and analyze one in the give-and-take of argumentation. When teaching this material, a presentation of the general account of each fallacy has to be quickly followed by exposure to lots of actual examples. And the students have to be required to prepare detailed critiques, in which they not only argue for their allegations of fallacy, but in which they also argue whether the argument can be saved or improved, and if so, specifically how.

A Handful of Informal Fallacies

To give you the flavor of our approach, let me introduce you to a small handful of informal fallacies as we define them, along with a brief example of each. Later, I will show how these fallacies can be applied in evaluating arguments.

Irrelevant Reason

1. The arguer has put forth a premise as a reason for the conclusion.

2. The premise, considered in conjunction with other premises, fails to satisfy the relevance requirement.

A Member of Parliament in Canada once charged in the Canadian House of Commons that the federal Department of Health and Welfare had been cooperating with the Kellogg Company (the manufacturer of breakfast cereals) in permitting the sale of a breakfast cereal (Kellogg's Corn Flakes) which contained "little or no nutritional value." The Minister of Health at the time, Marc Lalonde, seeking to rebut that charge, stated:

As for the nutritional value of Corn Flakes, the milk you have with your corn flakes has great nutritional value.

The nutritional value of an accompanying food doesn't have any bearing on whether the food it accompanies has any nutritional value. Mr. Lalonde's reply was irrelevant as a reason for the claim that corn flakes have nutritional value.

Hasty Conclusion

1. The arguer presents a premise-set as a sufficient basis for a conclusion.

2. The assertions constituting the premise-set taken together are not sufficient to support the conclusion because:

[a] They do not provide evidence which has been systematically gathered by an appropriate method; and/or

[b] They do not supply a sufficient sample of the various kinds of relevant evidence; and/or

[c] They ignore the presence of, or the possibility of, contrary evidence.

After visiting the Calgary (Alberta) zoo, a disgruntled tourist wrote this letter to *The Calgary Herald* newspaper:

> We arrived at the park gate at 19:25 hrs. at which time the cashier gleefully took money for admission. Upon our entering the zoo and walking across the bridge, the loud-speaker stated that the zoo buildings were closing at 20.00 hrs. and that the zoo itself would close at 20.30. We went to the ticket center and asked if we could get a pass for the following day. The answer was no. It is easy to see that Calgary is anything but a friendly city, but rather out to rake off the tourist for all they can.

The unfair attitude of the Calgary zoo (assuming the report is accurate) is relevant to the attitude toward tourists to be found in Calgary, but the zoo is just one of Calgary's tourist attractions, and there are many others. We need to have a much more representative sample of raking off tourists before the generalization to Calgary as a whole is supported. (In fact, more than one instance of such behavior is needed to conclude even that the Calgary zoo has a policy of raking off tourists.)

Questionable Cause

1.   A causal claim occurs in someone's argument, either as a conclusion or as a premise.

2.1   The person argues to the causal claim as the conclusion, but fails to provide adequate support for it; OR

2.2   The person argues from the causal claim, as one of the premises, without supporting it, and there are grounds for questioning the acceptability of the causal claim.

Here is an example from a *Time* magazine story some years back. The city of El Paso, Texas, was then about one-third the size of Dallas, Texas, but the number of El Paso residents found in state mental hospitals was one-seventh the number of Dallas residents in such institutions. Other things being equal, one would expect roughly similar proportions, so how might the difference have been explained? A University of Texas biochemist offered this explanation:

> El Paso's water is heavily laced with lithium, a tranquilliz-ing chemical widely used in the treatment of manic depres-sion and other psychiatric disorders. Dallas has low lithium levels because it draws its water from surface supplies.

That is an intriguing hypothesis: El Paso citizens were ingesting amounts of tranquillizing lithium with their drinking water, which helped to prevent or remedy the symptoms of mental disorders for which they might otherwise have sought treatment in a state mental hospital. But more investigation was needed. Were there other cities with high lithium levels in their water supply? If so, how did their mental hospital admission rates compare to those of El Paso? Also, how did admissions from Dallas compare with those of other cities with similar lithium levels? Furthermore, could there be alternative explanations? Did life in Dallas tend to put great pressures on its citizens? Did the considerably smaller El Paso have a more serene pace? Without investigating further the correlation between lithium intake and mental hospitalization and without checking alter-native explanations, the biochemist would be guilty of *questionable cause*.

As it happened, *Time* had come across a competing hypothesis:

> State mental health officials pointed out that the men-tal hospital closest to Dallas is 35 miles away from the city, while the one nearest El Paso is 350 miles away.

So quite possibly the higher incidence of mental hospital admissions in Dallas than in El Paso was simply a function of the much more convenient location of the mental hospital to Dallas than to El Paso. More research was clearly needed.

Causal Slippery Slope

1. Someone claims that if an action or policy is permitted, that will set in motion a chain of events that will eventually, through a series of (more or less fully elaborated) causal steps, lead to a particular outcome.

2. The person claims or argues that this outcome is undesirable and that therefore the initial action or policy that will set in motion the chain of events leading to it should not be permitted.

3. At least one of the alleged links in the causal chain—whether defended, just claimed, or assumed—is questionable or false.

When it was proposed to make the use of seatbelts in automobiles compulsory in Canada, there was a certain amount of opposition to it. The following letter was published in a newspaper:

> If they can make us swallow this infringement of personal rights, what's next? A seat belt law for the bedroom, so we won't fall out of bed and hurt our little selves? Boy, when Big Brother watches us, he really watches us, doesn't he?

The argument here seems to be that the seat belt requirement is the first step down an incline leading to a veritable Orwellian 1984 ("Big Brother watching us"). But how precisely was this horror to come about? The intervening steps were not mentioned, except for the sarcastic reference to seat belts in the bedroom. We are given the first and the last chapters, but nothing in between. Most would agree that if the legislation were the first of a series of steps leading inevitably to the abolition of all individual rights, then it should be rejected. From our vantage point many years later we can see that the writer's prediction has not been borne out, but even at the time the projected outcome was dubious. Yet the author offered no reason to expect it.

Vagueness

1. An argument contains a premise, or a conclusion, whose meaning is indeterminate.

2. The indeterminateness of this statement makes it impossible to assess its acceptability as a premise or its significance as a conclusion.

Coca-Cola used to have a couple of advertising slogans: "Coke is it!" and "It's the real thing." It would not be unfair to regard these as reasons offered for drinking Coke. But what do they mean? It's impossible to tell, they are just too vague.

Guilt by Association

1. The critic attacks the arguer on the basis of some alleged association between the arguer and some other person, group, or belief(s);

2.

(a) The alleged association does not exist at all; OR

(b) The alleged association does not provide relevant or sufficient support for the critic's attack.

Several years ago, when the president of the Canadian Medical Association, Dr. Bette Stephenson, pressed for liberalized abortion laws, her stance provoked this letter in response:

> Perhaps it is not the law which ought to be called into question but the arrogant attitude of the president of the medical society. Laws should be designed to afford reasonable protection for all human life. Statutes made and enforced by sensible, civilized societies should not provide for the thoughtless, wholesale slaughter of those considered to be less than human by some. Remember Dachau and Auschwitz.

Here the writer was trying to attach the horrors of the Nazi death camps to the policy of making access to abortions legal, and thereby invite condemnation of the latter policy. But the murder of men, women, and children because of their religion (Jews) or ethnic group (Roma) is undebatably immoral, whereas the morality of abortion is highly contentious.

Ad Hominem

1. The critic responds to the position of an arguer by launching a personal attack on the arguer, ignoring the arguer's position.

2. The personal attack on the arguer can be shown to be irrelevant to the assessment of the argument.

In the fall of 1989, when Allan Bloom published his book, *The Closing of the American Mind*, Bloom attacked rock music as an overtly sexual form of music that contributes to an overall climate of promiscuity. He mentioned Mick Jagger's "pouty lips and wagging butt" as an example of how rock promotes sexuality. In a review in *Rolling Stone* magazine, William Greider wrote:

> Bloom's attack on rock is inane. Still the professor is correct about one important distinction between the kids of the 50s and those of the 80s: in the 50s the kids talked

endlessly about sex; today the young people actually do it. This seems to drive the 56 year old Bloom—who is still a bachelor—crazy. Bloom denounces Jagger with such relish that one may wonder if the professor himself is turned on by Mick's pouty lips and wagging butt.

In this passage Greider attacks a motive he attributes to Bloom for criticizing rock and roll (fear of repressed homoerotic feelings), instead of Bloom's position that rock music is overtly sexual and contributes to promiscuity. But Bloom's point could be true even if he were turned on by Mick Jagger.

CONTEMPORARY EXAMPLES

What I would like to do in the rest of my talk is illustrate, using some contemporary examples, how we can use this fallacy approach to critiquing arguments and reasoning.

I'm going to draw most of my examples from a couple of articles that appeared recently in the American magazine called *Vanity Fair*. The first three examples are from an article titled "High Noon in Crawford" (November 2005, pp. 222–236). Its contents are explained by the first two sentences:

> President Bush's Crawford, Texas, ranch was intended as a perfect backdrop for his cowboy image. But a grieving mother, a deadly hurricane, and disenchanted neighbors have brought a dose of reality to his vacation retreat. (*Vanity Fair*, 11/2005, p. 222)

Example 1

The article goes on to describe the ranch and the attitudes of those who live nearby. One of these is a man called Bill Johnson who owns a gift shop in Crawford that sells, among other things, Bush souvenirs. In Johnson's shop there is a sign that reads, (1) "HITLER, STALIN, CASTRO AND QADAFFI SUPPORTED GUN CONTROL" (ibid., p. 224).

Why would such astonishing information be posted in a Texas gift-shop? To understand it, you have to know about the controversy in the United States over whether there should be any general restrictions on the private ownership of guns. Such restrictions are known as "gun control." The debate is so heated that it is not at all surprising to find signs related to it in shops or restaurants, especially in rural areas of the country, where farmers and ranchers believe their right to own the guns they use to shoot predators of livestock, and other pests, is under threat. You also have to know that, in the United States, Hitler, Stalin, Castro, and Qadaffi are widely regarded as paradigms of evil dictators—and all four are considered by many to be more or less on a par. The sign, in short, is an argument against gun control. Here is one way it might be reconstructed:

(1a)

Claim (conclusion, standpoint): There should be no gun control.

Reasons:

1. Hitler, Stalin, Castro, and Qadaffi supported gun control.

2. Hitler, Stalin, Castro, and Qadaffi are paradigms of evil dictators.

3. A policy supported by such evil dictators will be bad.

Can we assume that the sign is factually correct—that Hitler, Stalin, Castro, and Qadaffi supported gun control? I don't think we should accept this premise. To start with, the term "gun control" is too *vague*. In the United States, it can stand for anything ranging from a ban on private ownership of military assault weapons and ammunition to a ban on the private ownership of any kind of gun. What precisely are Hitler, Stalin, Castro, and Qadaffi all supposed to have supported? We call this the fallacy of *vagueness*, because it is unclear what premise we are being asked to accept. So this premise needs to be clarified and evidence for it supplied, before anyone should accept it.

But even assuming that the key premise can be shown to be true or probable, whoever might endorse this reasoning commits *guilt by association*. Gun control is opposed on the grounds that it can be associated with such evil dictators as Hitler, Stalin, Castro, and Qadaffi. But it would be easy to come up with examples of policies that these men also supported yet that no one would object to (for example, public education, medical care, pension programs, construction and maintenance of roads and highways). So the mere fact that they supported or support gun control seems just *irrelevant* as a reason to oppose it. If that's a relevant reason, then we should oppose public health and education policies too, which is absurd.

Can the argument be fixed? On this first interpretation, it doesn't look like it. However, perhaps the argument can be interpreted more charitably. Maybe

Mr. Johnson meant to be suggesting a connection between unrestricted gun ownership and liberty. Perhaps he meant the following argument:

(1b)

Claim (conclusion, standpoint): There should be no gun control.

Reason:

1. Gun control is a threat to political liberty.

    Supporting reasons:

    1.1 Hitler, Stalin, Castro, and Qadaffi supported gun control.

    1.2 By restricting the private ownership of guns, they prevented the people from rising up in arms to overthrow them and preserve liberty.

On this reconstruction it is a better argument, because the reasons are no longer just irrelevant. But further questions arise. There seems to be a *questionable causal* claim in this argument. It seems unlikely that any uprising by arms-bearing citizens would have overthrown or would overthrow the police and the armies of Hitler, Stalin, Castro, or Qadaffi.

Yet another possible interpretation is that Mr. Johnson thinks that gun control is just one more restriction of individual liberty that is part of a trend that will lead to less and less liberty until the United States becomes a police state like those led by Hitler, Stalin, Castro, and Qadaffi.

(1c)

Reason:

1. Gun control will lead to more and more erosion of liberty until the United States becomes a police state.

    Supporting reasons:

    1.1 Hitler, Stalin, Castro, and Qadaffi supported gun control and their regimes were and are police states.

But this argument is an example of *slippery slope* reasoning that flirts with fallaciousness. We need to see (1) that there is a gradual erosion of liberty occurring in the United States, and we need to see (2) how it is that some measure of gun control would increase that erosion of liberty. These seem hard to do. For instance, there are much greater restrictions on firearms ownership in other countries (Canada, for one) and yet these countries do not seem to be experiencing the erosion of their liberties.

I hope that you can see how identifying a fallacy in this example as originally analyzed, then seeking other analyses that treat the argument more charitably and still finding fallacies in it, results in a pretty thorough examination of the text and its possible meanings and a clearer sense of what the issues might be or are in thinking through to one's own considered opinion about gun control.

Example 2

Let me turn to another example from the same article. A Crawford, Texas, woman called Shirley Westerfield paid for an inaugural ball for President Bush. (Inaugural balls are gala events with drinks and dancing that are organized in Washington on the night of a newly elected President's inauguration, paid for by supporters of that President and his political party.) At an event at Baylor University, near Crawford, to mark the beginning of the Bush's vacation at his Texas ranch this past August, Mrs. Westerfield is quoted as having said of President Bush, "He's one of us. I just like him. He reminds me of my father. You know—blue jeans, 'Let's get in the truck.'" (ibid., p. 226).

I take Westerfield to be claiming that Bush is a regular, ordinary rural Texan, and that is so because he wears blue jeans, and likes to drive a pick-up truck. But that is fallacious reasoning because the evidence is insufficient. She commits *hasty conclusion*. Not only is the evidence slim: lots of wealthy and powerful Americans who are not regular country people wear jeans and drive pick-up trucks at their country homes. Westerfield also overlooks all the evidence against her claim—that Bush was born into a wealthy and influential family, attended an elite east-coast university, and before he bought his ranch, lived in the city, worked in an office, or vacationed at his parents' country estate in Maine.

Can Westerfield's argument be improved? If she were to modify the conclusion she draws, it could be. Had she said, "Bush acts like one of us when he's at his Crawford ranch," she would have been on much safer ground, though to be sure she could then not have as strong a claim to draw further conclusions from.

Example 3

Although there are more bad arguments supporting Bush reported in this paper, there were also some bad arguments opposed to Bush. The author describes another Crawford, Texas, resident called Larry Mattlage as, "the real Crawford cowboy—with land, goats, sheep, a white beard, legs that stretch a mile" (ibid., p. 230), and reports that "he believes that Bush has done nothing for his beloved town except exploit it" (ibid.). From a number of things he says it is clear that Mattlage resents the fact that President Bush is now his neighbor. His attitude is reinforced when he is going for a drive and is stopped by the Secret Service from traveling along a familiar road because the President is using it to go for a bicycle ride. (The Secret Service are the special police who guard the U.S. President and other dignitaries.) Complaining of this inconvenience, Mr. Mattlage says, "Bush has got a whole ranch to ride a bicycle on. He closes the road so he can ride a *bicycle*. See, this is like the military. They took a quiet community and turned it into a base" (ibid., p. 233).

It seems to me that Mattlage is reasoning that Bush is objectionable because his presence places restrictions on the citizens of Crawford and the immediate area around Bush's ranch. This reasoning has an *ad hominem* flavor to it. It strikes me that the impositions on the local population caused by a President's private retreat are not a reason to resent that particular President. If an American President is entitled to have and enjoy a private retreat, then wherever it is located, as long as there is any threat of assassination there will be inconvenience to the local citizenry caused by the need for security precautions. Since the source of the problem is not Bush himself or his policies as President, but the fact that he happened to buy a ranch outside Crawford, the problem is or should be *irrelevant* to one's attitude toward Bush himself. It's just bad luck for the local residents that he chose Crawford.

Example 4

My final example comes from a different article in another issue of *Vanity Fair*, titled "Watergate's Last Chapter" by Carl Bernstein (October 2005, pp. 290–297, 336–343). Bernstein and Bob Woodward were the reporters working for the *Washington Post* newspaper whose stories contributed to the exposure of President Nixon's dirty tricks and of the cover-up that led to his resignation. The article in *Vanity Fair* describes the steps that led to the decision by Woodward and Bernstein to acknowledge that former FBI deputy director Mark

Felt was the man called "Deep Throat" during and after the Watergate scandal that brought down Nixon. Bernstein's *Vanity Fair* article is also an essay about the current state of political journalism in America. I think it is a wonderful article, and recommend it to anyone.

However, it is not free of fallacies. At one point Bernstein, talking about the current Bush presidency, says:

> The Bush White House operates a media apparatus far more sophisticated in fighting and discrediting the press and political opponents than the little shop directed by Haldeman and Ehrlichman and Colson and Ziegler [presidential assistants in the Nixon White House]. (*Vanity Fair*, October 2005, p. 340)

Bernstein goes on to write in support of this claim that "[t]he reach of the White House's hirelings now extends even into the press itself" (ibid.). He cites as evidence the use of someone called Armstrong Williams, "a black conservative commentator" to promote one of the Bush administrations education policies. Bernstein says that Williams "was paid $241,000 by the Department of Education through a P[ublic] R[elations] firm" (ibid.).

Now, I want to say, "Wait a minute. What is Bernstein suggesting here?" Bernstein is giving the impression that something improper occurred. But what happened was that a department of the U.S. federal government, the Department of Education, hired a public relations company to promote its policies. That is standard practice in any government in contemporary Western liberal democracies. This public relations firm then hired Armstrong Williams, a commentator—that is, someone who makes his living by writing opinion columns in newspapers and magazines—to write columns favorable to the department's policies. But Williams was already a conservative and so presumably he was already disposed to approve of and promote these policies. So it seems doubtful that he wrote things he did not believe in just because he was getting paid to do it. What is objectionable here, then? It cannot be that Williams expressed, as if they were his own, views he did not share, since presumably he favored the policies that he wrote in support of. Was it illegal for Williams to accept payment for columns that he might well have written anyway, and that honestly represented his own opinions? I doubt that very much, and Bernstein certainly did not say so. If it wasn't illegal, just what kind of impropriety is Bernstein alleging?

What I am uncomfortable with is the *innuendo* in the passage. Bernstein describes the conduct in negative terms, but he never states what it is that he objects to. He conveys the impression that some impropriety or other wrong-doing occurred, because he is being critical of the reach of the "Bush White House media apparatus." But he leaves the reader to draw that inference. He never spells it out himself.

Did the White House media apparatus interfere in the operations of the Department of Education? Did it improperly pressure the Secretary of Education to hire that particular public relations firm? Did it then improperly pressure that public relations company to hire Armstrong Williams? Did it put the texts of the columns that Mr. Williams published under his name into his hands and pressure him to do so? If Mr. Bernstein can support these allegations, he should produce that support, and if not, he should withdraw his claim that the White House was responsible for the promotions of Bush's education policy that Williams wrote.

In Bernstein's defense, if the events occurred as he describes them, it can be argued that there was indeed some impropriety. But that impropriety consisted, if it is true, of Williams' failure to reveal that he had been hired to write in favor of the government's policies (assuming that he did fail to do so). He could have said that he took the job because he already believed in the policies, but he ought to have disclosed that he was being paid, ultimately, by the Department of Education. That way, his readers could decide for themselves whether the funding of his columns *poisoned the well* against any merit his views might have. However, by itself, this impropriety is not evidence of Bush's media apparatus reaching its tentacles out like an octopus (which is my metaphor, not Bernstein's, I need to add before you accuse me of a *straw man* fallacy).

Conclusion

If the fact that I have discussed two texts with bad reasoning by supporters of Bush, and two texts with bad reasoning by critics of Bush, leads you to draw any inferences, be cautious. I do not mean to suggest that there is equally bad reasoning and equally weak arguments on both sides. I am not trying to be politically correct and balanced. (Like everyone else, I think that those who hold views I disagree with reason and argue much more poorly than those who hold views with which I agree.) I just thought these were illuminating examples for my purposes.

In my experience, fallacies tend to be committed much more frequently when people are reasoning and arguing under pressure. One type of pressure is created when a point of view to which a person has a strong commitment comes under criticism. One kind of commitment to a viewpoint is created by the conventions of debate, where it is the assigned task to argue in support of a controversial standpoint, defend it and one's arguments from attack, and attack the alternative standpoint. If students can learn to identify fallacies in their opponent's thinking, and avoid them in their own thinking, then they have a tool that is useful in debating. Of course, if people in general can learn to reason and argue less fallaciously and to recognize and expose fallacious reasoning by others, we might hope for better judgments, better decisions and better policies in all areas of private and public life.

J. Anthony Blair was one of the founders of the informal logic movement in philosophy and the journal *Informal Logic*. He has been an active scholar in the fields of argumentation, informal logic, fallacy, theory, and critical thinking over the past 30 years.

The Issue of Terrorism in Public Debate in Russia[*]

Vadim Golubev

This paper is a study of the use of the issue of terrorism in public debate in Russia. President Vladimir Putin's address to the nation in the wake of the Beslan terrorist attack, on 4 September 2004, will be examined.

The study doesn't pretend to be an exhaustive treatment of the topic; rather its purpose is to present a logico-pragma-stylistic analysis of the speech whose objective will be to identify communicative strategies of persuasion employed by the speaker and to investigate how the Russian leader used the problem of terrorism to further his political goals. Terrorism debate is analyzed within a wider context of the democracy and governance debate between the President and a liberal opposition.

In seeking persuasion of his or her audience, a skilled arguer assesses the audience and the issues at hand. When composing the message, the speaker takes into account several factors: the medium of communication (electronic mass media, print media); the topic of discussion; the audience (gender, level of education, expertise in the topic under discussion, rationality/emotionality, degree of involvement in the problem, level of life threat presented by the problem, etc.); the nature of the discussion (i.e., whether it is a direct dialogue with an opponent in a studio or an indirect dialogue through electronic or print media); applicable conventions (e.g., parliamentary procedures); and, finally, a broader, cultural, and political context in which communication is taking place, including such elements as openness/restrictiveness of the political regime, moral dilemmas and cultural taboos existing in the society, and traditions of conducting discussions inherent in the culture.

The process of assessment and adaptation of the issues to the audience results in developing a communicative strategy of persuasion. The key ele-

*Research for this paper was supported by a University of Edinburgh research grant.

ment of a communicative strategy is to choose targets to appeal to and prioritize them. While there are a wide variety of targets of appeal, it is possible to identify three major ones: people's minds, emotions, and aesthetic feelings. An appeal to people's reason, or rational appeal, is based on the strength of arguments. Emotional appeal is based on arousing in the reader or listener various emotions, ranging from a feeling of insecurity to fear, from a sense of injustice to pity, mercy, and compassion. Aesthetic appeal is based on people's appreciation of the linguistic and stylistic beauty of the message, its stylistic originality, rich language, sharp humor and wit.

Rational appeal is effective in changing beliefs and motives of the audience because it directly affects human reason, where beliefs and motives are formed. Emotional appeal is persuasively effective because it exploits concerns, worries, and desires of the people; the arguer "speaks to people's hearts." Aesthetic appeal is persuasively effective because, if successful, it changes people's attitudes toward the message and through the message toward its author. By changing people's attitudes from disapproval or reserved observation to appreciation or even admiration of the language and style of the message, the author increases the recipient's susceptibility to persuasion. People will be more willing to accept the arguer's reasoning after they have experienced the communicator's giftedness as the author of the message (Goloubev 1999: 239). The three components of the logico-pragma-stylistic analysis roughly correspond to these three major appeals of argumentative discourse: rational, emotional, and aesthetic.

Let us now turn to the speech. The breakdown into paragraphs follows the version published on the official site of the President of the Russian Federation. The only amendments relate to the translation of some sentences to make the English follow more closely the original Russian, syntactically and semantically. The speech is divided into explicit parts; paragraphs are numbered to facilitate analysis.

4 September 2004

Moscow, Kremlin

Address by President Vladimir Putin

Part 1

1 Speaking is hard. And painful.

2 A terrible tragedy has taken place in our world. Over these last few days each and every one of us has suffered greatly and taken deeply to heart all that was happening in the Russian town of Beslan. There, we found ourselves confronting not just murderers, but people who turned their weapons against defenseless children.

3 I would like now, first of all, to address words of support and condolence to those people who have lost what we treasure most in this life—our children, our loved and dear ones.

4 I ask that we all remember those who lost their lives at the hands of terrorists over these last days.

Part 2

5 Russia has lived through many tragic events and terrible ordeals over the course of its history. Today, we live in a time that follows the collapse of a vast and great state. A state that, unfortunately, proved unable to survive in a rapidly changing world. But despite all the difficulties, we were able to preserve the core of that giant—the Soviet Union. And we named this new country the Russian Federation.

6 We all hoped for change. Change for the better. But many of the changes that took place in our lives found us unprepared. Why?

7 We are living at a time of an economy in transition, of a political system that does not yet correspond to the state and level of our society's development.

8 We are living through a time when internal conflicts and interethnic divisions that were once firmly suppressed by the ruling ideology have now flared up.

9 We stopped paying the required attention to defense and security issues and we allowed corruption to undermine our judicial and law enforcement system.

10 Furthermore, our country, formerly protected by the most powerful defense system along the length of its external

frontiers. overnight found itself defenseless both from the east and the west.

11 It will take many years and billions of rubles to create new, modern, and genuinely protected borders.

12 But even so, we could have been more effective if we had acted professionally and at the right moment.

13 In general, we need to admit that we did not fully understand the complexity and the dangers of the processes at work in our own country and in the world. In any case, we proved unable to react adequately. We showed ourselves to be weak. And the weak get beaten.

14 Some would like to tear a "fat chunk" of the territory from us. Others help them. They help, reasoning that Russia still remains one of the world's major nuclear powers, and as such still represents a threat to them. And so they reason that this threat should be removed.

15 And terrorism, of course, is just an instrument to achieve these aims.

16 As I have said many times already, we have found ourselves confronting crises, revolts, and terrorist acts on more than one occasion. But what has happened now, this crime committed by terrorists, is unprecedented in its inhumanness and cruelty. This is not a challenge to the President, parliament, or government. It is a challenge to all of Russia, to our entire people. It is an attack on our country.

Part 3

17 The terrorists think they are stronger than us. They think they can frighten us with their cruelty, paralyze our will, and sow disintegration in our society. It would seem that we have a choice—either to resist them or to agree to their demands. To give in, to let them destroy and have Russia disintegrate in the hope that they will finally leave us in peace.

18 As the President, the head of the Russian state, as someone

who swore an oath to defend this country and its territorial integrity, and simply as a citizen of Russia, I am convinced that in reality we have no choice at all. Because to allow ourselves to be blackmailed and succumb to panic would be to immediately condemn millions of people to an endless series of bloody conflicts like those of Nagorny Karabakh, Trans-Dniester, and other well-known tragedies. We should not turn away from this obvious fact.

19 What we are dealing with are not isolated acts intended to frighten us, not isolated terrorist attacks. What we are facing is direct intervention of international terror directed against Russia. A total, cruel, and full-scale war that again and again is taking the lives of our fellow citizens.

20 World experience shows us that, unfortunately, such wars do not end quickly. In this situation we simply cannot and should not live in as carefree a manner as previously. We must create a much more effective security system and we must demand from our law enforcement agencies action that corresponds to the level and scale of the new threats that have emerged.

21 But most important is to mobilize the entire nation in the face of this common danger. Events in other countries have shown that terrorists meet the most effective resistance in places where they not only encounter the state's power but also find themselves facing an organized and united civil society.

Part 4

22 Dear fellow citizens,

23 Those who sent these bandits to carry out this horrible crime made it their aim to set our peoples against each other, put fear into the hearts of Russian citizens, and unleash bloody interethnic strife in the North Caucasus. In this connection I have the following words to say.

24 First. A series of measures aimed at strengthening our country's unity will soon be prepared.

25 Second. I think it is necessary to create a new system of co-ordinating the forces and means responsible for exercising control over the situation in the North Caucasus. Third. We need to create an effective anti-crisis management system, including entirely new approaches to the way the law enforcement agencies work.

26 I want to stress that all of these measures will be implemented in full accordance with our country's Constitution.

Part 5

27 Dear friends,

28 We all are living through very difficult and painful days. I would like now to thank all those who showed endurance and responsibility as citizens.

29 We were and always will be stronger than them, stronger through our morals, our courage, and our sense of solidarity.

30 I saw this again last night.

31 In Beslan, which is literally soaked with grief and pain, people were showing care and support for each other more than ever.

32 They were not afraid to risk their own lives in the name of the lives and peace of others.

33 Even in the most inhuman conditions they remained human beings.

34 It is impossible to accept the pain caused by such loss, but these trials have brought us even closer together and have forced us to re-evaluate a lot of things.

35 Today we must be together. Only thus we will vanquish the enemy.

This message was delivered the day after the end of the standoff between terrorists and Russian security forces during a school siege in Beslan, in Russia's southern republic of Northern Ossetia. There were more than 1,200 people taken hostage during the three days of terror. Nearly 340 people died, 176 of them children. More than 500 were wounded. A message posted since on a pro-Chechen Website confirmed what many believed: that the architect of the violence was Shamil Basaev, the most notorious of the Chechen militants. Russia was in shock.

Obviously such an emotional subject demands an emotional response from the country's President. Rightly, therefore, the speaker gives emotional appeal a priority. The message is clearly meant to comfort and uplift, unify and instill confidence in the people. In Part 1 especially, and throughout the text, we see expression[s] of sympathy and condolence. But who must these words comfort and uplift, in whom must they invoke hope and confidence? Who is the audience the speaker addresses his message to? These questions are not as straightforward as they seem. The primary audience [is] not the people of Beslan whom the terrorist attack immediately affected, although they do come up in the concluding part of the speech. The primary audience [is] all the people of Russia. Even the town of Beslan is referred to as a Russian town rather than a Northern Ossetian town (2), which would have distanced it from the country as a whole. The recipients of the message are referred to *fellow citizens* (22), *Russian citizens* (23), and *friends* (27), but never as Ossetians.

This is done to achieve two objectives. On the one hand, it serves to indicate that Russians are a united nation (inspiring confidence). On the other hand, it acts to reinforce the identification of the speaker, the President of the country, with his audience, his fellow countrymen (expression of empathy). Several linguistic devices are employed to produce the said effect. One of them is the repetition of key words or phrases: the noun *Russia* and adjective *Russian* are mentioned nine times in the original Russian text, the personal pronoun *we* and the possessive pronoun *our* are used no less than 33 times.

An interesting case to examine is the use of the word *people*, which is found in the text both in the singular and the plural form. Used in the singular, (a) *people* refers to the whole Russian nation: *This is not a challenge to the President, parliament, or government. It is a challenge to all of Russia, to our entire people* (16). In the plural, the word *peoples* refers to various ethnic groups composing the Russian Federation: *Those who sent these bandits to carry out this horrible crime made it their aim to set our peoples against each other, put fear into the hearts of Russian citizens, and unleash bloody interethnic strife in the North Caucasus* (23). In this sentence, Putin takes great care to emphasize that different ethnic groups living in the Northern Caucuses are one nation. He does that by using an umbrella term *Russian citizens* to refer to the people belonging to these ethnic groups. The speaker not only talks about a united Russia but emphasizes the country's greatness: Russia is referred to as *the core* (5) of a great state, *that giant—the Soviet Union* (5), as a country *protected by the most powerful defense system along the length of its external frontiers* (10), [and] as *one of the world's major nuclear powers* (14).

Having built up the idea of unity in Part 1 and Part 2, President Putin, at the end of Part 2, introduces one of his main theses: *all of Russia is under attack* (16). Later on the speaker reinforces his claim: *What we are dealing with are not isolated acts intended to frighten us, not isolated terrorist attacks. What we are facing is direct intervention of international terror directed against Russia. A total, cruel, and full-scale war that again and again is taking the lives of our fellow citizens* (19).

The message contains an important juxtaposition: Russia versus her enemies. And that is the only juxtaposition. There is no division within Russia itself: the State and the People are one whole.

Let us examine the rhetorical images of the opposing parties. The speaker creates an image of the Russian people as caring, courageous, humane people, and juxtaposes this image with the enemies' image as *not just murderers but people who turned their weapons against defenseless children* (2), *terrorists* (4, 16, 17, and 21), *international terror[ists]* (19), and *bandits* (23). In fact, the speaker ends his message with the word *enemy* (35), which tells us of the importance President Putin attaches to the concept. Describing the enemy, the speaker avoids any mention of their demands to withdraw Russian troops from Chechnya. Interestingly, never once was the word Chechnya mentioned in the whole speech. This is done to remove any connection between Beslan and the ongoing conflict in the neighboring republic. The speaker creates the impression that Northern Caucasus is currently a peaceful region and the bandits who committed the crime strive to spark a bloody feud between the peoples of the region similar to bloody conflicts in Nagorny Karabakh between Azerbaijan and Armenia; in the Trans-Dniester Republic between this self-proclaimed, unrecognized state and Moldova, which it had been part of; and *other well-known tragedies* (18).

Putin's emphasis is on the international character of the threat that plagues the modern world, hence the mention of the popular term *the new threats* (20), the reference to other countries in the next paragraph (21), as well the implication that the bandits who carried out the crime did not act on their own accord but were sent by those abroad who masterminded the terrorist attack (23). Even more striking is the reference to world conspiracy of presumably foreign policy-makers who condone terrorism against Russia. Some of them condone it because they see an opportunity to chip away a "fat chunk" of Russian territory; others see in Russia, one of world's biggest nuclear powers, a threat to them, the threat that *should be removed* (14).

As we have noticed before, the message is of a highly rhetorical character. It abounds in stylistic devices, which enhance its aesthetic appeal. Note the use of repetition of the word *we* throughout the text, parallelism of expression in Part 2: *we live in a time* ... (5), *we all hoped* ... (6), *we are living* ... (7 & 8), and *we stopped* ... (9). This feature is even more pronounced in the original Russian. As William Strunk Jr. points out in his book *The Elements of Style*, a good writer should express coordinate ideas in similar form. "This principle, that of parallel construction requires that expressions similar in content and function be outwardly similar. The likeness of form enables the reader to recognize more readily the likeness of content and function" (Strunk and White 1979: 26).

Many important statements are expressed in very short sentences, which help attract the attention of the audience: *And the weak get beaten* (13); *It is an attack on our country* (16); *Today we must be together. Only thus we will vanquish the enemy* (35). The speaker deliberately breaks his sentences into two, which again allows him to repeat certain key words, achieve sharpness of expression, and thus increase the aesthetic and emotional effects of the message: *Speaking is hard. And painful* (1); *We all hoped for change. Change for the better* (6); *This is not a challenge to the President, parliament, or government. It is a challenge to all of Russia, to our entire people. It is an attack on our country* (16). The latter sequence is also an example of the aforementioned stylistic device of parallelism. Another stylistic device employed to enhance the aesthetic appeal is the rhetorical question *Why?* (6) The question allows the arguer to make a pause and draw the listener's attention to the points that follow.

Rational appeal appears to be the last on President Putin's priority list. This assessment could be argued based on the fact that the number of sentences containing argumentation is comparatively small. Plus, as we have already mentioned, the purpose of the message is not to convince but rather to empathize and explain. As far as specific proposals for a course of action are concerned, the speaker makes only a few blueprint points, leaving proper arguments for concrete proposals for a later message. However, it only looks so.

The message contains a clear argumentation whose purpose is to justify the tough line President Putin is pursuing toward Chechnya, vindicate his actions during the crisis, and propose reforms in Russia's governance. We have touched upon the first issue already. The "other" clearly receives a biased representation: the perpetrators are not Chechen terrorists or Chechen militants but international terrorists. Hence any connection between Russian actions in Chechnya and the Beslan events is invalidated. Consequently, the Russian authorities are cleared of any blame of at least provoking this atrocity. All the blame stays with the terrorists themselves. This constitutes the first fallacy the discourse contains, the fallacy of shifting the issue. Instead of presenting a true picture, the speaker provides an interpretation of the events convenient for him.

Another fallacy the arguer commits is that of a false dilemma in which a contrary opposition is presented as a contradiction (van Eemeren and Grootendorst 1992: 190). President Putin suggests in 17 that there only appears to be a choice: to strike back or to give in to the demands of terrorists and to allow the terrorists to destroy and split up Russia, hoping that in the end they will leave Russia alone. In 18, however, he continues that in reality Russia simply has no choice: if the Russian Government gives in to the blackmail of the terrorists and starts panicking, millions of Russians will be plunged into an endless series of bloody conflicts such as the Nagorny Karabakh conflict or the Trans-Dniester conflict. Therefore, only one avenue is open to Russia—hold strong and defend herself. The false dilemma is therefore contained in the assertion that there are only two options that are in contradictory relation to each other: to give up the fight and let the country be destroyed or continue fighting and keep the country from breaking up. However, as opponents of the war in Chechnya point out, there may be a third option, quoting at least one example of a peaceful resolution of a deep-rooted violent conflict through negotiations with terrorists, that of the Northern Ireland settlement. The British Government had made several attempts to enter into negotiations with the Irish Republican Army before finally reaching a compromise that brought peace to Northern Ireland. Northern Ireland has not broken away from the United Kingdom as a result of that; the UK is still a united country. It is this third way—negotiations with terrorists—that is branded by Putin as succumbing to the terrorists' blackmail.

Another fallacy committed by the author is evading the burden of proof by making an argument immune to criticism. The same paragraph 18 concludes with a statement, *We should not turn away from this obvious fact*, which means that the point made is an obvious one and does not need to be defended. Such a statement violates Rule 2 of the critical discussion rules developed in the pragma-dialectical theory of argumentation. "An obvious way of evading one's own burden of proof is to present the standpoint in such a way that there is no need to defend it in the first place. This can be done by giving the impression that the antagonist is quite wrong to cast doubt on the standpoint or that there is no point in calling it into question. In either case, the protagonist is guilty of the fallacy of evading the burden of proof. The first way of evading the burden of proof amounts to presenting the standpoint as self-evident" (van Eemeren and Grootendorst 1992: 118). As we have already noted, the claim the arguer makes in this paragraph is not self-evident at all.

Another point worth mentioning when discussing fallacies is a shift of definition. If we examine paragraph 21 we will see that by the term *civil society* the speaker understands something different from what his liberal opponents understand. For President Putin civil society doesn't mean an open, self-organized society, in which the government is accountable to the populace, but rather a society with a vigilant community closely cooperating with law enforcement agencies in preventing terrorist attacks, e.g. through community patrols. Obviously, this shift of definition isn't a fallacy; rather it is a different interpretation of a term. Thus, what would seem at first sight a sign of commitment to democratic values is in effect another argument for the tightening of security in the face of terrorism.

The structure of the argumentation can be represented in the following way:

Figure 1

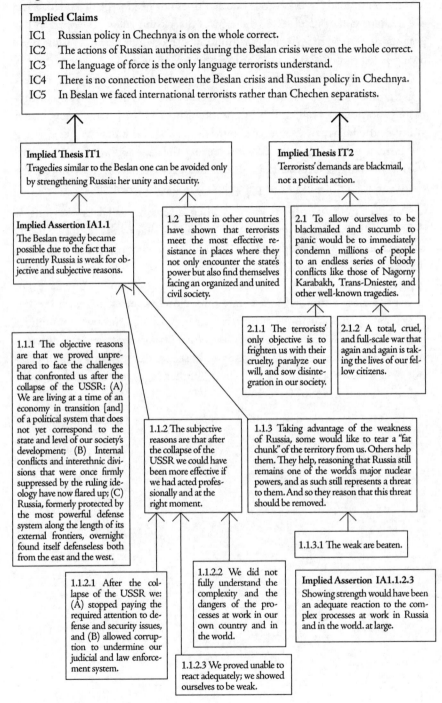

Implied Claims

IC1 Russian policy in Chechnya is on the whole correct.

IC2 The actions of Russian authorities during the Beslan crisis were on the whole correct.

IC3 The language of force is the only language terrorists understand.

IC4 There is no connection between the Beslan crisis and Russian policy in Chechnya.

IC5 In Beslan we faced international terrorists rather than Chechen separatists.

Implied Thesis IT1
Tragedies similar to the Beslan one can be avoided only by strengthening Russia: her unity and security.

Implied Thesis IT2
Terrorists' demands are blackmail, not a political action.

Implied Assertion IA1.1
The Beslan tragedy became possible due to the fact that currently Russia is weak for objective and subjective reasons.

1.2 Events in other countries have shown that terrorists meet the most effective resistance in places where they not only encounter the state's power but also find themselves facing an organized and united civil society.

2.1 To allow ourselves to be blackmailed and succumb to panic would be to immediately condemn millions of people to an endless series of bloody conflicts like those of Nagorny Karabakh, Trans-Dniester, and other well-known tragedies.

2.1.1 The terrorists' only objective is to frighten us with their cruelty, paralyze our will, and sow disintegration in our society.

2.1.2 A total, cruel, and full-scale war that again and again is taking the lives of our fellow citizens.

1.1.1 The objective reasons are that we proved unprepared to face the challenges that confronted us after the collapse of the USSR: (A) We are living at a time of an economy in transition [and] of a political system that does not yet correspond to the state and level of our society's development; (B) Internal conflicts and interethnic divisions that were once firmly suppressed by the ruling ideology have now flared up; (C) Russia, formerly protected by the most powerful defense system along the length of its external frontiers, overnight found itself defenseless both from the east and the west.

1.1.2 The subjective reasons are that after the collapse of the USSR we could have been more effective if we had acted professionally and at the right moment.

1.1.3 Taking advantage of the weakness of Russia, some would like to tear a "fat chunk" of the territory from us. Others help them. They help, reasoning that Russia still remains one of the world's major nuclear powers, and as such still represents a threat to them. And so they reason that this threat should be removed.

1.1.3.1 The weak are beaten.

1.1.2.1 After the collapse of the USSR we: (A) stopped paying the required attention to defense and security issues, and (B) allowed corruption to undermine our judicial and law enforcement system.

1.1.2.2 We did not fully understand the complexity and the dangers of the processes at work in our own country and in the world.

Implied Assertion IA1.1.2.3
Showing strength would have been an adequate reaction to the complex processes at work in Russia and in the world. at large.

1.1.2.3 We proved unable to react adequately; we showed ourselves to be weak.

Let us start our overview of the above figure with an explanation of the different designations applied to the various elements of the argumentation. As you can see from the figure, it contains two types of statements: expressed statements and implied statements. The latter are divided into Implied Claims [IC], Implied Theses [IT], and Implied Assertions [IA]. All these terms basically mean the same thing—an argued statement or point of view—but derive from different traditions of argumentation theory: the terms *claim* and *assertion* were introduced by [Stephen] Toulmin working within the framework of Procedural Informal Logic, while the term *thesis* was introduced by Aristotle and belongs to the tradition of Classical Dialectic (van Eemeren et al. 2001: 27–47). The purpose of assigning the implicit statements different names is to differentiate them in terms of argumentative importance and the degree of implicitness: ICs are the least apparent statements in the fabric of the message and therefore the justification of ascribing these statements to the speaker can be subjected to doubt more than any other implied statements; while the theses are hierarchically more important than the assertions because the latter are themselves arguments put forward in support of the former. Both the ITs and the IAs are but slightly paraphrased statements that are already available in the discourse.

It is also important to note that the ICs themselves form an argumentation which can be reconstructed so that any one of them can act as the conclusion following from the other ICs as its premises. However, in our opinion, the most crucial IC for President Putin is IC1, and thus, it is IC1 that crowns the whole argumentation of the message. As we have already mentioned, Putin is engaged in an implicit debate with the opposition over two main accusations. The first accusation concerns his actions during the siege that resulted in so many deaths: had the demands of the terrorists about the withdrawal of Russian troops from Chechnya been met, the school would not have been blown up. The second accusation concerns the overall policy in and around Chechnya: it is this policy that has incited the terrorist act. The Russian President's reasoning develops along two main lines of argument. While the two lines are interwoven, as is shown in Figure 1 in which both lines of argument lead to the same implied claims, and the arguments supporting one line of argument serve the other as well, we can say that the second line of argument is shorter and more clear-cut. It terminates in the text in IT2 and points indirectly to all the ICs but most directly to IC2, IC3, and IC5. The first line of argument is longer and the statements involved in it are better substantiated in the message than those of the first one. The second argumentation terminates in the text in IT1, and while pointing to all the ICs, most directly it supports the very important implied claims IC1, IC4, and IC5.

We have already touched upon evaluation of the two lines of reasoning and pointed out that the first one is weightier than the second one. It is precisely the problem of Putin's argumentation: his apologia is not well enough argued. IC1, IC4, and IC5 are not proven to be the case. They lack solid explicit arguments in the message. However, to make this conclusion, we must justify our reconstruction of the implicit elements in the argumentation, including the ICs.

In our reconstruction of the structure of the arguer's reasoning, we followed an informal logical approach to argument reconstruction, rather than a formal logical approach, for the following reasons. Van Rees points out that while both in informal logic and formal logic, reconstruction aims to isolate the premises and conclusion of the reasoning underlying an argument, the approaches differ in two major aspects: "First, for informal logicians, deductive validity is no longer necessarily the prime or only standard for evaluating an argument. One of the important issues in informal logic concerns exactly this question of the validity standard to be applied. Most informal logicians hold that some arguments lend themselves to evaluation in terms of deductive validity, while others may be more appropriately evaluated in terms of other standards. This issue has important implications for reconstruction. It means that not all arguments must necessarily be reconstructed as deductively valid. This is especially relevant in the matter of reconstructing unexpressed premises" (van Eemeren et al. 2001: 180).

For our purposes it means that we don't seek to fill in missing premises all the time in all individual argumentations (syllogisms) but only where necessary, e.g., in the argumentation consisting of the conclusion 1.1.2 and the premises 1.1.2.1–IA1.1.2.3. Implied Assertion IA1.1.2.3 is an unexpressed premise that goes together with the explicit premise 1.1.2.3, constituting a single argumentative support for 1.1.2.1. The weakness argument is central to President Putin's reasoning. In IA1.1.2.3, and especially in the explicit statement *And the weak get beaten*, the speaker emphasizes the necessity of strong action in dealing with Chechen separatists who resort to terrorist attacks on Russian troops and civilians (e.g., in IC3). According to our reconstruction, the statement *And the weak get beaten* lies at the very foundation of a long chain of arguments (1.1.3.1).

Moreover, "informal logicians view arguments as elements of ordinary, contextually embedded language use, directed by one language user to another in an attempt to convince him of the plausibility (not necessarily the truth) of the conclusion. For reconstruction, this implies taking into account the situated character of the discourse to be reconstructed" (van Eemeren et al. 2001: 180).

This aspect is especially important for reconstructing the ICs. To do that, we have taken into account not only the immediate context, i.e., the message, but also a broader context of public debate over Putin's policy in Chechnya, and therefore the need for the speaker to present some kind of *apologia*. Having taken into account the President's earlier statements concerning terrorism and the conflict in Chechnya, the quoting of which is outside the scope of this paper, we came to the above formulations of the ICs.

Let us now return to the pragmatic aspect of our analysis. According to the theory of argumentation, there are three types of propositions or statements: propositions of fact, value, and policy. "These correspond to the most common sources of controversy: (1) disputes over what happened, what is happening, or what will happen; (2) disputes asserting something to be good or bad, right or wrong, effective or ineffective; and (3) disputes over what should or should not be done" (Rybacki and Rybacki 1191: 27–28). In pragmatic terms, propositions of fact and value fall into the same category of utterances performed by way of assertive speech acts, and propositions of policy correspond to the category of utterances performed by way of directive speech acts. The argumentation structure represented above contains exclusively statements of fact and value, of which the latter are only IC1 and IC2. Meanwhile, the message contains utterances performed by way directive and commissive speech acts.

Commissive speech acts express the speaker's intention to commit himself or herself to a certain course of action. Such acts include pledges, promises, guarantees, etc. *A series of measures aimed at strengthening our country's unity will soon be prepared* (24) and *I want to stress that all of these measures will be implemented in full accordance with our country's Constitution* (26) are examples of commissives, while *We must create a much more effective security system and we must demand from our law enforcement agencies action that corresponds to the level and scale of the new threats that have emerged* (20) and *I think it is necessary to create a new system of coordinating the forces and means responsible for exercising control over the situation in the North Caucasus* (25) are examples of directives. In effect, the above directives are indirect commissives through which President Putin informs the country of his commitment to introduce new measures to strengthen Russia's security.

The pragmatic analysis shows that most speech acts performed in the discourse are assertive and expressive acts. The former include claims, assertions, and statements, and the latter include expressions of sympathy and condolence. Directives and commissives serve an extremely important purpose in the discourse, that of confidence building. However seemingly insignificant and secondary among the components of the arguer's communicative strategy of persuasion, they are still a valuable part of it. It is with the help of all types of speech acts that the speaker achieves his objectives: to explain the reasons of the Beslan tragedy, lift the spirits of the people, vindicate his policy in Chechnya and in the Beslan crisis, and justify the proposed reforms in Russia's governance. To quote President Putin, "And terrorism, of course, is just an instrument to achieve these aims."

References

Goloubev, V. 1999. Looking at Argumentation through Communicative Intentions: Ways to Define Fallacies. In *Proceedings of the Fourth International Conference of the International Society for the Study of Argumentation*. Amsterdam: Sic Sat, Amsterdam University Press.

Rybacki, K., and D. Rybacki. 1991. *Advocacy and Opposition: An Introduction to Argumentation*. Englewood Cliffs, NJ: Prentice-Hall.

Strunk, W., Jr., and E. B. White. 1979. *The Elements of Style*. New York: Macmillan

van Eemeren, F. H., and R. Grootendorst. 1992. *Argumentation, Communication, and Fallacies*. Hillsdale, NJ: Lawrence Erlbaum.

van Eemeren, F. H., et al. 2001. *Crucial Concepts in Argumentation Theory*. Amsterdam: Sic Sat, Amsterdam University Press.

Vadim Golubev is chair of the department of English for Journalists, St. Petersburg State University, Russia. Dr. Golubev's teaching and research interests are argumentation and debate in the media.

"Agree to Disagree" as a Cultural Practice: Examining the Functionality of Disagreement in Debate

Steven Woods and Jianglong Wang

This paper analyzes the American cultural practice of agreeing to disagree and examines how this practice functions in teaching debate and argumentation in the United States. Based on their analyses, the authors then advocate the need for those who teach debate and argumentation in Asian cultures to overcome the cultural barriers to agreeing to disagree, and suggest strategies for the teachers to accomplish the task. The paper concludes with a discussion of the implications for future research in the area of teaching debate and argumentation across world cultures.

INTRODUCTION

Most people in the United States take for granted the adage "agree to disagree." To Americans, particularly to American debaters, nothing seems more natural than being ready to disagree when it comes to dealing with different opinions in the process of developing one's argument. This, however, is by no means true across cultures worldwide. Many Asian cultures have minimum levels of tolerance for disagreement, especially from their in-group members (Becker 1991; Bond 1991; Gao 1998). The ability to maintain disagreement and feel comfortable in doing so is a culturally acquired skill necessary, perhaps, for all competent debaters.

This paper will examine debate training from an inter-cultural perspective, exploring the assumptions of Western debate training in contexts in which other assumptions about the nature of disagreement and conflict exist, in particular the contrasts provided in Asian cultures. A discussion of "agree to disagree" as cultural construct will start the paper, followed by a look at models of U.S. debate and then a consideration of the issues related to differing values toward public discussion and how to have exchange and interaction among cultures in relationship to debate training and teaching argumentation.

AGREEING TO DISAGREE AS A CULTURAL PRACTICE

Cultures in the world perceive individuals' argumentative trait and/or assertiveness quite differently. This divergence in perception sets cultures apart, and each culture's acceptance of individuals' argumentativeness is contingent upon the culture's positive or negative views regarding open expression. In North American cultures, for instance, open expression is encouraged, even if individuals' openness in presenting their views implies opposition or confrontation. Geert Hofstede (1991) believes that the cultural practice of speaking one's mind is considered a virtue in individualist cultures. In individualist cultures, he asserts:

> Telling the truth about how one feels is the characteristic of a sincere and honest person. Confrontation can be salutary; a clash of opinions is believed to lead to higher truth. The effect of communications on other people should be taken into account, but it does not, as a rule, justify changing the facts. Adult individuals should have learned to take direct feedback constructively. (p. 58)

Indeed, cultural behaviors are learned. Individuals acquire cultural behaviors while growing up, which Glen Fisher (1988) termed as cultural programming. In individualist cultures like that of the United States, confrontation as a culturally acquired behavior is accepted as a normalcy in life. The clash of ideas leading to what is seen as higher truth is valued and rewarded. Telling the truth, and telling it directly, even if it hurts other people has positive value for members in American culture.

Argumentation scholars, while admitting that Americans are programmed to confront at a very young age (Ziegelmueller, Kay̆, and Dause 1990), believe that argumentation per se is not confrontation, however. Instead, they hold that argumentation is a logical or philosophical activity that involves inquiry and advocacy, because the process of argumentation is the logical development of ideas (arguments) via proof (evidence) (Ziegelmueller, Kay, and Dause 1990). Thus, it follows, by logical reasoning, if one feels that his/her argument is attestable or he/she believes in the strength of the evidence gathered, then disagreement is desired and, in fact, welcomed, as the ultimate goal of engaging in argumentation is to seek out the higher level of truth. Following this line of thinking, it then becomes apparent and inevitable for debaters to agree to disagree in the process of seeking higher truth.

In academic debate, the basic starting point of the process is an understanding that there will be at least two sides to any proposition that is advanced. The concept of disagreement is based in Western cultures' assumption about the basis of all arguments of civil dispute (politics or the courts in particular) involve standard points where there will be dispute is known as "stasis." Hermagoras developed the concept in Greek rhetorical theory, and Cicero also developed a stasis doctrine (Murphy 1983; Ochs 1983). The idea that there are disagreements is so normal that there are specific points defined where disagreement will occur. Debate training provides a way to become proficient in those "natural" points of disagreement. In this way debate training is tied to a cultural acceptance of agreeing to disagree.

On the other hand, in collectivist cultures, disagreement--let alone confrontation--is generally frowned upon, because maintenance of harmony with one's social environment is a matter of higher order. Hofstede observed that "in the collectivist family children learn to take their bearings from others when it comes to opinions. 'Personal opinions' do not exist: they are predetermined by the group" (1991, p. 59). In collectivist cultures like those of China, Japan, and Korea, open expression of one's feelings and views is not encouraged. Instead, individual members are obliged to exhibit loyalty to the group. Regarding development of ideas and how group members resolve differences among themselves in China, Lin Yutang offered the following:

> The logical mind works with cut and dried distinctions. According to logic: If A is right, then B, which is opposed to A, is wrong. If you say to a Chinese, "A is right," he will say, "You are right." But if you say, "Perhaps B is right," the Chinese will say, "You are right." You say, "Evidently A and B cannot be both right. Mr. Lin, you are inconsistent." And the Chinese will say, "You are right." (quoted in Anderson 1975, p. 91)

In Lin's words, the most logical approach among the Chinese is not to show disagreement at any cost, because the relationship between the individuals in the conversation is of much more importance. Culturally, then, to people in collectivistic cultures, agree to disagree would seem to be a foreign practice that functions only to alienate the individual and hurt the harmony of the group. To people in collectivist cultures, agree to disagree is a blatant violation of their cultural norm for appropriate behavior within the group and, therefore, is shunned by members of the culture.

U.S. Models of Debate and Argumentation

The earliest version of U.S. debate models stems from Aristotelian views on forensic speaking. Determinations of extent of harm, responsibility, and justification, as outlined by Aristotle (Cooper 1960), form the core of what are considered "stock issues" in competitive debate. In fact, competitive debate teams are traditionally termed "forensics" teams. While there are variations in the actual practice of competitive academic debate, the framing of the overall essence of the activity as neo-Aristotelian would not be far off.

Debate is seen as a way to train for real-world disagreements that one might encounter in the courts, or even across a fence with a neighbor. The idea that one should be prepared to spontaneously engage in argument is central to the practice of training persons to argue. Topics for debate are based on current and ongoing controversies in society, with an acknowledgment that people will be on differing sides of those issues indefinitely. It is telling that often the resolutions from one era are repeated in another era, or show that even historical evolutions still leave issues as unresolved as ever (for example, debating the value of the League of Nations and then later the United Nations).

The structure of debate is set up so that those participating will have to argue from a variety of viewpoints on a variety of issues. Participants are assigned sides in competitive tournaments, and it is built into the structure that participants will be assigned an equal number of times to different sides. In preparation for tournaments, students get ready by finding arguments and supporting evidence to bolster a variety of differing perspectives on potential issues that might be debated. A survey of debate texts indicates that there is clearly a value in being able to establish good argumentative "ground" on both sides of a topic (Bartanen and Frank 1991; Freeley and Steinberg 2000).

Such training is seen as valuable in contributing not only to competitive success but also to participation in society. Better opportunities are available to the person who can debate and argue in areas such as business, law, and politics (Ross 2002). In fact, Urban Debate Leagues have been developed as a response to poverty and lack of enfranchisement of the poor and people of color in the U.S. (National Association of Urban Debate Leagues 2004). The importance of debate in society is highlighted by the expectation of presidential candidates to engage in such behaviors during the campaign.

The rewards for participation are also available in the present, ranging from simple awards and trophies at tournaments to public recognition of performance and financial rewards in the form of scholarships. Being in debate is encouraged and rewarded in academia and society in the U.S. Rather than something to be avoided, debate is embraced and prepared for, and those with particular talent in it are given positive feedback and encouragement to continue.

UNDERSTANDING THE VALUE OF DEBATE ACROSS CULTURES

Individuals' perceptions of things are often reflections of their cultural values. Individualists' positive perception of a person's argumentativeness is a manifestation of their cultural values of being open in expressing one's feeling and views. On the other hand, collectivists' negative perception of a person's argumentativeness is a revelation of their cultural values of maintaining group harmony. As cultures change over time, cultural values change as well, particularly when cultural exchange has reached a phenomenal level with the advancement of technology and international travel.

Recent research has well documented such changes of cultural values, as cultures frequently interact with each other. Jung-huel Becky Yeh and Ling Chen (2004) have found that the Chinese values toward being argumentative are beginning to show some significant changes in recent years. Their research on the cultural values and argumentative orientations of the Chinese living in Taiwan, Hong Kong, and mainland China demonstrates that, although the Chinese are still holding on to their traditional Confucian values toward being argumentative, more and more individuals are beginning to realize the importance of public debate in matters of social concerns. Yeh and Chen discovered that "mainland China has demonstrated a prominent pattern in perceiving 'being argumentative' as a positive and constructive action, and has shown a strong motivation for argument" (2004, p. 59).

Similarly, Gary Rybold (2001) found that his experience of teaching public speaking and debate in China was quite educational and rewarding. He believes that "China is changing in ways we simply can't predict" and "cultural exchanges were excellent learning experiences for the debaters [from the United States] and audience [those in China] alike" (2001, 18). According to Rybold (2004), the Chinese welcomed his Ted Turner debate training, and effectiveness of the training was obvious, as the Chinese were not only attentive learners but also efficient users of the knowledge they had acquired from the training.

Although Rybold's experience is rather encouraging to those who are interested in developing international debate, the challenges for teaching debate across cultures still remain, as one must overcome the differences in values toward being argumentative and the negative perception of public debate, which entails the practice of agreeing to disagree.

STRATEGIES FOR TEACHING DEBATE/ARGUMENTATION IN DIFFERENT CULTURES

The basic elements of the concept of agree to disagree are a place to start in teaching debate across cultures. By acknowledging that there is a difference of perspective on what is appropriate and ultimately what is "right," interaction can occur between those who are offering debate methods to those who are culturally uneasy with them. Rather than holding the belief that debate is the only way to conduct argument, debate should be seen as but one way to engage in discussion. There is no need to create a hierarchy in which one type of interaction is valued as more appropriate than another.

In interacting across cultures, remembering the platinum rule of interaction as described by Bennet as doing unto others as they themselves would have done unto them (Bennett, 1979), is more appropriate than the golden rule of treating others as you would have them do unto you. So while argumentation is a mutual goal of the training, it should not be the primary context for interaction of those doing the training. Offering ideas in a climate of respect and understanding of differences is a primary concern.

A beginning point could be to introduce the concept of agreeing to disagree within a context that de-emphasizes the personal nature of conflict and keeps a focus on the issues being discussed. Part of this introduction would be an explanation of the depersonalization of the argumentative context. In Asian culture the importance of status and the hierarchy of the speaker are inseparable from the argument itself. It is important to explain that, while the credibility of a speaker is important in Western argument, issues are routinely depersonalized in debate. Strong disagreement with another person in the West is not necessarily a challenge to that person's status. It is a matter of also understanding that Asian culture is high context in that there is a preexisting understanding of the relationships that exist between persons outside the realm of communication, so that even before people speak, their status and seniority are understood. For the West, while that may be a part of an argumentative context, it is not always the primary determinant of the quality or acceptance of an argument. While seemingly obvious, the need to explain that disagreement is not a challenge to authority is one of the cross-cultural translations that need to be made.

Interaction would also require the use of examples and issues that are of interest and within the knowledge base of those being taught. Issues that are considered well within the contemporary bounds of controversy from a Western perspective may not be appropriate in non-Western contexts. Finding issues about which disagreement can be expressed without violating community expectations would be important. For example, keeping the focus on good to the community might involve decision making relating to addressing an issue that impacts everyday well-being, such as water quality or noise control. It would be possible to construct a resolution for debate that might enable two good ideas to emerge.

For Western debate the idea of two good ideas in a debate raises issues of theory that are problematic, such as non-competitive counterplans, or "plan-plan" theories of argumentation. But it is important to remember that many of the constructs of Western academic debate are artificially contrived to suit the needs of game playing rather than ensuring good "real-world" decision making, nor do they aid basic understanding of beginning debate concepts. So the changes offered here may make reaching a decision about who wins or loses more complicated, but this very dilemma leads to the next change or alteration to the debate format that may be necessitated by offering it for cross-cultural training.

It may be necessary to offer non-competitive versions of interaction. While the U.S. version of academic debate is explicit in identifying a winner and a loser, and unabashed in rewarding just the winner, an emphasis on process over outcome would be more appropriate outside of the U.S. Making sure not to confuse method with outcome is important. While those teaching debate may be used to focusing on "how to win," an emphasis on "how to participate" would be a better choice. In discussing how a person did in taking part in a debate, an instructor would not need to dwell on what they did in terms of aiding or harming their chances of losing. Giving feedback that treats all participants as equals with valuable contributions to make to the discussion reinforces a sense of community, rather than the distinctions of right and wrong that imposing a decision might do in a purely competitive debate. A discussion after the debate can acknowledge the strong performance of all participants, not a delineation of what the debaters did that failed to be persuasive. The process must contribute to the reinforcement of community, and so should the assessment process. It is possible that the debaters may participate in the assessment process, not just the critic, reinforcing community and the cultural expectation of Asian society for consensus.

Conclusion

Given the discussion of this paper, a model for instruction would (1) include a means to introduce the topic of argumentation that presupposes cultural difference about the idea; (2) include a way to acknowledge the community present, such as an ice breaker activity before moving further into the training process; (3) have topics that address common concerns and community building outcomes; (4) alter the "rules" of interaction to allow for alternative forms of advancement of ideas instead of traditional "offensive" arguments; and (5) have a participant-based assessment process.

Further research and experience in this area will hopefully yield additional insights and more concrete means of building an effective model. As the international debate community grows, and as members of the U.S. debate community increase their participation in that community, great opportunity to further critical thinking will emerge, along with, and also requiring, greater cultural sensitivity and understanding.

References

Anderson, A., ed. 1975. *Lin Yutang: The best of an old friend.* New York: Mason/Charter.

Bartanen, M. D., and D. A. Frank. 1991. *Debating values.* Scottsdale, AZ: Gorsuch, Scarisbrick Publishers.

Becker, C. 1991. Reasons for the lack of argumentation and debate in the Far East. In L. Samovar and R. Porter, eds., *Intercultural communication: A reader* (pp. 234–243). Belmont, CA: Wadsworth.

Bennett, M. J. 1979. Overcoming the golden rule: Sympathy and empathy. In D. Nimmo, ed., *Communication yearbook 3.* New Brunswick, NJ: Transaction Books.

Bond, M. 1991. *Beyond the Chinese face.* Hong Kong: Oxford University Press.

Cooper, L. 1960. *The Rhetoric of Aristotle.* Englewood Cliffs, NJ: Prentice-Hall.

Fisher, G. 1988. *Mindsets: The role of culture and perception in international relations.* Yarmouth, ME: Intercultural Press.

Freeley, A. J., and D. L. Steinberg. 2000. *Argumentation and debate: Critical thinking for reasoned decision making.* Belmont, CA: Wadsworth Thomson Learning.

Gao, G. 1998. "Don't take my word for it."—Understanding Chinese speaking practices. *International Journal of Intercultural Relations* 22:163–186.

Gudykunst, W., G. Gao, K. Schmidt, T. Nishida, M. Bond, K. Leung, G. Wang, and R. Barraclough. 1992. The influence of individualism-collectivism on communication in ingroup and outgroup relationships. *Journal of Cross-Cultural Psychology* 23:196–213.

Hofstede, G. 1991. *Cultures and organizations: Software of the mind.* London: McGraw-Hill.

Johannessen, R. L. 2002. *Ethics in human communication*, 5th ed. Prospect Heights, IL: Waveland Press.

Murphy, J. J. 1983. The age of codification: Hermagoras and the pseudo-Ciceronian. In J. J. Murphy, ed., *A synoptic history of classical rhetoric* (pp. 77–89). New York: Random House.

National Association of Urban Debate Leagues. 27 Oct 2004. Impact of debate. Available at www.urbandebate.org/impact.

Ochs, D. J. 1983. Cicero's rhetorical theory. In J. J. Murphy, ed., *A synoptic history of classical rhetoric* (pp. 90–150). New York: Random House.

Ross, Sherwood. 3 June 2002. College debaters get head start on exec track. Reuters.

Rybold, G. Feb. 2001. Teaching public speaking to university students in the People's Republic of China. Paper presented at the Western States Communication Association Convention, Coeurd'Alene, Idaho.

Rybold, G. Feb. 2004. Expanding inclusiveness through international debate: International Debate Education Association training in the People's Republic of China. Paper presented at the Western States Communication Association Convention, Albuquerque, New Mexico.

Tannen, D. 2006. The roots of debate in education and the hope of dialogue. In J. Stewart, ed. *Bridges not walls: A book about interpersonal communication* (pp. 592–597). New York, NY: McGraw-Hill.

Triandis, H. 1995. *Individualism-collectivism*. Boulder, CO: Westview.

Yeh, J., and L. Chen, 2004. Cultural values and argumentative orientations for Chinese people in Taiwan, Hong Kong, and mainland China. In F. Jandt, ed., *Intercultural communication: A global reader* (pp. 51–64). Thousand Oaks, CA: Sage Publications.

Ziegelmueller, G., J. Kay, and C. Dause. 1990. *Argumentation: Inquiry and advocacy*, 2nd ed. Englewood Cliffs, NJ: Prentice Hall.

Steven Woods, Ph.D. is an associate professor in the Department of Communication and the Director of Forensics at Western Washington University. He teaches communication ethics and has research interests in rhetoric and debate.

Jianglong Wang, Ph.D. is a professor in the Department of Communication at Western Washington University. He teaches courses in intercultural and interpersonal communication, and his research interests include communication across cultures, Chinese American cultures and communication.

The Use of Topoi in Contemporary Debate[*]

Benjamin K. Sovacool

The ideas of economists and political philosophers, both when they are right and when they are wrong, are more powerful than is commonly understood. Indeed, the world is ruled by little else. I am sure that the power of vested interests is vastly exaggerated compared to the gradual encroachment of ideas.

—John Maynard Keynes

INTRODUCTION

It is often said that a proper investigation of history strengthens the understanding of any subject. When it comes to studying rhetoric, Aristotle laid the foundations of the discipline. Aristotle believed that speakers needed to understand themselves, their audience and its emotions, and the material itself to present arguments—in any rhetorical event—logically and convincingly. He defined rhetoric as "the faculty of discovering ... the available means of persuasion" (Wilson & Arnold 1969, 43). Aristotle suggested that this function belonged to no other art, and developed the *topoi*—often referred to as lines of argument or *loci*—as a systematic tool to aid rhetors in inventing their arguments.

The concept of universal lines of argument, or the notion that every audience reasons similarly, holds great promise to rhetoricians, communication scholars, and debate coaches. The concept suggests the existence of a rhetorical mechanism that functions independent of culture, discipline, and context. The discussion about topoi, despite their classical origins, is connected to a diverse and important set of modern rhetorical practices: preparation, adaptation,

[*]The Manuscript is derived from the author's graduate thesis at Wayne State University, which was directed by Dr. George Ziegelmueller.

invention, framing arguments, logical thinking, and refutation. Despite their potential value, however, modern rhetorical scholars have largely ignored or dismissed the concept.

While there is a considerable body of literature about the classical foundations of topoi, there is very little relating it to contemporary rhetorical practice. The works of Aristotle, Cicero, Quintilian, Francis Bacon, and Saint Augustine provide the foundation of the concept, but these ancient rhetoricians were obviously unaware of contemporary academic debate. Corbett (1965) suggests that the topoi are useful for teaching students about evaluating arguments, but never assesses if they are actually being used. Perelman and Olbrechts-Tyteca (1969) spend a considerable amount of time discussing lines of argument under their heading *loci*, but do not evaluate the extent that modern rhetoricians engage the concept. Wilson and Arnold (1969) develop different "lines of thought" in their argumentation textbook, but never distinguish between the different types of topoi. Wallace (1972) suggests that topoi may be useful in building political and ethical arguments, but never provides any examples of them. Vancil (1979) argues that topical systems are no longer relevant to contemporary rhetoric because of major changes in the function of logic resulting from Locke and Hume, and goes so far to suggest that the topoi are "untenable" for the modern age.

Furthermore, in his introduction to *Rhetoric*, Arnhart (1981) comments that the topoi are based on inferential reasoning—and thus illogical—and presented in an incoherent style. Barilli (1989) theorizes that the topoi are only "quasi-logical," that none of the topoi are "decisive or necessary," and that "the topoi serve little use in modern rhetoric, and it would do scholars well to look at other parts of rhetoric more useful" (333–334). And Zompetti (2000) agrees that the topoi have the potential to be a very important concept for modern debate coaches, but concludes that despite such promise they are not used by many practitioners.

The narrow approach taken by many of these works is unfortunate as understanding the role that topoi may play in contemporary collegiate debate can contribute to the more effective teaching of debate, and this, in turn, can result in better prepared and more effective public advocates. Because many students and teachers of debate come to the activity with little or no background in either argumentation or rhetorical theory, the focus of instruction and learning is often upon the specific substantive content of the topic being debated rather than on the more universal concepts of rhetorical invention. A broader conceptual awareness of the universal elements within the debating experience can make the learning easier and more permanent. The topoi offer the possibility of strengthening advocates' abilities to discover and develop arguments (Sovacool 2003). If debaters simply learn the substantive content of arguments on a specific topic they may not be able to generate arguments that are relevant to different topics. The topoi would seem to provide a conceptual basis for teaching less content dependent ways of arguing.

This discussion seeks to explore the relationship between the concept and elements of topoi and the teaching of collegiate argumentation and debate. Specifically, it explores the role of topoi in rhetorical and argumentation literature, the extent that students have the opportunity to study concepts related to topoi in argumentation and debate classes, the degree that contemporary college debate coaches are aware of generic tests of the formal aspects of argument, and the extent that contemporary college debate coaches are aware of field specific lines of argument. The paper is structured into four parts: a brief historical sketch of the foundations of topoi, the prevalence of topoi in current argumentation and debate textbooks, the degree that modern debate coaches use the concept, and the conclusions of the study.

THE HISTORICAL FOUNDATIONS OF TOPOI

Rather than trying to create an exhaustive discussion of the historical roots of topoi, this section will focus on the genesis of the concept in Aristotle's *Rhetoric*, Cicero's *Topica*, and Quintilian's *Institutoria Oratoria*. These three works are widely available and are the most frequently and thoroughly studied by rhetorical scholars.

Aristotle conceived of topoi as a "system for guiding intellectual explorations of a creative, rhetorical sort" (Wilson & Arnold 1969, 44). As one translator explained in an introduction to *Rhetoric*:

> To Aristotle *topos* means a place, and with him it is a live metaphor. He thinks of a place in which the hunter will hunt for game. If you wish to hunt rabbits, you go to a place where rabbits are; and so with deer or with pheasants. Each kind of game has its haunt to which you go when you wish to fetch that sort of creature out. And similarly with arguments. (Cooper 1960, 4)

Thus, Aristotle sought common and universal lines of argument that met this requirement, and classified them as topoi. Topoi direct rhetors to places where they can discover ideas to aid in amplifying or strengthening the particular case being argued. Often referred to as "storehouses" of argument, the topoi are the "stock formulas from which arguments can be cast" (Bizzel & Herzberg 2001, xxv). According to Aristotle:

> There are different kinds of argument, and the different kinds must be found in different places. Thus, topoi are places where arguments can be drawn from. They are commonplaces, where one can find universal forms of argument, used by everyone, in every science. (Cooper 1960, 5)

Aristotle discussed three different types of topoi: special topoi, general topoi, and refutative topoi.

Aristotle's special topoi are connected to the three different types of rhetoric: deliberative, epideictic, and forensic. While Aristotle develops special topoi for each of these branches of rhetoric, this project is concerned primarily with the special topoi Aristotle mentions for deliberative speaking. Aristotle suggests that deliberative—or political—speakers aim at "establishing the expediency or the harmfulness of a proposed course of action" (Bizzel & Herzberg 2001, 186). The political orator's domain is the "subjects of public business," and Aristotle classifies five distinct areas that fall under deliberative oratory.

> The main matters on which all men deliberate and on which political speakers make speeches are some five in number: ways and means, war and peace, national defense, imports and exports, and legislation. (Bizzel & Herzberg 2001, 187)

These five categories—ways and means, war and peace, national defense, imports and exports, and legislation—are the topics on which deliberative rhetors need to be prepared to argue and are the topoi of deliberative speaking.

In addition to the special topoi that are relevant to one of the three types of speeches, Aristotle identified general topoi that apply to any subject matter and are common to all speeches. According to Aristotle:

> The general topics, or commonplaces, are regions containing arguments that are common to all branches of knowledge; these are the topics of more and less, of

magnifying and minimizing, of past and future, and of possible and impossible—the four common places in the strict sense. (Cooper 1960, 155)

The topics of more or less deal with quantity, and assess how something is greater or lesser than another. Magnifying and minimizing are concerned with magnitude, or the degree to which something either is or isn't a significant problem. Past and future deal with causality, and question whether a thing has occurred or could potentially occur. Possible and impossible are concerned with probability, and include lines of reasoning that if two things are alike, and one is possible, so is the other. These four "special means" of persuasion belong to all three types of rhetoric. They are common, universal, and general.

The last type of topoi discussed by Aristotle is the refutative topoi. These topoi are concerned with common errors in the language, form, and psychological appeals of arguments. In his *Rhetoric*, Aristotle classified twenty-six different types of refutative "lines of argument," and these lines of argument include different tests of argument, premises, evidence, and language. For example, Aristotle urged orators to use utterances made by an opponent against them, "turning the tables," and the topoi of definition notes that one can re-define ambiguous terms to craft the various senses of the word.

While the discussion about general and refutative topoi in Cicero's *Topica* is almost identical to that of *Rhetoric*, the two differ over the scope of deliberative topoi. Cicero conceived of deliberative speaking more broadly than did Aristotle. Cicero broadened deliberative speaking to include the giving of advice in general, including private advice such as whether someone should marry and what type of life people should live. He clarified:

> Now let us pass on to the rules of deliberation. There are three kinds of things to be sought out; and an equal number to be avoided on the contrary side. There is something that attracts us to itself by its own force, not capturing us by its benefit, but drawing us by its dignity, such as virtue, knowledge, truth. There is something else, however, which is to be sought not because of its own force and nature, but because of its return and utility, such as money. There is furthermore something joined from parts of both these. (Cicero 1995, 201)

For Cicero, then, deliberative speaking involved both *honestra* and *utilia*, speaking about honor and virtue, and speaking about utility. Cicero did not outline a specific set of subtopics, like national defense or legislation, as Aristotle did. Instead, any proposed deliberation dealing with utility or honor was valid for a deliberative speech. Essentially, Cicero widened the arena of deliberative topoi to include virtue, utility, or a combination of the two.

For the most part, Quintilian's views here are identical to Cicero's. Quintilian emphasized honor and utility much in the same way of *Topica*'s treatment. Nevertheless, Quintilian also conceived of deliberative topoi as having a more distinct role. In the *Institutes of Oratory* he wrote:

> Consequently, those who propose to offer advice upon peace, war, troops, public works or revenue must thoroughly acquaint themselves with two things, the resources of the state and the character of its people, so that the method employed in tendering their advice may be based at once on political realities and the nature of their hearers. (Quintilian 1920, 443)

In contrast to Aristotle and Cicero, Quintilian believed that knowledge of state affairs—national defense, legislation, exports and imports—was not enough to be an effective deliberative speaker. Rather, deliberative speakers must also learn to argue about the character and composition of the public. Here, Quintilian included subtopics like expediency, popularity, and practicability as important deliberative topoi, in addition to the political topoi already developed by Aristotle.

Many modern scholars continue to recognize the usefulness of topoi. Perelmen and Olbrechts-Tyteca (1969) begin their discussion of topoi by urging teachers and students to use the concept. They devote many pages of the *New Rhetoric* to a discussion of the loci (topoi) of quantity and quality. Wallace (1972) believed that the topoi help rhetors better communicate arguments to diverse audiences, and he urged speakers to draw from various ethical and political topoi. Wilson and Arnold's (1969) discussion of invention in their introductory public speaking text begins with a comprehensive and systematic presentation of the topoi, which they reclassify in an attempt to make them clearer to modern students. Corbett (1965) took a similar approach in his work and emphasized the importance of topoi in inventing arguments when students have little or nothing to say.

THE PREVALENCE OF TOPOI IN MODERN ARGUMENTATION AND DEBATE TEXTBOOKS

Locating topoi within historical and academic literature does little to indicate whether the concept is being taught in argumentation and debate classes. What is often presented in journals and advanced books on rhetorical theory assumes an already developed understanding of foundational topics. For these reasons, basic argumentation and debate textbooks provide a better indication of whether the concepts of topoi are currently available to undergraduate students. An examination of the most popular texts should provide some insight into what elements of the argument process contemporary authors and teachers consider important for students to know and be able to use.

In a recent issue of *Argument & Advocacy* John Tindell (1999) selected and reviewed the twelve most recent argumentation and debate texts available at that time: *Logical Self Defense; A Practical Study of Argument; Argumentation: Understanding and Shaping Arguments; Logic and Contemporary Rhetoric; Patterns of Inductive Reasoning; Argumentation and Critical Decision Making; Argumentation and Debate; The Art and Practice of Argumentation and Debate; Strategic Debate; Critical Thinking and Communication; Advocacy and Opposition;* and *Argumentation: Inquiry and Advocacy.* His list of texts seems to provide a representative sample and is the one examined for the purposes of this study. When searching for topoi within these texts, three questions were asked. First, did the texts provide any direct references to topoi, topos, loci, or commonplaces? Second, did the texts mention invention, systems of topical invention, methods of refutation, argument fallacies, tests of evidence, tests of data, forms of argument, and fallacies and stratagems? Third, did the texts mention any of the special topoi or loci relating to deliberative, epideictic, or forensic speaking?

The examination of the twelve textbooks revealed that each provides different coverage, context, depth, focus, and terminology in their references to topoi. For example, Ziegelmueller and Kay (1997) classify the forms of argument according to deductive and inductive reasoning; others, like Freeley (1996), frame the discussion without this distinction; and some texts—like Johnson and Blair (1994)—do not mention the forms of argument at all. Similar inconsistencies also appear in the twelve texts' treatment of argument fallacies, methods of refutation, tests of evidence, tests of data, loci, special topoi, and general topoi. Thus, summarizing these various viewpoints into one concise, comprehensive list is difficult. Still, the texts' discussion of topoi can be classified into five categories: tests of argument, tests of data, refutative topoi, general topoi, and special topoi.

The first type of topoi identified are the tests of argument, also called "forms of argument," "methods of evaluating argument," and "techniques for analyzing arguments." While many of the texts, like Rybacki and Rybacki (1998), discuss the various forms of argument, they do not develop ways to test these forms of argument. These tests are discussed by three different authors. Moore and Moore (1998) note that argument by analogy can be tested for clarity, truth, relevance, and consistency; argument by causal correlation can be tested for sample size, randomness, specificity of the conclusion, and omission of evidence; and hypothetical arguments can be tested for their deducibility, testability, connectedness, simplicity, and explanatory power. Freeley (1996) identifies a number of the same forms of argument, but discusses how to test them in a different way. Freeley notes that all forms of argument can be tested for their cogency; arguments by example can be tested for relevance, quantity, time period, typicality, and non-critical negative examples; arguments by analogy can be tested for significant points of similarity, if those points are critical to the comparison, if the points of difference are non-critical, if the reasoning is cumulative, and if only literal analogies are used as logical proof; causal arguments can be tested for their sufficiency, undesirable effects, counteracting causes, capability, and necessity; and arguments by sign can be tested for their relevancy, inherent relationship, disruptive counterfactor, and cumulative reasoning. Finally, Ziegelmueller and Kay (1997) note that argument by example can be tested for typicality, negative instances, and sufficiency; argument by analogy can be tested for similarity and accuracy; argument by causal correlation can be tested for consistency, strength, time sequence, and coherence; argument by causal generalization can be tested for intervening factors, sufficiency, and other unspecified effects; and argument by sign can be tested for invariable indicators, sufficiency, and contradictions.

Similarly, the second type of topoi discussed—tests of data—are categorized differently by each text. Ziegelmueller and Kay (1997) note that there are general tests of data that apply to all forms of data and evaluate internal consistency, external consistency, and relevancy. Others develop their tests of data with respect to premises and evidence. Ziegelmueller and Kay and Freeley emphasize the tests of premises, also called tests of perceptual or value premises. These tests are concerned with validity, soundness, truth, clarity, utility, sufficiency, acceptability, and reliability. The most comprehensive techniques—discussed by over ten of the textbooks—are concerned with the tests of evidence. These are looking for: accuracy, reliability/competency/ reliability, consistency, timeliness/recency, context, precision/clarity, relevance, accessibility/verifiability, bias, sufficiency, cumulative strength, critical ability, representativeness, and the statistical tests of sampling, time period, and comparable units.

The most difficult type of topoi to summarize is the refutative topoi, also called the argument fallacies. The twelve texts create an amazing list of over forty refutative topoi. Each author categorizes these topoi very differently. In many instances, the authors may use similar names for different fallacies— hasty generalization is identified as occurring when the premises do not support the conclusion, possible or contrary evidence may exist, the premises are not sufficient to support the conclusion, and or the argument makes a generalization from too small a sample. Likewise, many authors use different labels for the same fallacy. "Begging the question" is identified as begging the question, circular reasoning, the problematic premise, arguing in a circle, and creating a non-falsifiable syllogism. Ad hominem attacks are called ad hominem, "attacking the man," guilt by association, poisoning the well, tu quoque, and the generic fallacy. Composition and division are mentioned together, separate, and sometimes not at all.

Nonetheless, once these discrepancies are consolidated, the following separate refutative topoi remain: begging the question, straw argument, ad hominem, appeals to authority, ad populum, appeals to tradition, appeals to newness, appeals to ignorance, appeals to personal interest, appeals to fear, appeals to humor, appeals to the emotions, red herring (including majoring on minors), two wrongs, faulty analogy (false consolation), questionable cause (including the backwards, coincidence, and common cause fallacies), ambiguity (including vagueness and equivocation), slippery slope (reductio ad absurdum), emotionally charged language, post hoc ergo propter hoc, composition, division, false dilemma, false standards (fallacy of extension), is/ought fallacy, fallacy of continuum, exaggeration, ridicule, arrangement, paralepsis, and technical jargon.

The texts discuss ten different types of general topoi. These are general techniques that rhetors can use in any speech regardless of its topic. They are: minimization, maximization, exposing inconsistencies, reducing to absurdity, denying a problem exists, identifying irrelevancies, establishing dilemmas, turning the tables, assessing probabilities, and defining time frames. Moreover, five types of special topoi are identified for use in deliberative situations. These are the loci of quantity, loci of quality, loci of essence (including the genetic, intent, function, and personal act loci), pragmatic arguments, and argument from principle.

When added up, there are more than fifty different types of topoi discussed in the twelve textbooks. Every text referenced at least some topoi, with a majority of texts discussing the concept in a systematic and comprehensive manner. It is important to note that the difference in how each text approached the topoi is related to the educational backgrounds of the authors. For instance, those with an academic focus in logic or philosophy tended to emphasize the argument fallacies and tests of argument. Those with an academic focus in argument placed more emphasis on the tests of evidence. And those with an academic focus in communication and debate tended to provide a more balanced emphasis of tests of argument and evidence, yet are the only ones to elaborate on the special and general topoi. However, while the approach each text takes may be different, this demonstrates that the topoi are still very much alive among the professors of communication, logic, philosophy, rhetoric, and argument who write introductory texts in argumentation and debate.

THE DEGREE TO WHICH MODERN DEBATE COACHES ENGAGE THE CONCEPT OF TOPOI

In order to determine whether the topoi are taught and practiced by modern debate coaches, this project also distributed an argument survey to college debates coaches at local, regional, and national debate institutes and emailed a copy of the survey to each of the directors of debate programs registered with the Cross Examination Debate Association (CEDA) and the National Debate Tournament (NDT). The survey asked a series of closed questions about the background and experience of the respondents and the nature of their programs and five open-ended questions about generic arguments and techniques they use. A total of fifty-one surveys were passed out manually, and 212 were emailed to coaches on the CEDA/NDT roster. A total of fifty-eight surveys, twenty-seven percent, were returned. Because there is a considerable overlapping membership between NDT and CEDA and because most of the coaches working at the summer debate institutes where the surveys were distributed are also members of NDT and/or CEDA, the percentage of surveys returned undoubtedly understates by a considerable margin the actual percentage of policy debate coaches who responded to the survey.

The first half of the survey asked demographic questions for comparative and interpretive purposes. The background questions asked were concerned with the respondents' major area of study, the experience level of the students entering the respondents' programs, classes in argumentation taken or taught by the respondents, classes in logic taken or taught by the respondents, and classes taken or taught by the respondents in both argumentation and logic. The second half of the survey sought to discover what topoi coaches were aware of and taught to their students. Five open-ended questions were asked. The first question was concerned with general and refutative topoi, and asked what generic techniques of refutation the respondents taught their students. The second question dealt with special topoi, or those specific to policy debate as a whole and asked what major, substantive lines of argument the respondents expected to find on any given policy debate topics. The final three questions were concerned with field specific topoi, and asked what major, substantive lines of argument the respondents expected in legal, foreign policy, and environmental topics. Open-ended questions were used in order to avoid suggesting topoi to the respondents.

The results of the survey as a whole are interesting because they reveal emerging trends in the debate community regarding argumentation and provide a broad list of many different lines of argument that one can expect to hear in policy debates. However, the survey also sought to explore any difference in responses between those trained in communication, argumentation, and logic, and those who were not. Thus, the results of the survey were correlated with the background questions concerning the training, academic focus, and experience levels of the respondents.

In examining the demographic backgrounds of the fifty-eight respondents, the majority can be clustered into two main categories: those with debate experience and an academic training in debate, argument, and logic, and those with moderate debate experience yet with no specific classroom training in argument and/or logic. The information did reveal a number of other mixed groups, but these categories were very small, and their responses were not significantly different. The first category of respondents were twenty-three people who had been communication majors, had taken or taught courses both in argumentation and logic, and had considered their programs to be those that recruited debaters with significant experience. In contrast to this group, the second category included thirteen people who had not been communication majors, considered themselves moderately experienced, but had received no formal training in argumentation and/or logic.

There was little significant difference in the results between the two groups regarding topic specific topoi. For instance, concerning the common lines of argument on an environmental topic, those formally trained in communication and argumentation listed arguments about economics, climate, politics, environmental critiques, and species extinction as their top five; those without a formal training listed economics, politics, regulatory effectiveness, species extinction, and international modeling. A comparison of the results from the second question concerned with legal topoi revealed a similar trend. The top five topoi listed for those with a communication and argumentation focus were critical legal studies, feminism, questions of legal process, politics, and critical race theory. The top five for those without communication and argumentation training were critical legal studies, social movements, politics, discrimination, and questions of legal process. In some instances, the results were identical. The top five topoi reported by those with communication and argument training for a foreign policy debate topic were United States hegemony, international relations, politics, economics, and international counterplans (alternative proposals advocated by the opposing team); the top five for those without communication and argument backgrounds were hegemony, politics, international relations, economics, and international counterplans.

Concerning topoi specific to policy debate as a whole, there was little substantial difference as well. The top five listed for those with communication and argumentation training were politics, counterplans, critiques, spending disadvantage, and economics; those without communication and argumentation training listed politics, counterplans, procedural arguments, economics, and solvency arguments. It might be expected that the topic specific topoi and topoi specific to policy debate would be the same for both types of coaches because both are professionally engaged in researching and debating specific policy debate resolutions. It could follow from this, then, that it is the refutative topoi that would have the greatest chance of disparity in responses between the two groups because knowledge of the refutative topoi is more closely linked with formal communication training. However, this was not the case. While it was true that the communication-trained coaches were able to list more topoi quantitatively, this group had more respondents. Proportionally, the results are almost identical. The top five techniques those with communication and argument educations emphasized when working with students were the fallacies, tests of evidence, comparison, pointing out contradictions, and turning the tables. Those without communication and argument training emphasized looking for inconsistencies, the fallacies, tests of evidence, comparison, and turning the tables.

These results indicate that the special topoi are widely used and practiced in policy debate. While they differ for each resolution, coaches frequently use many different types of special topoi. Regarding an environmental topic, the respondents identified twenty-seven different environment specific topoi. The most frequently mentioned environment specific topoi were concerned with politics and economics, and the most referenced type of topoi on an environmental topic was disadvantages. Regarding a legal topic, thirty-six different legal specific topoi were identified. The single most frequently mentioned legal topoi was critical legal studies, and the most common type of topoi on a legal topic was critiques. Regarding a foreign policy topic, twenty-nine different foreign policy specific topoi were identified. The two most frequently identified foreign policy specific topoi concerned Unites States hegemony and international reactions, and the most common type of foreign policy specific topoi was disadvantages. The respondents identified twenty-two different policy debate specific topoi, which coaches expected to find in any debate regardless of a specific topic. The most frequently mentioned policy debate specific topoi were concerned with politics and counterplans, and the most common type of policy debate specific topoi was disadvantages.

It is interesting to note that the coaches were generally able to list a greater quantity of topic specific topoi, and that their responses were less detailed regarding the general and refutative topoi. For instance, close to thirty different topic specific topoi were listed for legal and environmental topics. In contrast, only ten types of refutative and general topoi were mentioned. Moreover, not a single coach identified any tests for premises or the different forms of argument—example, analogy, cause, sign. The results also indicate that these topoi were used and practiced regardless of formal training in communication, logic, or argument. There was little significant difference between the responses for coaches who have taken, taught, and learned communication classes and those who have little to no experience in communication at all.

Conclusions

The above discussion reveals five interconnected conclusions. First, topoi continue to be a relevant and respected concept in the literature of argument and rhetoric. The genesis of topoi began with Aristotle, who provided a comprehensive and systematic approach to the topoi in his *Rhetoric*. It is here that we find Aristotle's three types of topoi: special topoi, which are particularized to the three types of rhetoric; general topoi, which are useful regardless of a particular topic; and refutative topoi, which provide useful tests of argument, evidence, and language. These concepts were further developed by Cicero, who expanded Aristotle's notion of the special topoi for deliberative speaking to include all things relating to utility and virtue. Quintilian emphasized the importance of public character and composition in the construction of the special topoi for deliberative speaking.

In contemporary times, Vancil has argued that the topoi are completely useless for the modern age. He noted that logic has fundamentally changed since classical times, and that these changes in logic make topical systems of invention—because he believes they are based on logic—untenable and insignificant for contemporary rhetoric. Others also have expressed concern about particular aspects of the theory of topoi or its application. Larry Arnhart, a translator of *Rhetoric*, critiqued both the substance and the presentation of the topoi Aristotle provided Barilli, another translator, believed that the topoi were unnecessary and unimportant for modern students.

However, Vancil's claim that the topoi are useless in the modern age is simply wrong because it is based upon the faulty assumption that all topical systems rely upon an outmoded concept of logic. Aristotle's special topoi, for example, are based upon the three kinds of rhetoric, not formal logic, and the general topoi are totally unrelated to any logical system. Furthermore, many of Aristotle's refutative topoi identify errors in the way language, rather than logic, is used. Even the overwhelming majority of the topoi that are related to reasoning and analysis concern errors in what, today, would be referred to as inductive reasoning rather than strictly syllogistic reasoning. Additionally, Vancil's criticism ignores the newer systems of topoi offered by Wallace, Perelmen and Olbrechts, Tyteca, Corbett, Wilson and Arnold, and others. All of these contemporary systems suggest that topoi are based upon more than just logic, and can be connected to values, commonplaces, language, and non-syllogistic forms of reasoning. Finally, Vancil's and

Barilli's claims that the topoi are unnecessary and unimportant are denied both by the extensive treatment given to topoi in contemporary argument and debate textbooks and by the coaches' survey.

Second, how thoroughly contemporary students come to know the topoi in their argumentation and debate classes depend upon the specific textbooks used. An analysis of twelve contemporary argumentation and debate textbooks revealed over fifty different types of topoi available to students. While different texts placed varied emphasis on the topoi, every text examined discussed at least some topoi, with many providing a comprehensive and systematic approach. However, because the texts placed particular focus on balancing argumentation theory and debate, no two books were alike in their discussion of topoi.

The two texts that provide the most thorough, clearest, deepest coverage of the topoi were Ziegelmueller and Kay's (1997) *Argumentation: Inquiry and Advocacy* and Herrick's (1995) *Understanding and Shaping Arguments*. Herrick's text is the only one to discuss the tests of the forms of argument, tests of data (premises and evidence), the refutative topoi (argument fallacies), and special topoi for deliberative speaking (loci of quality and quantity). Ziegelmueller and Kay do not mention any of the special topoi, but provide the most comprehensive list of the tests of the forms of argument as well as systematic discussions of tests of evidence and premises, refutative topoi, and a few of Aristotle's commonplaces (comparison, minimization/maximization). Other texts more narrow in their approach still provide students with reasonably thorough discussions of the topoi. Johnson and Blair's (1994) *Logical Self-Defense* discusses tests of premises and evidence and provides the most developed coverage of the argument fallacies—over two hundred pages—but never mentions the different tests of argument, general, or special topoi. In contrast, Freeley's (1996) *Argumentation and Debate* spends a great deal of time emphasizing the tests of the forms of argument and tests of evidence, but never mentions any special or general topoi. The text that provided the least comprehensive list of topoi was Moore and Moore's (1998) *Patterns of Inductive Reasoning*. While this text did focus on some, not all, of the tests of the forms of argument, it listed the least number of refutative topoi and never mentioned the different tests of evidence and premises, special topoi, or general topoi.

The twelve textbooks discussed do fall into three categories: those emphasizing critical thinking and argument, those emphasizing academic debate, and those that provide a more balanced emphasis. The results from this project seem to indicate that those emphasizing critical thinking and argument place greater emphasis on the argument fallacies and tests of premises. This explains Johnson and Blair's (1994) intense focus on evaluating premises and the refutative topoi. The authors of introductory argument and debate texts that provide a more balanced emphasis tend to emphasize a balance of fallacies and tests of data with tests of argument, general topoi, and special topoi. This tends to be the case with Ziegelmueller and Kay's (1997) text. And the authors that emphasize academic debate, like Freeley (1996), tend to emphasize the tests of argument and evidence with a less developed focus on fallacies and tests of premises than those trained in logic. While each type of author discussed some of the topoi, they did so with different emphases, contexts, and depth. These differences in emphasis seem to be a result of the different backgrounds of the authors and the different audiences for whom their works are directed. It is important to note that even though these scholars come from very different fields of study, all continue to find the topoi useful.

Third, college debate coaches appear to have a reasonable awareness of the generic tests of the formal aspects of argument. The research survey distributed to debate coaches revealed that that the coaches were aware of numerous generic tests of the formal aspects of argument. Every respondent named at least one type of general topoi or refutative topoi, although the coaches provided fewer of these topoi than they did special topoi. The open-ended nature of the research question did not allow any judgment regarding the extent to which the topoi relevant to the more formal aspects of argument were emphasized in the classroom and/or coaching. Refutative topoi were more frequently referred to than were the general topoi. Over half of the respondents mentioned using argument fallacies and various tests of evidence when instructing students, and a significant number of coaches also referred to contradictions, comparison, turning the tables, and ridiculing an opponent's argument. A smaller number of coaches referred to some of the general topoi. Minimization, maximization, and comparison were the only general topoi noted. None of the coaches mentioned any particular tests of argument or tests of premises.

Fourth, college coaches were strongly aware of field specific lines of argument. Here, the respondents to the survey identified more than one hundred and fifty different types of field specific lines of argument. These special topoi were divided into two types: those specific to policy debate as a whole, and those specific to the particular topics of environmental, legal, and foreign policy. When asked about topoi specific to policy debate as a whole, coaches' identified over twenty different lines of argument. The most frequently mentioned responses were concerned with assessing the political implications of a policy action, finding alternative solutions to a proposal, and evaluating the economic implications of a proposed plan. When asked about topic specific lines of argument for environmental, legal, and foreign policy topics, the coaches listed more than one hundred different topoi. The most common responses for environmental topoi dealt with economics and politics; the most common legal topoi were concerned with critical legal studies and legal process; and the most common foreign policy topoi addressed United States hegemony and the effect of U.S. foreign policy on other countries. These results tend to reveal that classical rhetoric is still an important tool for modern speakers, and that debate coaches are more aware of topic specific topoi than they are of general and refutative topoi.

The coaches' approach to the general and refutative topoi was much less systematic and comprehensive than that found in argumentation and debate textbooks. However, the coaches provided more comprehensive lists of special topoi for generic deliberative situations as well as longer lists of special topoi for the environment, law, and foreign policy. The only textbook to focus on special topoi at all was Herrick's (1995), and it limited its discussion to the loci of quantity, quality, argument from pragmatics, and argument from principle. In contrast, the coaches only referred to a few of the general topoi, and never mentioned tests of the forms of argument or tests for premises. This suggests that many debate coaches' training in argumentation and rhetoric is not as deep or broad as might be expected and that many students' debate training may be more relevant to public policy than to argumentation. In addition, these findings reinforce the relevance of field variant and field invariant approaches to argument. While the field invariant topoi of argument are more universally applicable, they may also require special training and awareness. Field variant topoi, on the other hand, may be "picked up" naturally and easily by those working within a particular field.

Fifth, despite the differences in the type of topoi taught, the survey supports the overall conclusion that classical concepts of topoi are still important to the modern age. The topoi developed by Aristotle, Cicero, and Quintilian occupy a large part of the topoi used by modern debaters. Aristotle's general topoi—especially minimization, maximization, and comparison—are emphasized by coaches when working with students. Moreover, Aristotle's five categories of special topoi for deliberative speaking (war and peace, ways and means, imports and exports, legislation, and methods of defense) are almost identical to some of the topic specific lines of argument used by modern policy debate coaches (international relations, cost, economics, politics, and military readiness). These findings seem to prove that classical rhetoric can still serve as an important guide for modern students.

This project has not claimed to be exhaustive, and much work regarding topoi and modern argumentation and rhetoric still needs to be done. Because the topoi consist of such a large part of debate practice and argumentation and rhetoric theory, a more focused study concerned with coaches as well as debaters and students could be useful. Additionally, more exploration regarding the extent that general and refutative topoi are taught in argumentation and debate classes and practiced by debate coaches would provide a deeper understanding of different methods of critical thinking available to students. And if one accepts that the notion that common, universal lines of argument can resonate with all audiences, a project attempting to locate them in other areas outside of policy debate like law, politics, and science would be useful because these are forums that go beyond the mere simulation of debate and into the real creation of policy.

Regardless, this project has demonstrated that the lessons of classical rhetoric strongly resonate within the modern argumentation and debate field. Zompetti's (2000) claim that the topoi should be used more by debate coaches is well supported. Because the topoi are so widely used in both argument and debate theory and practice, they can serve as an indispensable guide in the identification and construction of arguments. They can help students locate arguments within vast amounts of literature, and notice arguments they might otherwise miss. Because topoi are the places from which arguments can be built, they can help students in constructing and refuting arguments. The topoi can also assist in the development of critical thinking skills because they help students understand what makes a well informed and thought out argument. And since the topoi offer an easy approach to argument identification and construction, they are the building blocks to more advanced debate theory. The rich heritage of Aristotle, Cicero, and Quintilian leave many treasures for modern rhetors, and while the Greek and Latin terminology largely remain lost, the concepts remain widely used in both modern theory and practice.

BIBLIOGRAPHY

Arnhart, L. (1981). Aristotle on political reasoning: A commentary on the rhetoric. DeKalb: Northern Illinois University Press.

Barilli, R. (1989). Rhetoric. Minneapolis: University of Minnesota Press.

Bizzell, P., and B. Herzberg. (2001). The rhetorical tradition: Readings from classical times to the present, 2nd ed. New York: Bedford.

Cicero, M. T. (1962). De inventione (H. M. Hubbell, Trans.). New York: Loeb. (Original work published unknown.)

Cicero, M. T. (1995). Cicero on the genres of rhetoric (J. F. Tinkler, Trans.). Baltimore: Towson University Press.

Clarke, M. L. (1968). The Roman mind. New York: Norton.

Cooper, L. (1960). The rhetoric of Aristotle. New York: Appleton.

Corbett, E. P. J. (1965). Classical rhetoric for the modern student. Oxford: Oxford University Press.

Covino, W. A., and D. A. Joliffe. (1995). Rhetoric. Boston: Allyn & Bacon.

Freeley, A. J. (1996). Argumentation and debate: Critical thinking for reasoned decision making. Belmont, CA: Wadsworth Publishing.

Golden, J. L., and B. Goodwin. (1983). The rhetoric of Western thought (3rd ed.). Dubuque, IA: Kendall Hunt Publishing.

Govier, T. (1997). A practical study of argument, 4th ed. Belmont, CA: Wadsworth Publishing.

Herrick, J. A. (1995). Argumentation: Understanding and shaping arguments. Boston: Allyn & Bacon.

Hill, B., and R. W. Leeman. (1997). The art and practice of argumentation and debate. Mountain View, CA: Mayfield Publishing.

Hiz, H. (1967). Cicero. In P. Edwards (Ed.), The encyclopedia of philosophy. New York: Macmillan.

Inch, E. S., and B. Warnick. (1998). Critical thinking and communication: The use of reason in argument. Needham Heights, MA: Allyn & Bacon.

Johnson, R. H., and J. A. Blair. (1994). Logical self-defense. New York: McGraw-Hill.

Kahane, H., and N. Cavander. (1998). Logic and contemporary rhetoric: The use of reason in everyday life. Belmont, CA: Wadsworth Publishing.

Kennedy, G. A. (1991). Aristotle on rhetoric: A theory of civil discourse. New York: Oxford University Press.

Lawson-Tancred, H. C. (1991). Aristotle: The art of rhetoric. New York: Penguin Books.

Marty, M. E. (1996). Unsecular media: Making news of religion in America. The Christian Century, 2, 223–240.

McKeon, R. (1987). Rhetoric: Essays in invention and discovery. Woodbridge, CT: Ox Bow Press.

Moore, K. D., and E. Moore. (1998). Patterns of inductive reasoning: Developing critical thinking skills. Dubuque, IA: Kendall Hunt Publishing.

Perelmen, Ch., and L. Olbrechts-Tyteca. (1969). The new rhetoric: A treatise on argumentation. South Bend, IN: University of Notre Dame Press.

Prelli, L. J. (1989). A rhetoric of science: Inventing scientific discourse. Columbia: University of South Carolina Press.

Quintilian, M. B. (1920). The institutes of oratory (H. E. Butler, Trans.). Cambridge: Harvard University Press.

Rieke, R. D., and M. O. Sillars (1997). Argumentation and critical decision making. New York: Longman.

Rolfe, M. (1932). Cicero and his influence. New York: Longmans, Green, & Co.

Rybacki, K. C., and D. J. Rybacki. (1998). Advocacy and opposition: An introduction to argumentation. Boston: Allyn & Bacon.

Sovacool, B. K. (2003). The use of topoi in contemporary debate. Master's Thesis, Wayne State University, Detroit, MI.

Tindell, J. H. (1999). Argumentation and debate textbooks: An overview of content and focus. Argumentation and Advocacy: The Journal of the American Forensic Association, 35, 185–191.

Vancil, D. (1979). Historical barriers to a modern system of topoi. Western Journal of Speech Communication, 43, 26–37.

Wallace, K. R. (1972). The substance of rhetoric: Good reasons. Contemporary rhetoric: A reader's coursebook. In D. Ehninger (Ed.), Iowa City: University of Iowa Press.

Wilson, J. F., and C. C. Arnold. (1969). Public speaking as a liberal art, 2nd ed. Boston: Allyn & Bacon.

Wood, R. V., and L. Goodnight. (1995). Strategic debate. Lincolnwood, IL: National Textbook Company.

Ziegelmueller, G. W., and J. Kay. (1997). Argumentation: Inquiry and advocacy. Boston: Allyn & Bacon.

Zompetti, J. P. (2000). Revisiting topoi: Their use for contemporary argumentation and debate. Proceedings of the 1st Tokyo Conference on Argumentation. Tokyo: Japan Debate Association.

Benjamin K. Sovacool is a postdoctoral fellow at the Centre for Asia and Globalisation at the Lee Kuan Yew School of Public Policy at the National University of Singapore. He previously taught in the Government and International Affairs Program at the Virginia Polytechnic Institute and State University in Blacksburg, VA. He holds a Ph.D. in Science and Technology Studies from Virginia Tech.

A Problematic Politics: An Analysis of "Micro-Political" Arguments and Their Pitfalls

Keith J. West

"fiat"—Medieval Latin, from Latin, let it be done, *third person sing. present subjunctive of "fieri,"* to become, to be done.
—www.dictionary.com

An intellectual agreement between the participants in the debate to discuss the issue of "should" rather than "would."
—Dr. Catherine Palczweski

A concept that enables the participants in the debate to role-play the actor(s) in question, enabling them to debate the desirability of action by the actor(s) without sacrifice of personal integrity.
—Keith West

Academic debate in any format is a constantly evolving activity. It grows, changes, and experiments with various ways of improving itself and its participants. This experimentation is by definition dynamic, involving the actions and ideas of participants and critics alike, and invariably some changes are favored and rewarded over others, often leading to shifts in performance as the participants adapt to their audience—the critics. As such, it is incumbent upon those of us who occupy the community of critics to consider carefully what ideas and behavioral patterns we reward. Likewise it is incumbent upon us to remember that this activity is not ours, it belongs to those who do it—the debaters themselves, and we owe them the respect of hearing them out and allowing their discourse to sway our ballots. In attempting to resolve this dilemma, it is often concluded that the best way to promote positive performance and eschew intervention as much as possible is to make the arguments we find persuasive available to the debaters themselves, and such is the aim of this paper.

This paper will seek to examine the concept of fiat, as it is being used and indicted in contemporary NPDA-style [National Parliamentary Debate Association] American Parliamentary Debate. It will first identify and explain the concept of fiat and the "pre-fiat" and "post-fiat" worlds in NPDA debate. It will next examine the concept of "reflexive fiat" as postulated by Gordon Mitchell, which underlies the concept of micro-politics in NPDA debate. It will finally raise several independent objections to the use of micro-politics in NPDA debate.

FIAT

Much, though not all, of NPDA debate revolves around pragmatic instantiations, of the resolution; often incarnated as "plans." A plan is a specific, circumscribed statement of advocacy for the resolution that (usually) binds the government team to defending that action and only that action. Plans are usually only considered appropriate —or "topical"—if they fall within the scope of the resolution, i.e., they can be subsumed by the resolution in general. It is argued that from an affirmation of a specific instantiation, or case study of the resolution in action, we can induce the truth of the resolution. While the strength of this induction may be at times dubious, the concept of the plan is generally accepted because it is perceived to provide clearer debate and thus more direct clash. For example, under the resolution "The United States should change its foreign policy toward North Korea," any number of potential changes could occur. The plan perspective would suggest that a team identify one of those possible changes and advocate it. For example, "The United States will provide North Korea with two light-water reactors." This plan is but one instantiation of the resolution, but the breadth it takes from the debate is seen as an acceptable sacrifice for the focus and clarity of advocacy it provides.

Once the plan is established by the government (or proposition) team, then the concept of fiat is applied. Fiat may be defined many ways, but a generally agreed upon functional effect is to focus the debate on the desirability of the plan rather than the possibility that it would actually be adopted. For the purposes of the debate we assume that the government represents the body with the power to enact the plan, and the opposition represents the body with the power to defeat it. The critic (or Speaker of the House) is assumed to possess the deciding vote and, based on the persuasive abilities of both sides, chooses to either endorse or reject the plan of action and—by extension—the resolution. Fiat, I would advance, constitutes the decision to enter into this role-playing conception such that the individuals involved no longer represent themselves, but instead the factions of the agent in question, thus insulating them as individuals from the responsibility to make their arguments consistent with their personal beliefs, enabling them to "take the other side" and advance the debate.

PRE-FIAT VS. POST-FIAT

Initially with regards to topicality (an argument that the proposition's plan does not fall within the purview of the resolution) and more recently the rise of critical argumentation (arguments based largely on objections to rhetoric and/or mindsets), the concept of a split between the pre-fiat and the post-fiat worlds has arisen. This concept would contend that while most arguments we make (case arguments, disadvantages, etc.) have weight in the role-playing world of debate, some arguments (critical arguments and, more recently, micro-political arguments) have weight in the "real world." The real world is said to occur before we apply fiat and enter into the role-playing realm. The "pre-fiat world" involves the people in the room as individuals, and perhaps others as well. It is distinct from the "post-fiat world," where the game of debate takes place. Arguments such as criticisms of objectionable rhetoric and/or mindsets are sometimes articulated to claim that "rhetorical violence" has been inflicted upon the individuals present, and that the importance of the judge taking a stand against such violence personally (often via the ballot) trumps any significance of arguments within the post-fiat, or role-playing, world. It may be argued that fiat is merely an illusory concept, and thus the events that can or do occur in the world without fiat are more significant by definition, and thus should be preferred a priori.

The micro-political case attempts to take advantage of the primacy granted to the pre-fiat world by placing its impacts exclusively within this realm. The micro-political case would argue that the individuals present ought to take action rather than engaging the role-playing game. For example, under the resolution previously mentioned, "The United States should change its foreign policy toward North Korea," the following micro-political plan could be offered by the proposition: "If you give us the ballot, my partner and I will write letters to our senators requesting that they provide two light-water reactors to North Korea." In addition to merely speaking for oneself, it is not uncommon for individuals using this strategy to attempt to propose action for all individuals in the round, for example, "Everyone in this room should write letters to their senators urging them to give North Korea two light-water reactors." It is also possible for individuals to propose a micro-political alternative to the proposition's case. For example, in response to a plan that states, "The United States will provide North Korea with two light-water reactors," the opposition could indict the concept of fiat as merely illusory and claim that, if given the ballot, they (the opposition) would go back to their campus and write letters to their senators encouraging them to support the contribution of two light-water reactors to North Korea. They may contend that such action, since it functions in the real world, or pre-fiat world, trumps any advantages the proposition may claim, since their advantage[s] all lie within the imaginary post-fiat world. Often in cases of this type the function of the ballot is transformed from a method of deciding a winner in the round and/or allowing the speaker of the house to decide on which side of the aisle to sit, to instead functioning as a tool of the critic's personal intellectual endorsement. The critic is often asked to use the ballot to endorse a certain team's "movement," or ideology, as opposed to using it to evaluate the outcome of the round.

REFLEXIVE FIAT

In a presentation at the Southern Communication Association conference in 1995, later published in the *Rostrum* in 1998, Gordon Mitchell argues for what he terms "reflexive fiat," or the application of fiat to one's self. Whether the current proponents of micro-political advocacies know it or not, Mitchell's arguments form the foundation of much of what they assume when making micro-political arguments; thus an overview and examination of his arguments seems appropriate.

Mitchell begins with several indictments of the contemporary conception of fiat, each of which merits discussion and review:

> One problem with approaches to fiat which feature such a
> structural separation between advocate and agent of change
> is that such approaches tend to instill political apathy by in-

culcating a spectator mentality. The function of fiat which gives debaters simulated political control over external actors coaxes students to gloss over consideration of their concrete roles as involved agents in the controversies they research. The construct of fiat, in this vein, serves as a political crutch by alleviating the burden of demonstrating a connection between in-round advocacy and the action by external actors defended in plan or counterplan mandates.

A second manner in which the structural features of this sort of fiat tend to circumscribe active political involvement is through the containment of fiat action within the spatio-temporal boundaries of the contest round. The fiction of simulated authority evaporates when the judge issues his/her decision and the debaters disband and head to the next round. Advocacy, resting on the ephemeral foundation of simulation, is here a casual and fleeting phenomenon that carries with it few significant future ramifications or responsibilities. By cultivating an ethic of detachment from the actual polis, this view of advocacy introduces a politically regressive dynamic into the academic debate process. (1998, 12)

It seems that Mitchell raises several troubling arguments here. If academic debate in the United States, in its current form, does indeed fail to energize, or worse yet hinders attempts at social change, then we must indeed consider a change. There do appear to be two areas of difficulty with Mitchell's analysis—the first with his description of the problem and the second with his solution.

Both of Mitchell's indictments seem to underestimate the pervasive nature and power of education, especially given that debate in the United States is situated within the academy. As debaters role-play these external actors, they learn more about the perspectives that help to dictate policy within our governing structures. Beyond that they learn about the problems that plague our world and various solutions to them. Whether they intend it or not, that knowledge will help inform those around them and indirectly energize them toward social action. When a debater contributes to a class or writes a paper based on the knowledge gleaned from participation in academic debate, she or he has acted to assist in the spread of the very thing that helps to tear down oppression—knowledge.

Furthermore, given the fact that debate is but an activity that participants move through, and not the terminal result of their endeavors (by and large), it seems important to consider how the experiences of these people will affect their future. Many debaters go on to careers in law and politics, and the ideas they discuss during their participation in academic debate may well help them to shape the world in the future. Robert C. Chandler and Jeffrey Dale Hobbs's work demonstrates that there is broad consensus among those in the legal, political, and educational fields regarding the benefits of debate for them in pursuing their careers (1991, 5). In many ways these true ends are sidelined when we begin to see the debate round itself as the end as opposed to seeing the debate experience as a means to later development and societal change.

With regards to the solution Mitchell proposes—reflexive fiat—several additional problems arise. Earlier in his paper Mitchell cites the action of a team from Wake Forest in the United States.

> This year, a Wake Forest team advocated a counterplan which promised that they would personally contact human rights NGOs and plead for them to better value and respect Palestinian people and culture. The Wake Forest debaters, Sean Nowak and Armen Nozarabhian, secured a negative ballot in a round against Texas with this counterplan, but have apparently not yet implemented its mandates. (1998, p. 20)

At the time of Mitchell's writing, Wake Forest had yet to contact the NGOs as they had claimed they would. This seems to indicate that the shift to reflexive fiat does not necessarily lead to a shift in individual action and/or societal change. In fact, this situation prompts one to wonder if this shift leads to further pacification by promoting the idea that we *have* taken real action and are thus absolved of our responsibility to act otherwise. At least within the contemporary conception of fiat we are able to step clearly out of the role we have played and we can realize that, with the exception of some education we may have gained or enabled, the real world is still in need of change.

Mitchell anticipates this "hollow promise" objection toward the end of his paper; however, it seems his response is in some ways insufficient. He states the following:

> While this "hollow promise" strategy might pay short term dividends, eventually, lack of follow through could

be presented in future rounds by opponents to downgrade the credibility of reflexive fiat advocacy. Nozarabhian and Nowak from Wake Forest currently face this contingency; having yet to have followed through on their reflexive fiat proposal to contact Middle Eastern NGOs (made at the Kentucky tournament), the credibility of their next attempt at reflexive fiat may be in jeopardy. (1998, 20)

Indeed, it is possible that these individuals could theoretically be called to task for their lack of action, but even if that happens, it does not prevent this strategy from being used successfully the first time, even if it is insincere. Furthermore, it takes particular advantage of smaller or less well traveled teams that may never have encountered these individuals before, or become aware of the promises they have made. If this practice became commonplace, every team would be required to keep an entire file on every pair of debaters in the country in order to effectively counter the practice.

Furthermore, this issue is complicated by its lack of transparency. Many potential promises are largely non-verifiable. If a team offers to go back to their campus and put up flyers and protest about a given issue, how is a team half way across the country (much less any other team) able to verify their compliance? This matter becomes even more troublesome in parliamentary debate, as pre-prepared evidence is not allowed into rounds, making verification all but impossible. It seems that this well-intentioned avenue could quickly and easily be exploited by the unscrupulous for their own competitive gain at the expense of true activism and fairness, not to mention education.

OBJECTIONS

There are two major objections to the micro-political framework beyond the rejoinder presented above that I would like to address. The concerns of fairness and the lack of a mutual constituency both bear independent analysis.

Fairness

The micro-political act is, by definition, premised upon the action of the individual. Furthermore, since it claims implications outside of the game world, it must also rely on implementation not guaranteed by the power of fiat. Indeed the micro-political claim not only declines to utilize fiat, but also often indicts it. Fiat functions, under Catherine Palczweski's interpretation, to focus the debate on the question of "should" rather than "would." Without fiat present, the question of would again becomes relevant. Thus, to address this question the opposition deserves access to information regarding the likelihood that implementation will actually occur. Unfortunately, the only individuals with unfettered access to that information are the members of the proposing team, who have a compelling interest not to accurately divulge that information if it undermines their cause. Thus, we have a situation where the lynchpin of the proposition's case is placed beyond the pale of discussion, inherently disadvantaging the opposition. Furthermore, any attempt to indict the propensity of the proposition to enact their proposal amounts to an ad hominem attack, problematic in its own right.

Additionally, once the government chooses to abrogate the role-playing format of fiat, they force the opposition (if they wish to be able to compete in the "trump-card realm" of the pre-fiat world) to abandon the role-playing environment as well. The key difference here is that while the government can choose the issue and the side they wish to defend and advocate as individuals, the opposition cannot. The distance which the role-play nature of fiat provides has been ripped away, and the opposition is now forced—upon pain of punitive sanction via the loss of the ballot—to personally advocate against views that they themselves may hold. This is analogous to asking an atheist actor who plays a priest on stage to perform a live Catholic Mass. We adopt and argue for positions we do not hold because, like actors, we realize that that while we play the role, it is the synthesis between our viewpoints that the audience receives that truly matters—not the viewpoints themselves. The decision of one team to abrogate the role-playing nature of fiat forces the other to follow suit and risks placing them, as people, on morally untenable ground.

Mutual Constitution

The concept of mutual constitution would say that it is important in any debate for there to be a point of shared concern, and that it is this shared concern that best generates clash. Michael Janas tells us that mutual constitution occurs when "the actor of the resolution is in some way constituted by the teams in the debate; that all parties to the debate help to make up the actor."(1996, 14). This perspective seems quite sound. So long as we have overlapping interests and the capacity to affect—in some way—the actor in question, we all have an equal stake in the debate. However, this is not so in the case of micro-political action. When such action is restricted to only the advocating team, rather than all persons present, it lacks mutual constitution. The opposing team in no way makes up the decision-making body of the proposing team and has no access to shaping the actions that team takes, and likewise no responsibility for those actions. When the proposing team opts to shape the round in this way, they define the opposition out of equal access to, and interest in, the outcome of the debate. It is this very form of exclusion that is most likely to lead to the pacification Mitchell fears. So long as the debate centers around an actor that we all have a stake in and share responsibility for, we understand that our actions can help to lead to the policy changes we propose; however, when individuals are excluded from that responsibility, it becomes much easier to claim that things are not our problems, nor our obligation to mend.

Conclusions

While the contemporary move to micro-political action, founded on Mitchell's concept of reflexive fiat, does illuminate some problematic faults in the reigning paradigm, its solution is insufficient and undesirable. Debating within a micro-political framework is both unfair to one's opponents, and possibly counterproductive to the ends of the movements it seeks to foster. It invites the unprincipled to take advantage of others and, in its own way, fosters the same kind of complacency it seeks to correct. I see no place for micro-political argument—proposition or opposition—within NPDA debate.

References

Chandler, Robert C., and Jeffrey Dale Hobbs. "The Perceived Benefits of Policy Debate Training in Various Professions." *Speaker and Gavel* 28, nos. 1–4 (1991): 4–6.

Janas, Michael. "Give Me Some of That Old Time Religion: Constitutive Agents and the Problems of Fiat." *Speaker and Gavel* 33, nos. 1–4 (1996): 9–20.

Mitchell, Gordon R. "Reflexive Fiat: Incorporating the Outward Activist Turn into Contest Strategy." *Rostrum* 72 (January 1998): 11–20.

Keith West has been involved in academic debate, first as a competitor and then as a coach, for over a decade. He is currently completing a master's degree in communication studies at Texas Tech University.

Chapter 2
Training Young Debaters

Teaching Younger Debaters in Hong Kong: A Program Overview

Sam Greenland

There is a substantial program in Hong Kong to teach debating to junior secondary students. By eliminating many of the technicalities of competitive debating, and building up to full debates via other forms of presentations, these students can readily develop the same skill set as that of older students. These skills also read across very effectively to their performance in other academic areas. This paper details some of the methods used to teach younger students, and explains the approach taken in more detail.

Introduction and Background

The English Schools Foundation (ESF) comprises 17 fee-paying, but partly government-subsidized, schools (5 secondary) in Hong Kong. The ESF is very active in organizing student debating, both in its own schools and in the wider community. Its range of activities includes organizing tournaments, teaching workshops, and coordinating the national debating team. Its activities are open to students from all educational backgrounds at secondary school level, whether they attend international, government, or ESF schools.

Hong Kong has 9 years of compulsory (and free) education. Many students then attend a further 2 years of school, culminating in public examinations. Roughly 40% of those students go on to take Hong Kong's A-level examinations after another 2 years, and, of these, about half will go on to tertiary education. The system is due to change over the next few years, with the post-compulsory cycle becoming a single 3-year program, and with tertiary education beginning a year earlier.

The vast majority of Hong Kong students speak English as a second language (ESL). The majority of government schools use Cantonese as the medium of instruction ("CMI" schools). Approximately 20% of government schools at the upper end of the academic spectrum, if their students have passed the relevant aptitude tests in English, are entitled to become "EMI" schools, using English as the medium of instruction. The government curriculum remains the same in both types of school. ESF schools use English as the medium of instruction and are currently undergoing a switch from the British curriculum to the International Baccalaureate (IB). The various international schools use English and/or other languages and teach a range of national curricula from their home countries or the IB.

DEFINITIONS

For the purposes of this paper, "junior secondary" students are those in their 7th to 10th years of education, who in Hong Kong are usually from ages 11 to 16.

PROGRAM BACKGROUND AND DESCRIPTION

The ESF offers a wide range of debate activities to the students of Hong Kong, as detailed below. All of these activities are open to both junior and senior secondary students. An approximate breakdown of attendance by school type and by age can be found under each heading.

School-Based Activities

The ESF's Debating Officer is available to visit schools to teach debating, either as one-off sessions or as a series of multiple workshops. These either can be extra curricular events or can form part of the English curriculum. A teaching plan has also been developed in one ESF school to teach debating as part of the British Key Stage 3 English curriculum.

Most schools that request single or multiple workshops as part of their English curriculum are government schools. In general, the CMI schools will target their senior secondary classes with such courses, whereas EMI schools tend to use debating for junior students.

One-off extra curricular events are taught in the full range of Hong Kong schools and are usually aimed at junior students irrespective of the language used as the school's medium of instruction, although some government CMI schools will also target their senior students as part of their preparations for the A-level examinations (even though the content being taught is not directly linked to the syllabus).

Teacher Training Events

The ESF offers professional development courses on debating for its own teachers and has also begun to offer these to teachers in government schools. The workshops are aimed at English teachers and are intended to give the teachers tools with which to teach their students basic debating skills, and also to demonstrate to teachers the value of encouraging their students to take up debating. A handbook for teachers on this subject is currently awaiting publication.

All teacher training events to date have been produced for teachers of junior secondary students. The emphasis of the workshops has therefore been on helping teachers to develop their students' generic debating skills, rather than on the competitive aspects of debate.

Open Events

The ESF organizes after-school and weekend debate training courses, open to all Hong Kong students. Some of these are taught courses with a specific curriculum, running for a set number of sessions with the same student body. Others are one-off workshops, which anyone may attend, followed by opportunities to put into practice (in adjudicated debates) the skills covered in the workshop.

Most of the taught courses are attended by junior secondary students from a wide range of schools, with a slight bias toward the EMI government schools. The one-off workshops, on the other hand, are overwhelmingly attended by students from CMI government schools, with a mix of junior and senior students.

PROGRAM OBJECTIVES

Only a small minority of students attending ESF workshops are doing so to prepare for competitive debating. The vast majority come to develop the broader academic and presentation skills that debate teaches, and to improve their oral English ability. In that light, the programs are designed to focus on the first two of these areas—academic and presentation skills—while it is accepted that exposure to debating, and to the kind of English-language environment that it creates, will naturally contribute to the third—oral English ability.

The overall program objectives are therefore to provide as many students as possible with the basic skills needed to participate in a debate, with the expectation that the next steps will then be taken outside the program, in the students' own schools.

These conditions make it easy to accommodate, and to target, junior secondary students. Since the debating topics used at workshops tend to be simple, drawing largely on issues related to school and adolescent life, there are very few knowledge barriers to participation by younger students. Furthermore, the Hong Kong government curriculum does not place much emphasis on developing analytical and reasoning skills, so there is not much of a gap in these areas between junior and secondary students.

The remainder of this paper will focus on the content of the programs aimed at junior secondary audiences, and on some of the practical activities that are used as teaching tools to achieve these objectives.

Debate/Presentation Techniques

We do not focus on any one particular format of debating when we teach beginners. Nor are we trying, particularly with younger students, to focus too heavily on the technical aspects of debating. We do not introduce scoring by adjudicators, or competitive results, until well into the programs. Instead, we focus on individual feedback, improvement, and attainment.

All skills that we teach are equally appropriate to any format of debating, or indeed to most situations of presentation and discussion. The skills listed below are, for the sake of convenience, broken down into the three areas of content, style, and structure (also known as matter, manner, and method).

Content

The primary focus of teaching content to younger debaters is to make them aware of the need for both argument and evidence to support an opinion, and of the relationship between the two.

We begin with the statement of simple arguments, and then work on developing those into substantive reasoning. The model of statement, explana-

, supporting evidence, and consequence works well with this age group, as y can understand and appreciate the different (but equally necessary) role t each element plays in supporting an opinion.

Working on rebuttal skills comes next, again beginning with simple state-ents of counter-argument and moving on to development of rebuttal argu-ents in exactly the same way as a constructive argument.

The comparison of arguments, and the relative strengths and weaknesses f each, is somewhat more advanced and often stretches the ability of younger debaters, since they do not necessarily have the breadth of experience and nowledge to be able to view arguments objectively. However, since the de-ates and discussions usually take place within a peer group of very homog-enous background and experience, this is not always a barrier to development: he same limitations that cause speakers to use juvenile arguments are present in their audience.

We therefore aim to have our junior debaters able to develop arguments into solid debate-worthy content, and to enable them to measure different ar-guments (supporting different opinions) on a comparative scale. This is clearly a highly useful skill in the broader classroom context, let alone in the world beyond the classroom.

Style

Since the vast majority of our junior students are not native speakers, and dif-ferent debate formats have different expectations in terms of rhetoric, humor, and so forth, we do not attempt to train these skills. Instead, we focus exclu-sively on confidence-building and presentation skills, since these are both the most useful areas in a broader academic context and also the basic building blocks for future stylistic development.

Hong Kong government schools have a tendency to teach English in phrase blocks rather than encouraging students to build their own sentences, which tends to result in students who have difficulty with impromptu speaking in any format, even conversation. We therefore emphasize the skills of speaking from notes, rather than fully prepared speeches, and we prioritize the trans-mission of information over linguistic accuracy. This is highly unusual for most of our students and takes some time to develop.

We also work on physical aspects of presentation: body language, eye contact, gesture, and voice control. We avoid the more stylized aspects of public speaking and focus instead on simple, informal confidence-building techniques. This is because progress for many of our students is hampered not by a lack of reasoning ability, but by a lack of confidence when speaking English in public. Empirical evidence shows that it is probably the major limitation for the majority of our students, and thus confidence-building activities require a great deal of attention in order to maximize their potential.

Finally, we work more generally on encouraging students to focus on their audience during a presentation, rather than on their own personal idea of what the presentation should cover or sound like. This appreciation of audience response is again something that is foreign to many of our students, and takes time to develop and to practice.

Structure

Since structure is by nature quite rigid, it is simple to teach the basic rules to even the youngest of our students. We use schematized speech structures to assist them with preparation and confidence. Part of the curriculum development in one ESF school went as far as preparing worksheets for students to write their own speeches, with a basic speech structure already set out for them to use as the grammatical framework for their ideas and with blanks for them to fill in.

Students are encouraged to repeat structure and phrasing from speech to speech, which builds their confidence and removes some of the nervousness that they experience, particular for the non-native speakers. They are also taught to use note cards to help them structure their speeches more effectively.

Once students have progressed to simple debates, we introduce team structure, in particular the team introduction and summary roles. This mirrors speech structure, and most students find it a very straightforward concept. However, we do not attempt to teach the skills of summary speeches beyond the simple basics.

Broader Academic Skills

There s a significant lack of emphasis on critical thinking and logical analysis in the current Hong Kong government curriculum, which is being addressed through changes to the system to come into effect over the next few years. In the meantime, debating is being used in some schools as a means to bridge this gap. These schools, however, tend to focus these benefits on their senior students, as part of their preparation for tertiary education.

In terms of junior students, though, we see plenty of support for this aspect of our programs in applications for the taught extra curricular courses that we run during weekends and school holidays. Most parents tell us that they have enrolled their children with us, or have encouraged them to take up debating, because it fosters in them the skills which are not taught at school, but which the parents see as necessary for their future.

Debating forces participants to develop key academic skills such as research, logic, and critical analysis of information. Because superior knowledge of debating topics confers a distinct advantage in competition, we also find that many of our more driven students develop much more intense individual learning patterns. This can only be of benefit to them in their broader studies.

Through debating, students also have to learn the presentation, listening, and discussion skills that are vital for successful group work. As classroom curricula shift increasingly toward group learning, and assessment covers more diverse forms of presentation and achievement, these skills come increasingly to the fore. We have also found, through empirical feedback, that students who have learned to debate subsequently participate to a greater extent in classroom discussion and are more prepared to ask questions and seek out information from their teachers.

However, we do still encounter a prevailing assumption, among teachers in the government schools we work with, that these skills are either too complex or unnecessary for junior secondary students, particularly those who are not headed for A-level or tertiary education. One aim of our program is to educate the teachers as well about the benefits that debating can bring to all ages of secondary students.

Language Skills

Many schools and parents in Hong Kong encourage students to debate because of the benefits that it will bring to the level of their linguistic achievement. However, the language skills that we seek to develop are not related to the acquisition of new vocabulary, grammar, and similar skills. Instead, we focus on helping ESL students to make better use of the language that they already possess.

We seek most notably to build their confidence when using English in situations where they are required to give a public presentation. In doing so, we draw a clear distinction between debating and public speaking, which is not often made in Hong Kong (where debating is seen largely as a particular format for public speaking). Most notably, debating requires an ability to give a large portion of a speech in a fairly impromptu manner, since students cannot fully predict the course of the debate before it begins. The criteria for assessing debates are therefore quite different. This difference requires students to change their approach, moving from a scenario in which they prepare—and often rehearse—their speeches well in advance to one in which they have to improvise a great deal more.

Debating constructs situations in which speakers need to use natural sentences, rather than relying on previously learned formulae. Although this is initially a barrier for many of our debaters, who are uncomfortable with the notion that they will not be corrected every time they make a mistake (which still happens all too often in the classroom), once the adjustment is made their fluency tends to increase rapidly.

Once this step has been achieved, students shift their focus to the primary objective of conveying meaning and information, rather than that of avoiding mistakes. This has the benefit of removing their inhibitions when speaking in English in public situations, and anecdotal evidence suggests that this benefit subsequently extends to non-debate scenarios, such as classroom discussion and social situations.

DESCRIPTION OF ACTIVITIES

This section of the paper covers some of the activities used in the program as part of the lead-up to "full" debates. The main aim of these activities is to allow students to work on individual skill areas of debating without having to worry about the full range of skills right from the start.

Argument Game

Rules

Students are divided into two teams of equal numbers. Two rows of chairs are set up, one facing the other. Each team sits on one row, such that each student is facing a member of the opposing team.

One team is designated the affirmative team, and the other the negative. The teacher announces a topic. Each student must then hold an argument with the opposing team member sitting opposite (i.e., all the pairs are talking at once), until the teacher announces that time is up. There is no preparation time, and the argument time is usually limited to 1–2 minutes.

Everyone then moves one seat to their left, with the students on the end of a row moving round to its other end. The teacher then announces another topic, and the game begins again. There can be as many iterations as desired, with opportunities for review and teaching in between each iteration.

Teaching Opportunities

The game can be used as a simple warm-up activity to increase students' participation or as a teaching tool in its own right. Successive iterations can run with

- the same topic each time, with or without changing the teams from affirmative to negative each time. In between iterations, students can reflect on the arguments used by their opponents, and deploy better rebuttal arguments in the following argument.

- different topics in each iteration, with the teacher focusing on different aspects of content skills in between each iteration (e.g., use of examples, development of consequences, etc.) for the students to apply in the subsequent argument.

The game is a very efficient training tool, since all students are participating in every iteration. It is not possible for a teacher to follow every student's performance, so peer feedback and reflection on individual performance are vital tools for students to assess and improve their skills.

The use of simple and familiar topics and the short time allotted to each argument eliminate the need for preparation and research. Instead, the focus is on the core dialectic element of debate, with its basic cycle of argument and rebuttal. The game is suitable for all levels of debaters, is repeatable and flexible, and can accommodate unlimited numbers of participants.

Balloon Debates

Rules

A balloon debate is set in a hot-air balloon, in which a number of people are travelling. The balloon's envelope has been punctured, and the weight of the passengers is causing the balloon to fall too quickly. One or more travelers must be thrown out of the balloon in order to slow its descent and save the remaining passengers.

Students are divided into teams of 2–4 members. The optimum number of teams is 5–9, although more (or less) can be accommodated. Each team is given a traveler in the balloon to represent; the traveler can be any fictional or real character. One member of each team must then present the case for their character to remain in the balloon, and point to one (or more) other traveler who should be sacrificed for the safety of the remainder.

After each team has been given an equal opportunity to present its case, each student is given a ballot paper on which to write the name of the character who they feel should be thrown out of the balloon. The team whose character receives the most votes is eliminated. Successive iterations, if desired, can eliminate further characters.

To increase participation, teams can (in the first round) be given two opportunities each to make a presentation, one focusing on the positive case for their character to remain in the balloon and the other addressing the reasons for eliminating one or more of the other travelers. Successive iterations of the game increase participation opportunities for all team members. Speeches should ideally be kept short.

Teaching Opportunities

The format is simple for students to grasp, and the lack of formal adjudication or assessment by skill categories makes this a very suitable activity for beginners and younger students. The competitive element is very straightforward, yet can be exploited in a number of different approaches in order to avoid defeat. The basic structure of the game can be effectively recycled by using different characters.

Using characters as the subject of debate, rather than theoretical positions for or against a topic, makes it easier for students to develop arguments and provide supporting evidence. Characters can also be researched more easily, making this a useful activity to introduce such skills to younger participants. The teacher's choice of characters can tie this activity in to other curriculum areas, e.g., history (using historical figures) and literature (comparing fictional characters).

Every student is both a participant and an audience member, with the opportunity to influence the result in both roles. The simple feedback from peers, through the voting system, is an effective method for teaching students how to appeal to audiences without artificially breaking down performance into skill categories.

The game can be scaled to allow participation from a large number of students in a short time. Students have to develop teamwork skills, and stronger students can pass on their skills to weaker ones through peer-to-peer teaching within teams.

Simple Debates

Rules

The debating format used is stripped down to the essentials. There are two teams of equal numbers, one affirmative and one negative. The debate begins with the first member of the affirmative team, and speakers are thereafter taken alternately from each team until everyone has spoken once. All speakers are given the same time limit, and there are no reply/summary speeches. There are no interruptions, questions, or points of information. All speakers after the first affirmative are encouraged to use both rebuttal and constructive argument in their speech.

Teaching Opportunities

Using simple rules and simple topics removes the technical barriers to entry for beginners, allowing them to focus solely on developing their basic skills of content, style, and structure. Feedback can be used as a training tool for participants and audience alike.

Time limits for speeches can start off very short, and then be extended as students' abilities increase, without altering the basic flow of debates. Technical additions such as summary speeches, points of information, etc. can be added subsequently, once students have reached a level where they can adjust to the increased requirements.

BENEFITS ASSESSMENT

We have not conducted any formal assessment of our programs, beyond surveying participants after they have participated in our activities.

However, feedback from teachers suggests that students who have participated in debate classes become more confident in participating in other classroom activities. This is particularly the case for ESL students, whose increased confidence in their language ability removes a major barrier to academic success, and especially for students of subjects other than language, whose results may suffer from a lack of linguistic aptitude rather than a lack of ability in that particular subject.

On a pure debating level, we have found that younger students tend to develop the core debating skills more quickly than the ability to discern reasoned arguments and logic. However, as they mature and gain knowledge, the skills that they have learned help them to formulate ideas and analyze information more quickly and concisely. The concepts of structuring and planning a speech can also be transferred very straightforwardly into both written and oral presentations.

Sam Greenland has taught debating in Hong Kong since 2001, and is also the coach of the Hong Kong national schools' debating team. He is currently studying for a master's degree, at Sydney University, for which his thesis will investigate differences of approach in school debating programs between Hong Kong and Australia.

The Middle School Public Debate Program: Design and Function*

Kate Shuster

The Need for Middle School Debate

Claremont Colleges National Debate Outreach (CCNDO) is the community service and educational outreach program of the Claremont Colleges Debate Union. The Debate Union is part of Claremont McKenna College, in Claremont, California (about 45 minutes east of Los Angeles). The Debate Union has conducted outreach programs in primary, middle, and high schools for more than a decade.

I was hired as program director for Claremont Colleges Debate Outreach in the spring of 2002. Although our high school debate program continued to grow, it became clear that we would have to supplement our existing debate outreach programs with some new strategies. We simply were not reaching enough students, and there were so many needy students that we had not yet served.

Part of the new outreach strategy we adopted was the Middle School Public Debate Program (MSPDP). In part, this was a response to a mounting demand. The Debate Union had received calls from many high school coaches asking for help recruiting from middle schools.[1] We had also been approached, separately, by community activists asking for our public debating programs to be implemented in their local middle schools. After some investigation, I determined that there was in fact a tremendous need for debate and public speaking instruction in the middle grades. California, like many states in the United States, has "content standards" for education. These standards are set out to make sure all students receive the same, sophisticated education

* Parts of this paper previously appeared in *Idebate Magazine*, volume. 4, no. 2.

regardless of their specific location. Many of these standards, particularly in the area of language arts, are met by practicing debating and its associated component skills. Young adolescents, we discovered, are particularly eager to participate in debating activities.

There is a serious need for debating and public speaking programs in the middle grades. Most middle schools do not have extracurricular programs, particularly academic extracurricular programs. Students rarely have a chance to interact with students from other middle schools, particularly students from other communities. Further, middle school may be the last chance to productively reach students who are classified as "at-risk." These students are usually tracked into programs for low achievers by the time they advance to high school. As a result, they are often not reached by high school debate programs, which normally attract students who are able to spare the time for elective courses or extracurricular clubs. If we can reach students in the middle grades, they can benefit from debate training and use the skills developed by debate training once they get to a high school and beyond. Since young adolescents are also less likely to be concerned about appearing "smart" in front of their peers, students in the middle grades are particularly open to involvement in debate and public speaking activities. In addition, parents are more likely to be actively involved in the education of their children in the middle grades than they are in high school. This is primarily because children are less independent in young adolescence than they are in later adolescence. Parental involvement is an essential part of program sustainability and expansion, as I will explain later.

Given the demonstrated importance of oral literacy in high school and beyond, it is particularly important to train young adolescent students in public speaking and debate. Young adolescents are quite talkative and argumentative, especially when compared to their counterparts in high school. This makes debate a natural fit for the middle grades. When I speak to teachers about debate education, they often remark that the challenge they face with middle school students is not how to get them to debate, but how to get them to listen. Fortunately, debate does teach students how to be active and critical listeners. Listening skills are increasingly important in state or locality-mandated content standards inside and outside the US. Listening skills are critical to success across the curriculum, because if students do not develop sophisticated listening skills, they will not be able to fully process and engage other aspects of curricular instruction. In addition, debate creates an incentive structure to build listening skills as well as providing the infrastructure upon which such skills can be effectively constructed and developed. Such learning tools as "flowing," the system of taking notes in a formal debate, can help students to immediately focus on listening and critical engagement with an ongoing discussion. It is worth noting here that flowing bears a strong similarity to the Cornell system of note taking, which has demonstrated success in college preparatory programs such as AVID (Advancement Via Individual Determination).

Debate practice in the middle grades allows students to build skills they will need in high school and beyond. Debating is "active learning," understood as a process of involving students in an activity while they reflect critically about what it is they are doing. Active learning strategies help students to master content and develop thinking skills. This skill acquisition means that students are more likely to succeed in classes, particularly smaller and more challenging seminar-style classes, where students are normally called upon to discuss a wide variety of subjects on relatively short notice.

Although debate programs in the middle grades can help build and sustain high school debate programs (and this has been borne out in our outreach program), it is important to note that the purpose of middle school debate outreach should not be the expansion of high school debating. Middle school and middle level education should be seen as ends in themselves, rather than as instrumental to some further program. If students choose (for whatever reason) not to debate in high school and beyond, our programs can still be successful if they convey to students the skills they need for success in high school and beyond. In other words, we should design programs *for* middle school students rather than for high school students by way of middle school students. This approach, which sees middle level education as its own end, is consistent with the mission statements of organizations like the National Middle School Association, and is essential to understanding and taking action to meet the unique needs of young adolescents, their teachers, and their parents.

Indeed, the purpose of debate education should not necessarily be the indefinite continuation of formal debate practice. If debating is genuinely cross-curricular, students will not need to participate on an interscholastic debate team in order to reap the benefits of training in academic debate.

Academic debate is a valuable exercise because it trains students to employ various component skills. In this respect, participating in a debate is much like writing a research paper. When students write a research paper, they use a variety of component skills such as spelling, grammatical construction, argument construction, evidence analysis, organization, outlining, persuasion, word choice, and citation. Similarly, when students engage in a debate, they are exercising a variety of component skills, practicing their oral literacy in a laboratory environment, which enables careful and refined practice (Table 1).

Table 1: Some skills learned from debate in the middle grades

Skill	Acquisition
Research Competence	Students research constantly throughout the debate season. Because topics change and are announced in advance, special impetus is created for students to learn about current events. Changing topics encourage students to constantly research through the season. Topics are designed to be interesting and accessible for students, creating additional incentives. Students research in a variety of accessible media and learn to share their research with other teammates through synthesis and summary, thereby exercising writing skills as well.
Media Literacy	Because students must consult and evaluate information from a variety of media, they develop media literacy skills as part of research. The debate process amplifies this learning, as students must find evidence and arguments to support multiple sides of given topics. Media literacy is developed in tandem with its companion skills: reading comprehension and argument literacy. Students learn to analyze arguments for their validity and the strength of evidence, thereby developing the leverage to critically analyze sources of information.

Reading Comprehension	Through debate participation, many students confront sources of information that they would never otherwise consume. Debate provides a series of incentives that challenge students to read materials that are often considerably above their customary reading levels. As students develop argument literacy, they gain tools to increase their reading comprehension because they can analyze difficult texts in terms of their more recognizable component parts. Reading comprehension is also aided by the development of summarization and outlining skills.
Argument Literacy	Students gain argument literacy as they learn to identify the constituent parts of arguments (including assertions, reasoning, and evidence). Argument literacy is a key skill for building reading comprehension and media literacy. Students learn to identify and compare arguments for their relative validity, using understanding of logical fallacies and other failures of reasoning. These skills apply across the curriculum, as students learn to evaluate systems of proof, critically engage difficult texts, and construct persuasive essays—often significantly above the expected abilities for their grade levels.
Evidence Evaluation	Associated with argument literacy development, debate helps students learn to critically evaluate many types of evidence, including historical and contemporary examples. Debate fosters a sensitivity to bias (student bias as well as author bias), assisting students in developing critical thinking skills.
Summarization and Outlining	Students summarize and synthesize their research. This summarization, necessitated by the extemporaneous demands of the format, helps students refine recall and reading comprehension skills.

(continued)

Table 1 (*continued*)

Public Speaking	The debate format helps students to develop an optimal mix of impromptu and extemporaneous speaking skills. Oral literacy is developed through informed practice and repetition. Students gain confidence in otherwise intimidating speaking situations by preparing in advance, by learning speaking techniques, and by conducting research on issues.
Floor Management and Civility	Students engage each other throughout the debate using points of information. This teaches skills associated with civil engagement. Students also learn a skill unique to parliamentary debate formats: floor management. Students learn to manage engaged discussions when multiple parties are seeking to enter the debate. This management skill is applicable to multiple educational and professional settings.

The creation of a new middle school outreach program presented unique opportunities to rethink existing debate education practices and outreach strategies. The challenge was to maximize student participation while maximizing skill acquisition. As a first step in designing the new program, I worked to cultivate a network of school administrators, teachers, and parents whose input was critical to program design, evaluation, and revision. This process of consultation resulted in a unique outreach model and debate format that were designed especially to meet the needs of middle school students while maximizing the acquisition of skills associated with debate. The program also vastly exceeded our projections of student participation—in the pilot year of the program, almost 2,000 students participated in classroom and competitive debates.

The MSPDP is now entering its sixth year, serving six formal leagues of schools and partnering with many dozens of schools that are not participating in competitive interscholastic debating. Based on our best estimates, we project that this year the program will serve more than 9,000 students in class and competitive debating. More than 1,000 of those students participated in competitions in 2006–2007, with the average student attending three tournaments. This is a participation rate that compares favorably to those of programs that cost millions of dollars, such as the Urban Debate League (UDL) initiative.

PROGRAM DESIGN: THE FORMAT

The MSPDP uses a unique debate format that draws from many sources to maximize student participation as well as skill acquisition. This format was developed in consultation with professional educators. The format is outlined in Table 2. It is designed to maximize skill development, including student investigation and collaborative learning, while emphasizing public accessibility and age-appropriate rigor. In this section, I will briefly highlight some key features of the program.

Table 2: The Middle School Public Debate Program Format: A Summary

There are two sides in the debate: the **proposition side** and the **opposition side**. The proposition team makes a case for the motion for debate. The opposition team opposes the case made by the proposition team.

There are three debaters per side. Everyone gives one speech. This is the order of the speeches:

First proposition constructive—5 minutes

This speaker makes a case for the motion for debate, providing a proof of the topic with three or four major points.

First opposition constructive—5 minutes

This speaker makes several arguments against the proposition team's case and refutes the proposition's major points.

Second proposition constructive—5 minutes

This speaker should rebuild and extend upon the proposition's case. This means that this speaker must extend and amplify the original proposition points and refute the opposition's major arguments against the case.

Second opposition constructive—5 minutes

This speaker amplifies the opposition arguments against the case, providing

(continued)

Table 2 *(continued)*

new information about why the opposition team should win the debate. This speaker should answer the proposition's answers to the opposition team's original arguments.

Opposition rebuttal—3 minutes

This speaker must put the debate together and explain why, given all of the arguments in the debate, the opposition team should still win the debate. Should finalize refutation of the proposition's major points.

Proposition rebuttal—3 minutes

This speaker should summarize the issues in the debate and explain why, even with the opposition's arguments, the proposition teams should win the debate. Should refute the opposition's major points.

Points of information

May be a statement or a question. Can be attempted only during the middle three minutes of each constructive speech. May not be more than 15 seconds long. The speaker must recognize you to make your point. If the speaker does not recognize you, you must sit down.

Three-Person Teams

After consultation with middle school teachers, we decided to use three-person teams for the MSPDP format. The primary reason for this decision was to enable more students to participate in the program. We knew that many students would want to debate, and that we might thereby run into a shortage of rooms and judges. Allowing six people per debate would permit more students to debate than the standard American four-person format. Further, the three-person format follows standard models for three-student work groups commonly used in curricula for young adolescent students. Many teachers prefer to use three-person work groups in learning situations, as these groups challenge students to manage interpersonal relations in a more complex environment than a simple two-person dyad. In fact, students report that they enjoy the three-person format more than the two-person format.

Points of Information

We borrowed points of information from the standard parliamentary debate format used all over the world. An application for a point of information is a request to the speaker that holds the floor to yield the floor to a statement or question from a member of the opposing team. Middle school debate incorporates points of information into all constructive speeches. After the first minute and before the last minute of each constructive speech, members of the opposing team have the opportunity to apply for points of information. The speaker who holds the floor has the option to accept or reject all attempts. If the speaker accepts a point, she will say, "Yes, I'll take your point," or something similar. If she does not accept the point, she will say, "No thank you," or something similar. The speaker is under no obligation to accept a specific number of points, although it is in her interest to accept as many points of information as she can.

The value of incorporating points of information is that such interactivity in the debate format teaches civility and floor management skills, abilities that students will use in future endeavors, as they must learn to manage attempted interruptions and the thorough engagement by other participants in debates and discussions. Many debate advocates are currently trying to find a way to incorporate elements of civil discussion into debate formats; our experience with using points of information in the middle grades suggests that this element of debate practice can be an effective way to teach the desired skills while still engaging in formal debate practice.

Points of information are particularly useful for debate in the middle grades. Young adolescents are particularly engaged in formats that allow them to participate throughout. Students in the middle grades are easily bored and enjoy the ability to engage throughout any given debate. This is true whether students are involved in a formal debate or in a panel discussion.

Topic Variation

In the middle school program, students debate a different topic in each debate. The topics for each tournament are chosen in advance of the event by teachers and league administrators, and are released up to one month before each competition. This process allows teachers to integrate research, preparation, and practice into class and after-school sessions. Teachers and students overwhelmingly report that they enjoy having students debate a diversity of topics over the course of a tournament or a season.

Since topics are selected by teachers, teachers can include instructional subject matter as part of competitive preparation. This practice reverses traditional ideas about "debate across the curriculum"; rather than simply bringing debate to the curriculum, curricular materials can be exported as debate topics. Teachers, in my experience, strongly prefer to be actively involved in topic selection for debating.

Further, teachers and students can adapt topics to contemporary political and social crises or issues of immediate concern to the community as they arise. In some debate formats, the topic is selected well in advance of competition and does not change when events change. This can make topics less relevant to students and teachers. For a list of sample topics that were debated in the 2005–2006 school year, please refer to Table 3. Notice that the topics used are simple and direct. In addition, they address a diverse array of issues.

Table 3: Some topics used in the 2005–2006 school year

- The U.S. should eliminate farm subsidies.
- Zoos do more harm than good.
- Soccer players should wear helmets.
- The U.S. military should leave Iraq.
- Fried foods should have warning labels.
- The United States Federal Government should ban the domestic production of genetically modified organisms (GMOs).
- Television is a bad influence on children.
- All schools should provide students with music and art education.
- Performance enhancing drug testing should be required for all student athletes.
- The federal government's response to Hurricane Katrina was appropriate.
- Cell phones should be allowed in schools.
- All students should be required to say the Pledge of Allegiance.
- The U.S. should not send humans into space.
- The United Nations has failed at its mission.
- Iran should be allowed to develop nuclear energy.
- Californians should approve Prop 74.
- The United States should close its Guantanamo prison.

  Middle schools should have mandatory drug testing for participation in extracurricular activities.
- Food aid does more harm than good.

Debate on flexible topics teaches students about a wide variety of events and policies over the course of a season. This practice mirrors the aims of liberal arts education in that students inform themselves about many issues as part of integrated instruction. Further, debate on multiple topics encourages students to adapt their arguments to the subject at hand, relying on original research on a continuing basis. Students reported that the variety of topics encouraged them to seek out teachers in different departments at their schools, looking for information to help them debate issues of interest. Interestingly, this increased the spread of debate in partner schools, as different teachers became involved in working with the debate program. The breadth of topics demanded that students continually expand their knowledge base. All of these factors combine to create strong motivators for research.

Based on my observation of middle school students at work over the last three years, I have found it interesting that these students appear to be doing more original research than similarly situated high school students engaged in other debate formats. This observation has been confirmed by teachers who have experience in multiple formats, including administrative directors of other debating programs.

Finally, debate on flexible topics teaches a unique skill set to needy students. The associated skills include impromptu argumentation and interdisciplinary learning. The ability to debate on changing topics mirrors and amplifies classroom competence, as the ability to speak in an informed way on a variety of topics is critical to success in high school and beyond. In a world that increasingly demands that students consume information conveyed in thousands of media messages every day, debate on flexible topics trains students to think critically in a way that amplifies the media literacy learning associated with many forms of debate. Interdisciplinary training, in fact, may be necessary to ensure that students are able to transfer knowledge from one cognitive domain to another.

Empowering Student Voice

The MSPDP format is designed to encourage students to speak out in an informed way. Students are expected to develop expertise on an issue and then be able to debate either side of that issue.

At a competition, students arrive and register for debates. They come to a central location, where the "pairings" for debate are posted. The pairing sheet gives students information about the upcoming debate, including what side (proposition or opposition) they will be representing, who their judge will be, and what the room number is for their debate. Once all students have had a chance to see the pairing sheet, the topic for the debate is announced. Students are given 20 minutes of preparation time to create their notes for the debate. At the conclusion of the preparation time, the debates must begin.

The preparation time is usually one of the most exciting periods of any competition. Students transcribe or summarize relevant parts of their notes, outline speeches, and work with other students on their team or squad to gather last-minute ideas for arguments and speaking techniques. The time pressure of the preparation period encourages students to work together in a dynamic way. Students construct arguments and organize themselves and others into ad hoc collective learning communities. Materials created prior to the preparation time are not permitted in the debate itself. This means that students cannot read a speech that someone else wrote for them, for example. Students must have enough information about the issue and have done enough research to be able to debate in an extemporaneous and effective manner.

This practice "levels the playing field," in some respects, as once the debate begins, it is the student's voice and the student's ability to accurately characterize and defend her research that counts most of all.

Program Design: Administration and Function

The MSPDP model is designed to promote classroom debating and local competitive debating. In this section, I will lay out the basic design features of the program as well as explain how it is administered and projected to grow.

Central Administrator

The middle school model emphasizes sustainable local competition. In the pilot year, what is now the Inland Valley Debate League was run by a central administrator (myself). My primary duties included:

- Recruiting and retaining member schools;
- Training and supporting teachers;

- Soliciting and releasing topics for competition;
- Arranging for tournament sites and trophies;
- Building constituencies with district and school administrators;
- Establishing a league infrastructure;
- Training and certifying judges for competition; and
- Holding faculty workshops to promote curricular integration at partner schools.

As the central administrator, my goal was to cease being the central administrator of the pilot league after its pilot year. Now that we are in year four of the pilot league, that goal has been realized. In the spring of 2003, the league teachers met and elected officers to run the league. They decided on an administrative model for the league after consulting with the president of our local high school league, Bob DeGroff (of Colton High School, in Colton, CA).

The pilot league renamed itself the Inland Valley Debate League (IVDL). The president of the league, Townsend Junior High School debate coach Paul Bates, is primarily responsible for mentoring new teachers and schools, as well as soliciting and releasing topics. The league has chosen a tournament director to tabulate and administer competitions, using our new tabulation software. The secretary takes minutes of meetings but is also in charge of picking up trophies and bringing them to competitions.

In the last two years, we have undertaken a program of substantial expansion of the MSPDP. We have successfully created two new leagues here in Southern California—the Independent Schools Debate League (ISDL) and the Desert Valleys Debate League (DVDL). In addition, we have partner programs in New York City, California's Bay Area, and the District of Columbia. In Washington, D.C., the District of Columbia Debate League (DCDL) operates as a program of the District of Columbia Urban Debate League (DCUDL). The DCDL, now in its second year of operation, has more than a dozen new schools participating in MSPDP format tournaments. The New York City league, the Big Apple Debate League (BADL), was started with support from the International Debate Education Association (IDEA), and is our fastest growing league. Our newest league is the East Bay Debate League (EBDL), serving Oakland area schools in Northern California. We will announce those new leagues as they begin competitions.

One of the many lessons that we have learned as we have gone through the expansion process has been that expansion works best if teachers take a leading role. The most effective expansion drives we have had have been those led by teachers, where they contact and train other teachers directly, using our materials. This year, DVDL president Greg Paulk (of Desert Springs Middle School) has recruited and trained six new coaches for his league. Diane Parker, of Canyon Lake Middle School, recruited and trained teachers from three other middle schools in a workshop she staged at a conference sponsored by her school district. ISDL president Katie Ward has trained several new teachers to expand her league. She also designed and hosted an instructional workshop that trained more than 20 parent judges and 250 students to kick off the league's season in September. Teacher-sponsored initiatives are the most effective, least costly, and most credible mechanisms for expanding the program. If teachers relied on us for all their training, we would simply not have the staff or the time to meet the demand for training. We have strongly depended on teacher empowerment for the success of the program, and we will rely increasingly on teacher empowerment as the program continues to grow.

Teacher Empowerment

The MSPDP format, instructional materials, and supporting videos are all designed to make an extremely rigorous form of debate immediately accessible to middle school teachers. In the pilot program, no teacher had previous debate training or experience. Yet all teachers were able to pick up the program after brief training sessions. In subsequent years, we have refined our materials to include the following:

+ The MSPDP Website, at www.middleschooldebate.com, featuring a full array of free materials for teachers and students.

+ A textbook designed specifically to serve teachers using the MSPDP format in their classrooms and clubs. The textbook, titled *Speak Out! Debate and Public Speaking in the Middle Grades*, is published by IDEA Press.

+ Sample debates available on DVD and VHS, demonstrating best practices for both novice and advanced debaters.

Mastery of the format has empowered teachers to connect with other teachers. The MSPDP model puts teachers in both an administrative and instructional role, which allows them to design a program that meets the specific needs of their school site. Since the program supports classroom debating, contest debating, and ancillary public speaking and argumentation training, teachers can serve as team leaders and trainers at the site and in their communities. The MSPDP model supports site innovation. All MSPDP teachers have developed innovative teaching strategies using debate. These include school-wide debate tournaments, public debates, integration of debate format elements into the classroom, and other intrascholastic events.

Teachers are the individuals who are best positioned to direct debate instruction. They are on-site, they are able to continually recruit and discuss the participation of students, and they are able to garner administrative and district support. Also, teachers have sophisticated knowledge of the educational needs of students and much more teaching experience than any "knowledgeable" debate proxies that might be placed in the classroom.

Relying on teachers as instructional and administrative leads in the program also guarantees that program expansion will be easy and rapid. Once a league is established, the outreach coordinator's focus can turn to recruiting new schools for the pilot league and subsequent leagues.

MSPDP staff rarely conducts formal "trainings" for teachers. Generally, when a school expresses interest in the program, we will send the lead teacher a "starter packet," which includes materials available on the Website. We will also send a DVD or VHS sample debate. Then, we ask the teacher to read the materials, watch the debate, and contact us afterward with any questions they may have. This strategy helps to ensure that teachers look at the materials and approach their "training" with specific, targeted questions for MSPDP staff or their local league administrator or president. It also encourages teachers to learn the material on their own so that they can then teach it on their own,

Emphasis on Class Participation

Although many hundreds of students competed at league tournaments last year, the vast majority of students served were reached in classroom debating and speaking activities. As I have already mentioned, the program is designed to empower teachers to combine information they already possess (how to teach, how to encourage students, etc.) with new information given to them by Claremont Colleges Debate Outreach staff as part of the MSPDP.

Almost all MSPDP teachers were called upon to serve as "debate and speech" consultants at their school sites. Some even set up formal training sessions to help their colleagues use debate and speech in their classes. Others used a more informal process, disseminating documents and instructional guides to other teachers at staff and department meetings. Our initial teacher training sessions have replicated themselves as many more dozens of teachers have begun to use debate in their classrooms.

As part of the program, we sponsor training sessions for faculty interested in using debate in their classrooms. I have conducted workshops at dozens of schools for teachers who did not want to be debate coaches, but wanted to learn techniques for meeting content standards and exciting students about learning. These workshops and others conducted (formally and informally) by teachers have really been the heart of the program in its first three years. Promoting classroom debating has been critical to maximizing skill acquisition and student participation.

Judge Training and Certification

One stumbling block for many debate leagues has been a lack of qualified judges. One stumbling block for student success is a lack of parent participation in their schooling. Our judge certification program has been designed to overcome these two obstacles to league success.

I train coaches and tournament directors to become judge certifiers. These coaches, in turn, certify parent and community judges to judge debates at middle school competitions. College student volunteers are also eligible for this training process. The certification process includes the following steps:

1. The trainer gives prospective judges the MSPDP judging manual. Prospective judges are asked to read the manual in advance of their training. If this is not possible—for example, if the training is happening at a tournament—judges are given an abbreviated version of the manual as a "tip sheet." This "tip sheet," which was designed by teachers, is available on the "Judges" section of our Website, as is the judging manual.

2. The trainer shows prospective judges a sample debate on videotape.

Prospective judges are asked to take notes in the suggested manner (a standard flowsheet) and fill out a ballot after watching the debate. Then, prospective judges are asked to deliver their decision and comments as they would have to after a debate. If the training is happening at a tournament, prospective judges are sent to watch a debate with a certified judge.

3. Following the sample decisions, the trainer offers helpful feedback to each prospective judge. If the training is happening at a tournament, during Round 2 the tournament director or head judge trainer will have a question-and-answer session with prospective judges.

4. In order to receive a judging certificate, a prospective judge must judge a debate by herself/himself. We emphasize strongly that prospective judges should not judge by themselves until they are ready to judge by themselves. One thing that I say at judge training sessions is "If you think it is easy to judge, you are not ready to judge." We really want judges to work hard at judging.

5. The names of certified judges are submitted to the central administrator or league president for inclusion at tournaments.

In addition to the judge certification program, there is considerable "on-the-job" training for judges in the league. In the MSPDP, all judges are required to reveal their decisions and explain the reasons for their decisions. This process accelerates judge education as well as student learning.

We found that the judge-training program encouraged parents to become constructively involved in their students' debate participation. When parents judge debates, they recognize how difficult the process of debating and judging is. We also found that the certification process increased the numbers of available judges, allowing us to accommodate the sheer size of some of our competitions.

Finally, the certification process improved the quality of judging across the board in our competitions. It is our hope that some of the trained judges will "trickle up" to judge at high school competitions as students graduate, and move on to participate in high school speech and debate events.

Sustainability

One of the challenges that has faced debate outreach programs in the US and around the world is the question of sustainability. Leagues that are formed around a central administration with a centralized funding structure are particularly vulnerable to dissipation if the central administrator leaves, if the sponsoring institution decides to go in a different direction, or if the centralized funding pool dries up. Several debate leagues that started in a centralized manner in the US have suffered from these problems and collapsed in recent years. Others have struggled with issues of sustainability. Still others appear to have no interest in moving toward sustainability.

The MSPDP has successfully developed a protocol for transferring complete fiscal, administrative, and instructional responsibility to the leagues we have helped to start. I want to briefly explain how this has occurred:

+ Fiscal Responsibility. Leagues have not been financially supported by Claremont Colleges National Debate Outreach in four years. Schools are expected to pay dues into a central league fund that is used to buy trophies for league competitions. Although leagues set their own dues structure, generally dues are $75 for new schools and $200–$300 for returning schools. These funds are used exclusively to buy trophies, and are sufficient to fund competitions for the year. The dues cover school participation at all tournaments for all students for the year. Schools are responsible for their own costs for transportation to tournaments.

+ Tabulation. One major obstacle to league sustainability has been tabulation. In debate leagues that have been started by a central administrator or administering organization, the league tournaments must be tabulated by central administrators. The MSPDP has successfully transferred tabulation and tournament direction to teachers and school administrators. It is, as far as I know, the only such program in the US that has successfully transferred this control. Danny Cantrell, the assistant director of debate at Cerritos, CA, in Southern California, designed a tabulation program specifically for MSPDP competitions. The program, MSPDP Tab, is easily operated by novices and is available on our Website along with a manual for the program.

♦ Administrative Responsibility. MSPDP leagues, after the first year, are fully administered by their elected officers. In the first year, it is necessary to have someone (possibly a teacher) function as the central administrator for the league. After the first year, control is completely transferred to the league.

CONCLUSION

I have been involved in debate outreach in one form or another since 1997. In all this time, I have never had the privilege of participating in a program like the MSPDP—a program that has been an unbridled success and that has brought the skills associated with debate to such a large number of students for so little money. It has been a privilege to be associated with the program and with the teachers and students who have made it their own. I can remember pleading with schools to join our debate outreach program. But now, the schools call us. The word of mouth about the program has been so positive that even in an era of tight budgets I receive phone calls from several schools *every week*. These schools just want to know how they can be involved.

It would be my pleasure to help any school in any country that is interested in developing a MSPDP league or program. Please feel free to contact me with any needs for information or answers.

Note

1. In the US, the term "middle grades" refers to students in grades 5–8. Students in the middle grades are typically ages 11–14. In this paper, I will use the term "middle school" to refer to schools that serve these grades, even though these schools may be called middle schools, junior high schools, or even elementary schools, depending on school district designations and other factors.

Kate Shuster is the director of Claremont McKenna College's Middle School Public Debate Program, and is a Ph.D. candidate in the School of Educational Studies at Claremont Graduate University. She is the co-author, with John Meany, of three debate textbooks published by IDEBATE Press.

Chapter 3
Debate and the Public Sphere

"Let's Talk": A Methodology for Participatory Community Discourse

Kory Harvey and Steven Woods

INTRODUCTION AND BASIC PURPOSE OF THE PROJECT

For the past 4 years, the Western Debate Union (WDU) of Western Washington University (WWU) has developed and maintained an active and vibrant public debate dimension. The WDU is committed to the active promotion of public discussion and dialogue. While a successful intercollegiate competitive program is a fundamental aspect of our role on campus, providing a means to translate skills learned in competition to non-competitive contexts is a natural extension of what we do. It also allows us to reach a pool of interested students and community members that would otherwise be beyond the reach of just the competitive debate team. Both the students and coaching staff feel strongly that having a high degree of training in research and speaking skills are advantages that can and should be channeled into building discourse and action in the community at large. Our public debate dimensions have been efforts to capitalize on our strengths as advocates, and to provide space for others to engage in advocacy as well.

One of the primary means by which we attempt to facilitate public dialogue is through the "Let's Talk" open forum discussion series. "Let's Talk" is a campus and community forum organized to promote public discourse by bringing students, faculty, and community members together for a meaningful exchange of ideas and perspectives. The project is now entering its fourth year, averaging four events per quarter of the academic year. Attendance averages 60–80 persons per session, and has served well over 1,000 total participants.

The basic format of "Let's Talk" is to meet bi-weekly on campus to discuss a topic of contemporary interest. These topics have covered a wide range of issues on the campus, community, national, and international levels. While the series has utilized the specialized knowledge of a few campus and community members on particular topics, the emphasis is placed on facilitating an open forum wherein all persons in attendance are encouraged to be equal and active participants by asking questions, answering questions, making comments, and generally sharing their opinion or perspective. The events are free to the public, with broad-based and diverse attendance always encouraged.

Overview of the Project

The genesis of "Let's Talk" began as part of an overall assessment of what WWU's forensic program should entail. The coaches felt strongly that focusing solely on winning awards may not be the best use of the time and effort of the team members, or the best way to use the resources and opportunities available. Debaters had also talked about their frustration in just "talking" about change and social movement in academic debates and not really ever contributing their efforts toward it. It was rather ironic that some of the best trained advocates for social movement were being utilized in ways that served to isolate them from real advocacy contexts through the single-minded pursuit of individual awards in artificial contexts like tournament debating.

"Let's Talk" stemmed largely from the academic endeavors of the coaching staff, who are responsible for the teaching of argumentation classes in the Department of Communication. While there was certainly class time devoted to discussion, it was truncated both by time constraints and the formal academic atmosphere of the classroom. Free discussion was seen as desirable and encouraged, but there were content-related goals that could not be ignored in the course curriculum. These limiting factors associated with the classroom seemed to be inhibiting the frank discussion of some issues, as students felt uncomfortable speaking absolutely freely in a setting that involved graded participation and concern about the reactions of both classmates and the instructor.

The thoughts about starting the project were also a response to the departmental mission statement, which included an objective to "teach effective communication that nurtures civil discourse and encourages cooperative solutions in our diverse society." The faculty at WWU are concerned about contextualizing communication training in ways that not only prepare students for meaningful and successful careers, but also about making sure that the pursuit of a "liberal arts" degree is not just University sloganeering. Many courses in the Department are service-learning focused and have an expectation that the student will not simply become a faceless economic entity after graduation, but will be an active citizen of a community—both locally and beyond.

There was also an interest in going beyond the campus community to reach a larger potential pool of participants rather than limiting the program to just WWU students. It seemed important to make an attempt to bridge the gap between campus and the surrounding community, to offer a public forum that would appeal to anyone of interest. Granted, the most immediate audience and people participating in the program were WWU students, but developing an open enough forum and structure to accommodate anyone was an important consideration from the beginning. As is the case in many "college towns" the students are somewhat disconnected from the happenings of the town or city which surrounds the school they attend. It was hoped that by bringing the two together we could encourage collaboration and networking, thus not only increasing the diversity of dialogue at the forums but also creating an opportunity for interested parties on each side to become more familiar with one another. A guiding theme in this regard was that a genuine education involved extending the student's practical experience beyond the confining walls of the academy.

There were also two contextual elements related to the formulation of the "Let's Talk" series: first, the status of all the coaches being new to the program and having the opportunity to define the program based on their ideal forensics experience; second, the events of September 11, 2001. As faculty members new to campus, we were essentially given a blank slate to create a direction for the program that we felt was most appropriate. While the motivation for maintaining the competitive aspect of the team was obvious, supplementing that part of debate with a more community oriented element was also a strong desire. We felt that a greater engagement of both the larger student body and wider community were invaluable in the development of meaningful and effective advocacy skills for the students involved in the debate program.

Perhaps the most significant contributing factor influencing and spurring the formation of the series were the events and aftermath of 9/11. It is important to note that the tragic events of that day took place almost two weeks before the first day of classes at WWU. In many ways our students did not have a chance to react publicly to those events as a student body. They came to the first days of class, and beyond, still very much in a state of shock and anxiety. It was clear that those events were weighing heavily on the minds of students, but it was so out of context with the classes they were taking that they were largely left without an avenue to discuss them. There was a strong sense that people had things to say, questions to ask, and feelings to express but lacked an outlet to express them. The masses of confused and mixed emotions were just bottled up inside of them.

Given this background, we perceived a clear need for greater opportunities to participate in public discussion both to inform and to create an outlet for those suppressed emotions. People were scared, confused, and looking for answers to their many questions. We heard a number of students voice their concerns that they didn't know where to turn. They needed both an opportunity to express their many concerns and, perhaps most importantly, they needed a space where they could simply talk to other people about these issues and find some support, some sense of community.

At the same time, there was a rapidly growing intolerance toward public expression that was anything other than the predominant notion of anger and resentment. It was widely perceived to be unpatriotic and anti-American to question our own role in the tragedies of that fateful day. The climate of fear was so strong and widespread that people were afraid to raise any question that might possibly be interpreted as anything other than nationalistic fervor. The attacks of 9/11 had raised some very serious questions about the relationship between American policy and the growing insecurity in the world, yet, because the nation was so gripped with fear and animosity, these questions were largely being brushed aside. This climate was pushing careful and critical consideration out of the sphere of public dialogue and replacing it with a fear-based repetition of patriotic slogans and jingoistic rallying cries. Rather than asking how and why such a terrible thing could have happened, thoughtful examination of the issue was ignored in favor of calls for revenge and retaliation. Emotion had, quite understandably, won the day, leaving students with critical questions about the nature of this scary new world with nowhere to turn.

It struck us that our nation was facing grave new challenges that had caused a great number of people to commit to strongly polarized views. Many others were still debating within themselves where they stood on issues like war and peace, individual liberties, and security. Students needed a safe place where they could express their thoughts and concerns without fear of reprisal. In a university setting, we have a responsibility to encourage the intellectual development and understanding that occurs through civil and thoughtful discussion. One of the hallmarks of higher education is academic freedom and the free exchange of ideas in an environment that emphasizes civil liberties, values intellectual freedom and respects the rights of all. As a part of this commitment we are obligated to facilitate the right of free expression that is so fundamentally vital to the democratic process.

Coming up with a program that allowed for attendees to present ideas they were interested in, contextualized into real world issues, and creating a "safe" space for expression and interaction served all the aforementioned interests. In formulating "Let's Talk" it was also understood that not all who attended the sessions would want to participate by actively speaking out but rather by listening and contemplating the many divergent views offered. There was an emphasis on providing information and helping those people who just came to observe become more educated about the topics that were being discussed. So an overarching premise was to offer something for attendees to feel like part of a community by taking part in the broaching of contemporary controversies in ways that people could feel empowered and safe to talk about, and to make that space for discourse available in a way that would be easy to participate in whatever way someone would want to, either by speaking out, observing, or both.

One of the goals of the "Let's Talk" series is to offer students some practical experience in advocacy and public dialogue. The intent of the project is to serve as a resource for the community to help build critical thinking, problem solving, and communication skills. By making the opportunity available for students to actually engage in real public discourse, as opposed to the more "artificial" nature of staged debates in a classroom setting, the "Let's Talk" program can assist students in their efforts to become more effective advocates and to more meaningfully participate in public policy and community decision making.

All of these elements were developed into a theme that was also a method. The idea that people should come together and discuss ideas led to a title of "Let's Talk" and also suggested a basic way to facilitate that discussion. Essentially a topic would be chosen that people had expressed interest in, a location and time would be set, and people would show up and talk. The theme and method served as invitation as well. There were no promises of solutions, truth revelation, or expertise. The idea was to get people together and let them talk.

While such a basic premise may seem antithetical to a competitive debate program, the relationship has been a beneficial and positive one. Logistically it has been helpful to have persons who are trained speakers available to outline ideas on issues. It also helps that debaters are familiar with a broad range of issues, and find it easy to discuss them. Moreover, it offers students differing ways to participate on the team. Some students do not have the goal of competition driving them to be on the team, but still want opportunities to be able to discuss ideas and issues. The "Let's Talk" series provides a way for those individuals to be a meaningful part of the team without having to engage competitively. As coaches we have found that having debaters participate in a more "real world" non-competitive speaking forum rounds out their rhetorical skills. By speaking to an audience that is not made up of people familiar with the conventions of formal academic debate they must learn to apply the thinking and cognitive skills of debate into a format that requires differing presentation technique and skills.

Logistics

Topics for the forums are drawn from a pool of compelling current events. They are chosen by both the faculty and students involved, with suggestions from many different interested parties. A core group of 3–4 people take the various issues that people suggest and come up with a set of 3–4 topics for each school term. We have tried to keep things balanced and varied, with an effort to include issues on the local, regional, national, and international scales. We also try to cover a broad range of topic areas, such as environment, economics, cultural divisions, social justice, war and peace, etc. As such, the series has covered such wide-ranging issues as the war in Iraq, US–North Korean relations, the USA PATRIOT Act, reproductive rights, same-sex marriage, and federal Indian policy, right down to local watershed policy, campus safety, and tuition rate hikes. There is a deliberate effort to include at least one national or international issue and at least one local or regional issue per academic term. The diversity of topics not only keeps the interest level high with fresh ideas and discussions, but also helps people understand that they can engage in public discussion both about the major problems facing the planet as well as the local issues that affect them on a daily basis. While some of the more compelling topics end up being repeated in subsequent terms (Iraq, the local watershed, and the USA PATRIOT Act, for example, have all been discussed more than once), the discussion itself is always as different as the people who attend.

While promotion often seems to be a problem for these types of events, we have been rather fortunate in that regard. Logistically, we have effectively used both the official avenues of the university for promotional purposes (the University Calendar, bulletin boards, and press releases) as well as word-of-mouth advertising. The real difficulty, however, is not necessarily in the production and distribution of flyers, posters and notices, but rather in the very real challenge of getting people to actually show up. In today's modern society people are both too busy and too preoccupied with other things to dedicate the time and energy necessary to attend a public debate forum. In addition to plain old apathy, a lot of people simply feel helpless in the face of the many challenges our society confronts. Today's college students are overwhelmed with information, but often feel there's just nothing they can do to change the situation. We see the "Let's Talk" forums as offering progress on that front. It is an important chance for people to have educated conversation, to express opinions, and hear differing perspectives on important issues. We've discovered that people are often eager to participate when they learn that such an opportunity is available. As with any good or service, if people like what they get they come back for more.

In addition to existing in a university setting, we are fortunate to live in a part of the country where a large portion of the populace tends to be interested in such things. As such, attendance has not been a problem for us. Further, being loosely associated with a course or two where students can earn some degree of credit toward a grade for participating in the events is very helpful. Selecting topics that will have broad appeal to people's interest and entice them to participate, as well as scheduling the events at a regular and consistent time and in a convenient location are also very important. There is no single best way that we have found to encourage participation. In the end, a wide variety of efforts must be put forward to ensure both initial and repeat attendance.

FACILITATION

The usual tone of the forums is open, respectful, and attentive. Efforts are made at the beginning of each session to ensure everyone understands that the purpose and intention of the event is to generate civil and meaningful discussion wherein all attendees are encouraged to share their varying perspectives on the issue at hand. Participants are reminded that argumentative discourse need not devolve into partisan bickering or turn into a simplistic shouting match, but are rather encouraged to follow a line of reciprocity—if they expect others to listen to them, they must also be willing to listen to others. The facilitators, in particular, work to maintain a level of objectivity and openness which allows people of divergent points of view to comfortably voice their perspectives. Great effort is put forth to ensure that all opinions are heard and that no one monopolizes the discussion. Anyone who wishes to make an observation, statement, or ask a question feels quite free to do so. In this context, people begin to realize that disagreement is not only acceptable but also even healthy if it is used to facilitate a clearer understanding of the many different perspectives possible on any number of controversial issues. To respectfully hear out an opposing view contributes to the critical thought process with respect to major social and political issues of the day.

To increase exposure to ideas and the practice the critical thinking needed to engage those ideas are aspirations of the "Let's Talk" open forum project. The forums rely largely on a process of participatory discourse, and the facilitator's role might be somewhat loosely associated with certain aspects of the style of pedagogy known as the Socratic Method. Many people have had experience with this method in some form or another. Some may recall the sheer terror of a particularly scary instructor's class where students were ruthlessly drilled with a steady stream of difficult questions in front of their peers. This type of performance, popularized in any number of films about life at a private school, is both an exaggerated and outdated caricature of a methodology that can, when effectively employed, be used to invite and challenge students to think critically, analyzing an issue for themselves. Such methods as fear and embarrassment may force students to be prepared to regurgitate memorized bits of trivia upon command, but do very little to foster either a genuine development of critical thinking skills or a healthy desire to learn. The "Let's Talk" forums offer a more useful, and perhaps more accurate, picture of the positive and constructive potential for interactions between the facilitators and participants of public discussion.

Facilitators who seek to foster experiential learning will rely upon the tried and true methods of open and participatory discussion with participants to explore controversial social questions and to resolve complicated problems. The effort is a cooperative one in which the facilitator and participants work together to understand the many angles of an issue more completely. The goal is to learn how to analyze complicated matters, to reason effectively, to think critically about one's own arguments as well as those put forth by others, and to persuasively advocate for one's position. Participatory discourse helps students to articulate, develop, and defend positions that may at first have simply been ill-defined inclinations or random political leanings.

Humans being are, by nature, problem solvers, and one of the primary tasks of educators is to equip students with the tools they need to solve problems. Society will inevitably change over the course of our lifetimes, and the challenges that arise as a result of those changes will vary tremendously. Educators cannot provide students with an exact blueprint for certain answers that remain constant, but we can help them develop skills that might be applied and adapted to confront a wide variety of situations.

Well-informed experts could endlessly lecture to an audience about any number of issues, but the participatory nature of the "Let's Talk" forums prefers to foster as much active and experiential learning as possible. Just as an instructor who immediately answers a student's question loses a valuable opportunity to help that individual discover the answers on their own, the facilitator who simply dispenses their wisdom in soliloquy will limit others' opportunities to engage in the independent critical thought that likely could lead them to a deeper and more thorough understanding of the matter at hand. The objective is to encourage in students the habit of rigorous and critical analysis of the arguments that they hear, as well as the practice of assessing and revising their own ideas and approaches in light of new information or alternative reasoning.

A fundamental aspect of these forums is the teaching of reasoning skills, and the process of discovering a right answer is often more important than the answer itself. This is especially the case when the topic of discussion does not neatly conform to "right" and "wrong" answers. In this environment, students are encouraged to apply reasoning, as well as their own political and value judgments, to questions that lack clear answers and problems that defy simple solutions. This lack of certainty can, at times, be frustrating to students who have become accustomed to being spoon-fed by instructors, political pundits, and the media. They may feel uneasy at first because they are confronting a new dynamic, unfamiliar critical evaluation, and the uncommon form of interaction found in an open forum. It is vital for a facilitator to be aware of these feelings and to take them into account during their interactions with participants. While it may be a difficult transition for some away from their comfortable experience in rote recitation of lecture material, to provide certainty where there may be none is to teach dishonestly. Such a disservice limits the potential growth one might experience if encouraged to assess the issues for themselves. Using a model of participatory discussion provides students with greater confidence to talk to large groups, allows them to develop the ability to argue forcefully and persuasively, and teaches them to think critically.

EXPERIENCES

We have been pleasantly surprised by the substantial turnout to this series. Over the past three to four years, these events have averaged around 75 people, with our largest gathering nearing 150 participants. These numbers have definitely surpassed our original expectations. The dedicated efforts of the coordinating students and faculty to get out and pound the pavement in order to spread the word have apparently paid dividends. Such numbers also suggest a healthy appetite on the part of the student body and surrounding community for public discussion. While most concern tends to focus on the problem of getting a large number of people to turn out for such events, there are also unique challenges in the other direction. It can be rather difficult to have meaningful and inclusive discussion with any group larger than a 15–20, especially in an open and participatory forum. However, in spite of the large numbers, our experience has typically been very positive, with ample opportunity for all who wished to adequately share their views. The fact that the discussions have flowed so smoothly is testament not only to the many participants' eagerness to learn about and share opinions and perspectives on important public issues but also points to the general willingness of thoughtful individuals to interact civilly and to show their peers a level of respect one might not have expected in a "public debate." Discussions about issues like abortion, the war in Iraq, gay marriage, and local environmental campaigns can easily get caught up in emotion and become shouting matches, yet these forums have remained remarkably civil. That is not to say that strong opinions have not been expressed or that there has never been a heated exchange or emotional outburst. But these typically negative expressions have been the rare exception rather than the rule. Further examples of these positive outcomes are offered in narrative form at the end of this paper in Appendix A.

RESULTS AND RECOMMENDATIONS

The attempt to identify any particular thing that we have done to ensure the successful development of this community forum and thus offer it as a model for emulation by others has been a mostly futile one. We have really done nothing special; we've found no magic bullet nor discovered the much-sought-after solution to an elaborate Byzantine puzzle. We enjoy no secret knowledge. If there is any key to our success, it has been the engaging nature and positive attitudes of the participants themselves. We owe a great debt of gratitude to the many students, faculty, and community members who have so enthusiastically engaged in this project of open, civil, and participatory dialogue.

If we have contributed anything to the overall picture, it may be the spontaneity by which we decided to simply jump in and do something. Rather than endlessly theorizing and planning for the perfect scenario, hammering out the most appropriate theoretical approach, and clarifying the philosophical underpinnings, we decided to learn by trial and error. We had no real plan or methodological framework at the beginning, preferring imperfect action on the ground to endless pontification about the most optimal manner in which to proceed. While the pedagogical foundation of the project has more or less developed and taken shape over time, we started quite simply with the desire to bring people together to exchange perspectives and talk about important issues. We are learning experientially, progressively, and our approach is constantly evolving and changing. However, we hope that by offering a few things we have learned in our experience it may help others in their own efforts.

One of the things we have come to clearly understand through our involvement in the "Let's Talk" experience is that although we may be considered "debate professionals" we possess little, if any, exclusive or special expertise. We are part of a larger community made up of varying levels of knowledge, skills, and ability. So as we offer ideas about how to start a program like "Let's Talk," we acknowledge that at best they are suggestions to be tried, not the ultimate blueprint on how to proceed. There are a variety of contexts and differences among campuses, debate clubs, and interested persons in pursuing such endeavors; clearly we can only speak from our experience. Our suggestions are more intended to spark ideas about how to proceed, and not a specific template on how to operate. We look forward to borrowing the good ideas that others generate and utilize in establishing their own participatory community forums. Of course, even given the disclaimer, we do feel that we can offer some ideas to get people who are interested started, and to assure them that no matter what the initial product looks like they can achieve great accomplishments.

As mentioned previously, one of the first things to consider is the value of impulsive action. It is very difficult to determine which techniques, formats, and promotional efforts will be effective in different situations. No one thing will work in all cases. It's important to trust yourself and go with what you know. Start wherever you feel you have the most potential then be open and flexible in adopting new strategies and tactics as they present themselves, constantly reviewing and evaluating your progress. The old practice of trial and error is, interestingly enough, tried and true.

Financial considerations must also be taken into account. It would be inaccurate to say that "Let's Talk" costs nothing, but it does cost virtually nothing. We are fortunate in that we can reserve space on campus at no charge. There are also a variety of means to publicize the events that involve no expense: announcements in class, e-mail lists, posting in campus calendars, campus radio announcements, etc. We do pay for the copying of flyers that can be handed out on campus and around town as reminders (a single sheet of paper cut into quarters works quite well) and for larger size posters to hang up in high-traffic areas. But copy costs are relatively cheap, so very little financial resources are actually expended. We are fortunate enough to have people volunteer to participate in "Let's Talk" discussions to provide background information, so no honoraria are involved even when "experts" join the discussion. It would be nice to offer refreshments to guests, but in our case the complications of state law in providing such amenities are more of a factor in not offering them than the cost. Of course, food and beverage items that might be donated are a possibility. The power of free food to entice college students should not be underestimated!

Finding space if getting rooms on campus is not possible (perhaps your group is not affiliated with a college or university, the school charges to reserve them, etc.) could be a challenge. In some instances, agreeing to meet at a public location outdoors or in a park may be possible. It is also possible that some space in the community may be available such as civic buildings, churches, or libraries. It could work to meet at commercial establishments that serve food or drink, such as a coffee house or local diner. Clearly the size of the event dictates which options to pursue, but the many options available provide an opportunity to build partnerships with organizations that may have the requisite space and are interested in building community as well. They may appreciate the chance to network with energetic and organized people working to facilitate the shared goals of promoting discourse and public participation. Such cooperative efforts often offer many additional intangible benefits besides simply finding a place to hold your event.

Even if cooperating over meeting space is not an issue, pursuing community groups and other organizations as partners is a good idea. Another important message we have discerned in staging the "Let's Talk" forums has been that we are not the only people interested in building community and promoting discourse. Pre-existing forums and organizations may be available that can be utilized as a resource and ally to promote even more public discussion. We have cooperated with academic departments, student organizations, community organizations, and ad hoc groupings of persons on a variety of topics. Upcoming elections are a great reason to approach candidates or groups behind referendums for forums involving the public. It is usually very flattering to people when you contact them and share that you value their contributions and efforts and would like to help facilitate their ability to express their ideas to an even larger audience. We have also found that building networks has helped to generate topics, locate people to assist in coordinating events, and even builds a base of persons to attend your forums.

While we have had good luck by setting a standard time to hold the "Let's Talk" forums, it may be necessary when starting out a new program to experiment with a variety of times to find what is most convenient or practical for people in your area to attend. We have also varied our start time in response to concerns about security and having to walk in the dark on campus, and having alternate times for people who just could not make the regularly set time. Ultimately we have gone to one standard time, which has worked out for us, but other situations may require greater flexibility.

SUMMARY

For thousands of years, public debate and civil discourse have been important parts of our society. From antiquity to the present, people have gathered to engage in public dialogue. Whether it is the neighborhood association, the local school board, political figures, or an organized group of students, public deliberation can be an effective tool in accommodating social change. There is truth to the old adage that knowledge is power, and the more people involved in broad-based and participatory discussion, the more empowered the public becomes. When information and knowledge, and thus power, become concentrated, the door to potential abuse swings wide open as there are fewer and fewer checks on accountability. Conversely, the more people who know the facts, the harder they are to hide. The more widespread the information, the more difficult it is to manipulate.

A democratic and free society is best served by what the original founders of this nation called a diverse and robust "marketplace of ideas," wherein information is widely accessible and all views are to be heard by the people for their discussion and deliberation. Such free-flowing and accessible information is vital to a healthy and stable democracy. Public debate forums are one promising way in which such a marketplace can flourish. In our experience, it has been inspiring to see so many people willingly gather together to engage in meaningful dialogue and investigation. That, we believe, is what the "Let's Talk" discussion series is all about.

Appendix A: Narrative Highlights

TUITION RATE HIKE

The threat of a possible 15% tuition increase proposed for the following year brought students together to become more informed about tuition issues and to express their thoughts about it. Over 80 students, including several representatives from student government and other campus groups, participated in the discussion.

This particular forum was an effort to bring students closer to campus politics. Students had become concerned about tuition rates because the state's budget proposal was set to cut funding to higher education the following year. If cuts were to be made, the school would likely increase tuition by 15% to fill the budget gap. As might be expected, a fair amount of controversy had stirred in response to the proposal for such a substantial tuition hike. The student government was taking a position in defense of the hike but much of the student body was fairly upset by the possibility. It seemed that there was a need for both the student leaders and the student body to make a renewed effort to reach out to one another in an effort to not only express their differing points of view but also to build some student solidarity in seeking a mutual understanding. It was hoped that by facilitating such an exchange a sense of student empowerment might emerge.

Unlike the typical session wherein the facilitator offers 5–10 minutes of background information on the topic and then suggests a few questions for the participants to tackle, this session was begun with a very brief welcoming statement and the floor was immediately opened for discussion. It was assumed that those in attendance were relatively familiar with the topic and would have plenty to say without any need for prompting. It proved to be an accurate assumption. What ensued was a dynamic exchange of students engaging in a textbook example of deliberative discussion. There was no need for the facilitator to call upon students or to referee the debate; they simply waited respectfully for their own turn before offering a rebuttal to the previous speaker. It was amazing that the discussion was so orderly without even the slightest bit of outside intervention or direction. Although they had clearly divergent views on the matter, they all seemed to understand innately the value behind taking turns and hearing each other out in an effort to better understand one another's positions.

The result of this civil exchange was not only a much higher level of understanding regarding differing perspectives but also a greater appreciation for the complexity of the issue. Upon hearing alternative views and a very productive point-counterpoint between the various constituencies, most students left the forum with a different attitude than they had come with. The level of respect was impressive and the feeling of real communication was unmistakable. The students were left with a sense that they had really impacted the final decision through their discursive participation. As one student noted, "We need to start taking charge and listening to each other. We really can join forces and make a difference. We each assume that someone else is going to do it. We all need to be that 'someone else.'"

Campus Safety

The recent housing of 3–4 Level III sex offenders just a block off campus, the controversial declaration of "rape-free" zones on campus, and concerns over inadequate lighting brought together a group of about 60 to discuss issues of campus safety. Although the majority of attendees were students, there were also representatives from the University Police, WWU's Wellness and Prevention Services, the local rape crisis center, and faculty members from the Women's Studies Department.

The main problem students and faculty members discussed was that most people present were not aware of important campus safety information, such as the phone number for the greencoats (a campus organization), where to obtain a rape whistle, and how to enroll in a self-defense class on campus. In particular, there was a great deal of discussion about how to raise awareness without also raising fear. The goal was to provide education that promoted confidence and security rather than anxiety. Students suggested an advertising campaign similar to the one seen around campus to educate students about the dangers of excessive drinking, the creation of a mandatory session for first-year students that addresses important campus-safety information, and encouraging enrollment in one of the self-defense classes offered on campus.

This forum was a great example of a discussion that was not so much about dispute resolution with two opposing sides—one would hopefully have to search far and wide to find someone that was actually pro-sexual assault, but rather was a cooperative effort in problem solving. Such collaborative deliberation brings people together to increase awareness and understanding as well as to encourage common action toward a common problem.

The positive nature of discussion at this event, especially considering the gravity of the topic, was inspiring. The group seemed encouraged by the collective belief that such meaningful dialogue itself helps to create change in both individual behavior and social norms. Participants left the discussion feeling empowered by their interaction and dedicated to correcting the misconceptions about the gender gap in our society and, more specifically, the commitment toward working together to raise the positive level of awareness on campus. Despite their very real concerns, the participants seemed largely optimistic that the situation would change because students were becoming more aware of the safety concerns and taking steps to challenge them.

USA PATRIOT Act

In cooperation with the school's Associated Students board of directors and a coalition of student groups, a forum was organized to address a pending resolution before the student senate to defend civil liberties from the USA PATRIOT Act. The student government representatives wanted to see what the student opinion was about the Patriot Act and their response to the resolution. The resolution dealt primarily with students' financial and educational records, but also stated that the act violates personal rights, including Internet usage, e-mail tracking, and search warrants.

The opinions were varied, and the discussion covered a broad range of political perspectives. Some defended the act as providing the necessary law enforcement tools to effectively fight terrorism. Others responded that if we were to give up our freedoms and move toward a steadily more repressive government then we would lose the very things that America stood for. There was also some concern over the value of the resolution being only symbolic in nature, while others defended the symbolism as an important first step toward greater solutions. While some made references to George Orwell's seminal novel *1984*, others decried such references as an overreaction.

Certain members of student government suggested that repercussions could occur if the resolution were to pass. It was suggested that the state legislature might look negatively upon such a resolution and that could affect their decisions when voting for funding measures. Others disregarded this concern as a scare tactic, pointing out that opposition to the infringement of civil liberties came from both ends of the political spectrum.

In the end, the claim that it is possible to have both security and freedom seemed to hold sway. The majority of students seemed to be taking a stand for liberty. Several members of student government later reported that the forum had really helped them to understand students' concerns and to offer guidance on their decisions. The resolution passed on a 4-2-1 vote. As Associated Students President Paul Graves later recalled, "I think the forum was a really good way for the university community to come together and talk about these issues that are not only central to our school but to our society."

Appendix B: Instructive Commentary from Campus and Community

As this paper is about participatory discussion and dialogue, it seemed rather appropriate to include a selection of comments and feedback about the series from some of its various participants.

STUDENTS AND COMMUNITY MEMBERS

I wanted to thank you for taking time out of your day/night to have discussions like this. I think it's a tremendous help to people who have very little idea of what goes on in the world and in our own region. It's also extremely inspiring to hear someone talk so intelligently and so passionately about politics and real issues in the world. It inspires me to want to know more and constantly keep myself updated in a time in my life when it's easy to brush off the news. So thank you again for caring about the world we live in and caring enough to want to share your thoughts and knowledge with others. —**Chelsea M.**

I learned more from the Let's Talk discussions than in all the rest of my college experience combined. I like how it helps us to stay up to date on current events, especially because of the way the world is changing. It gave me a chance to voice my opinion and learn more about important issues. There's not a lot of other opportunities to do that. —**Carrie M.**

What I liked about Let's Talk is that it is an open event for students and community members to speak freely. It helps us to get several views on a topic, not just what the press may write. It was a great way to learn about what is going on in our community and how to really get involved. —**Devon H.**

I really enjoyed the Let's Talk discussions. They were an excellent forum for thoughts, opinions and facts on very relevant issues for today's society and I found them very informative. The opportunity to hear both sides of an argument was very educational. The discussions taught me how to have an opinion, and how to support it. —Greg Q.

The Let's Talk forums were awesome. I love being able to sit and listen to arguments/debates and to learn more about each subject. Let's Talk gave us an opportunity to express potentially controversial opinions in a safe and friendly environment. I liked how everyone felt comfortable in giving their own opinion without being judged. —Leah B.

Let's Talk gave me a better perspective on many hot topics and was a chance for greater campus participation. I liked that you didn't just listen to the side you supported, but had to listen to the other side as well. —Brooke L.

The Let's Talk forums have been very beneficial for me. They have helped me to understand issues a lot better and to think more critically about controversial topics. I definitely read the news with a much different attitude these days. I'm actually questioning the things I read and hear and looking for more complete answers. —Stefan S.

The Let's Talk discussions helped people learn to solve disputes, look at both sides of an issue and learn about things they probably wouldn't have otherwise. I am now much more aware of things going on around me. It's such a great way to get involved with the community ... we learn from one another. —Lindsay D.

I thought the Let's Talk discussions were VERY informative and interesting to go to. I think they are a very good idea for people of college age, especially, because otherwise it is hard to know about and understand what is going on in the world. This is a great way to get involved. I definitely would not know as much about these important issues without the discussions. —Sadie W.

I enjoyed listening to what others thought. It definitely broadened my horizons and made me think more deeply on a lot of issues. I learned a lot of useful information that is really relevant to my life and to my society. I even changed my views a few times. —Lisa K.

I really enjoyed the Let's Talk discussions. I was able to learn a lot about many different issues, things I definitely would not have learned by watching the evening news. Even when a topic initially seemed a little dry, I found that once I was there it was always an interesting exchange. —Neil D.

I really liked discussing topics that are very important in our lives. I liked being able to actually participate in the discussion rather than just sitting and listening. That made it a lot more meaningful to me, and also helped me to better understand my own position on things. It really helped me to see how valuable information is to my life. —Teresa F.

I thought it was the best thing ever. It gave me a chance to hear what other people thought about controversial topics and to clear up a lot of the haziness I had about things going on in the world. It gave me some valuable insight, and just made things simple and clear. —Tanvir S.

I think the Let's Talk discussions are great because they open up a unique form of dialogue in the community that is often lacking. It puts a lot of people with diverse opinions together in the same place and gets them to talk about their differences. People actually take the time to listen to each other, and that's a very powerful thing. —Mark H.

The beauty of the Let's Talk series is that everyone is allowed to speak freely and share their thoughts, feelings and questions with everyone else present. It is easy to become passive about most issues and never really understand or participate in intelligent discussion with others regarding the controversial issues. Let's Talk is not only about learning current events; it's about crossing the gap between reading the news and shaping the news. —Dean S.

I would like to take this opportunity to express my thanks and appreciation for helping WWU (Western Washington University) NARAL (National Abortion and Reproductive Rights Action League) hold a public forum on reproductive rights, particularly on the issue of the Partial Birth Abortion Ban. The discussion went very well and as a result WWU NARAL was able to increase their membership due to the exposure we received from the forum.

In addition to the help you gave us as a campus organization which experiences much resistance, I believe that what you are trying to do with the Let's Talk Open Forums helps the campus overall. It seems today that the idea of discussing (beyond the classroom) pertinent issues on college campuses is a dying notion. Many students have to work and many simply see it as unimportant. This places a large burden on clubs to do all the awareness raising. But the WWU Debate Union, I believe, has filled a unique and much needed niche on our campus; your efforts have reminded the student body and much of the faculty that a college experience should entail more than doing your homework and coming to class. A college experience should involve thinking, questioning, and becoming involved with the academic community that surrounds you. You provide a unique unbiased space to do this because you are not devoted to one particular theme or issue; you are simply devoted to the importance of critical inquiry and discussion.

I am so happy and filled with hope to see debaters taking the skills that they have gained through competition in an adversarial framework and developing them further in the community. As a former debater, I understand and value the power of the words we speak and the research we perform, and I cannot think of a better use for our skills as critical thinkers than to move beyond the competition to educate those around us; and thus, help the people on our campuses and in our communities to become aware of the issues *and* to be able to question these issues in order to make our world a better place.
—Breana Forni, WWU NARAL President

A Word or Two from the Chair

I want to thank you for all the time and dedication you have put into the educational growth of students through sponsoring the Let's Talk Series. Having attended several of the sessions I was greatly impressed by the numbers of students who attended the series and the articulation of their viewpoints on the major issues presented at each of the sessions. This kind of forum is particularly meaningful as an activity of the Communication Department. The common interests of students and others regarding such major issues as a safe and sustained water supply, a responsible and responsive government, and citizens' responsibilities in creating social harmony and health are especially important to share in public discussions. This is a scarce kind of activity on campus. What I saw during this series was intelligent, informed, respectful discourse. It was like a series of communication skills labs, only students were freely working. You offered very effective input to students across these sessions. You provided enough information, raised enough questions at the beginning of each discussion to encourage thought and interaction. The fact that the sessions were so lively yet orderly and respectful validates your positive influence on all who attended, hundreds of our students as well as nonstudents. My sincere thanks for this excellent series.

Thank you so much for sponsoring the excellent forum for the discussion on the Iraq/US situation. I was very impressed to see so many students attend. Most, if not all, appeared to be highly engaged even if they didn't make statements. It is reassuring to me as a faculty member to see young people speak up with such balance, insight, and concern. I found the time speeding past and the thoughts expressed very stimulating. As a facilitator, you did an excellent job of opening the discussion, making all feel very welcome, keeping the forum moving along, and avoiding obstacles of dominating or rambling participants. You were highly attentive, and very focused on the topic. I think that session really gave students a great deal to think about, and raised many important questions for them to investigate further. —**Sue Hayes, Communication Department Chair.**

Korry Harvey is assistant director of forensics, Department of Communication, at Western Washington University.

Steven Woods, Ph.D., is director of forensics, Department of Communication, at Western Washington University.

Thwarting Civic Skepticism: Nontraditional Pathways to Promoting Civic Virtue

Candace Williams

This paper investigates the trend of skepticism about traditional forms of political engagement in the youth populations of the United States and Hungary by examining how civic knowledge, community involvement, and trust in government correlates with democratic participation. Additionally, the paper explores nontraditional ways that students in both countries engage in democracy, and offers new alternatives to educators and community leaders trying to bolster youth participation in local government.

INTRODUCTION

The history of democracy provides us with the answer to the question "Can a people rule themselves?" The question for the future is "Can a people remain free?" National turmoil and international threats test the boundaries of democracy every day. Terrorism, AIDS, poverty, and violence are just a few of the complex issues that threaten the stability of governments everywhere. Civic participation is not an important element in the democratic system: it is the democratic system. If citizens do not participate in their government, future generations will find themselves coping with a new system of government, which may not guarantee the same personal freedom as democracy. Emerging democracies and long-standing democracies face the same issues. Declining civic participation has been an issue for three decades in the United States, while in the emerging democracy of Hungary, it has been an issue for the past 10 years. This paper will investigate the state of civic virtue in both countries to show that the core issue is the peoples' rejection of deliberative institutions. The paper will provide new ideas that use the school setting to combat this problem.

THE STATE OF CIVIC VIRTUE

Civic virtue refers to the personal habits of citizens that are necessary to maintain democracy. This section will use various studies to assess the state of civic virtue in Hungary and the United States. For structural purposes, the measure of civic virtue will be broken into two subcategories: civic knowledge and civic attitudes.

Civic Knowledge

Civic knowledge is both a measure of how well students understand the basic principles of democracy and a measure of the critical thinking skills necessary to interpret information. For example, a student proficient in civic knowledge would understand how democracies work and have the skills to interpret information about current events and civic principles. Civic knowledge cannot be disentangled from civic virtue. The Civic Education Study (CivEd) sponsored by the International Association for the Evaluation of Educational Achievement (IEA) found that the civic knowledge of 14 year olds is a positive predictor of their expressed willingness to vote as adults. This means that civic knowledge is positively linked to civic attitudes and participation. It is clear that citizens of democracies must understand how their government operates, and master critical thinking skills so that they can apply themselves as empowered voters.

Although the United States was founded on democratic principles over 200 years ago, its students do not have full mastery of the knowledge or skills necessary to maintain the democracy. The 1998 Civics Report Card for the Nation, an assessment guided by the National Standards for Civics and Government, reported civic educational progress for students in grades 4, 8, and 12. The results indicated students who had attained partial mastery of knowledge and skills deemed required for *competence* in civics comprised 69% of 4th graders, 70% of 8th graders, and 65% of 12th graders. Yet only 23% of 4th graders, 22% of 8th graders, and 26% of 12th graders had attained partial mastery of skills and knowledge deemed necessary for *engagement*. For example, an item in the 4th grade assessment asked students to correctly identify the three parts of the federal government. Only 24% could identify all three branches. Eighty-five percent of 4th grade respondents could not name two services that the government pays for with taxes. In the 8th grade assessment, only 6% of respondents could give two reasons why constitutions are useful to countries. Ninety-one percent of 12th grade respondents could not explain two ways that a democratic society benefits from citizens actively participating in the political process. Students in all three grades lacked the skills necessary to answer questions about the basic principles of democracy. These results make it clear that the youth of the United States are not acquiring the skills and knowledge necessary to engage in democracy.

In the previously cited CivEd study, Hungarian students performed slightly above the international average for civic knowledge, but it is clear that this is no indication of mastery of civic knowledge. In the total results for civic content, a measure of knowledge of democratic principles, Hungary scored slightly higher than the international average, with a score equal to that of the United States. As the 1998 Civics Report Card for the Nation illustrated, students in the United States do not exhibit basic proficiency or mastery of civic content. In the CivEd study, only 45% of Hungarian students were able to identify "people [being] prevented from criticizing the government" as the correct response to a question about why a government would be considered nondemocratic (Figure 1.1). Fifty-three percent of respondents from the United States answered the question correctly. Hungary scored just at the international average in the civic skills section. Figure 1.2 shows an item from the IEA assessment that tested interpretative skills. Seventy-eight percent of Hungarian students could interpret a political leaflet. When compared to civic content, civic skills are a relative strength for Hungarian students. Although the CivEd study demonstrated that Hungarian students performed well relative to students in 27 other countries, the study shows that its score and even the scores of top-ranking countries denote weakness.

It is clear that both countries are struggling when it comes to inculcating civic knowledge in their citizens. Although each nation does well on civic knowledge assessments in comparison to other countries, results from the assessments show that students in neither country have mastered concepts necessary for participation in democracy. As noted above, civic knowledge is linked to civic attitudes and participation. The sub-par levels of civic knowledge in the United States and Hungary have dangerous implications regarding the attitudes of citizens and the willingness of citizens to vote and participate.

Figure 1.1 Item example: Identify a nondemocratic government

Example 3 (Item #17) Type 1: Knowledge of Content
17. Which of the following is most likely to cause a government to be called nondemocratic? A. People are prevented from criticizing the government.* B. The political parties criticize each other often. C. People must pay very high taxes. D. Every citizen has the right to a job.

Source: IEA Civic Education Study, Standard Population of 14 year olds tested in 1999.

Figure 1.2 Item example: This is an election leaflet

Example 6 (Item #23) Type 2: Skills in Interpretation
We citizens have had enough! A vote for the Silver Party means a vote for higher taxes. It means an end to economic growth and a waste of our nation's resources. Vote instead for economic growth and free enterprise. Vote for more money left in everyone's wallet! Let's not waste another 4 years! VOTE FOR THE GOLD PARTY 23. This is an election leaflet which has probably been issued by . . . A. The Silver Party. B. A party or group in opposition to the Silver Party.* C. A group which tries to be sure elections are fair. D. The Silver Party and the Gold Party together.

Source: IEA Civic Education Study, Standard Population of 14 year olds tested in 1999.

Civic Attitudes

Civic attitude refers to the degree of trust and belief that citizens have in democratic principles. Trust is a key element of democracy. Citizens who do not believe in the efficacy of the democratic process shirk from participation and voting. This section will examine the trends of civic skepticism in both countries.

In the United States, increasing civic skepticism has been documented in both the youth and adult populations. A publication by the Center for Information and Research on Civic Learning and Engagement and the Carnegie Corporation reports that young people in the United States are "less likely to vote and are less interested in political and electoral activities such as voting and being informed ab out public issues than either their older counterparts or young people of past decades." The CivEd study found low levels of political trust in adolescents, especially when it came to the national government and political parties: 72.7% of students trusted local governments, while only 65.1% trusted the national government. Political parties were distrusted the most: only 35.1% of students reported trust. Youth disengagement is highlighted by the statistic that only 20% of eligible voters between the ages of 18 and 25 bothered to vote in the elections between 1990 and 2000. The full issue becomes clear when the voter-turnout statistics are analyzed for the adult population: the turnout-rate for all eligible adults ranged from 47% to 56%. In the United States, both the younger and the older generations are disengaging from politics.

Hungary is also plagued by decreasing democratic participation In a 1999 study of Hungarian trust, Hungarians gave political parties, the government, Parliament, and the trade unions 22 to 32 points of trust; these institutions were on the bottom of the 100 point confidence scale. Voter turnout has been declining since the beginning of democracy in the country: 76% of eligible voters voted in the parliamentary elections of 1990, 70% in 1994, 60% in 1998, and 44% in 2002. Civic skepticism is on the rise in Hungary. A 1996 study reported that 46% of adults were interested in politics. The same study found a decreasing interest rate as younger citizens were added to the representative sample: 2% of 25 to 35 year olds and 15% of 18 to 24 year olds reported interest in politics. A representative sample study done in 1995 found that 72% of the respondents were dissatisfied with the work of democratic institutions.

It is striking that both an entrenched and a transitioning democracy have the same problems when it comes to civic skepticism. A significant amount of adults in the United States and Hungary turn from the responsibilities of citizenship. Research shows that youth are even more disengaged from politics than their parents.

FORCES OF POLITICAL SOCIALIZATION

Political socialization is the process of guiding a child toward becoming an ideal citizen. Political roles, values, behaviors, and norms are all instilled via socialization. Current socialization theories conclude that adult political values, which are formed between ages 17 and 25, are based on early childhood experiences. Socialization institutions can contradict and corroborate political messages. For example, rhetoric heard in the home may give children one view of political leaders, while the school curriculum gives an opposite message. Peer groups, the media, political parties, customs, power structures, traditions, churches, the education system, and the family unit are just a few of the many socializing institutions that exist in society. It is hard for political powers to ensure that new generations learn social ideals that ensure survival of democracy. This section of the paper will focus on how the political socialization that occurs in homes and schools has led to a rejection of deliberative institutions.

The Home

In order to understand the Hungarian family home as an institution of socialization, it is necessary to study the history of politics in the home. Until 1990, Westerners, fellow Soviets, and Hungarians called the region "the merriest barrack" because the regime respected the sovereignty of private life. Tight controls were maintained over the political sphere. The softening of dictatorial rule in 1956 brought about a tacit agreement between the regime and the people. Personal freedom was exchanged for civic silence. The regime stayed out the personal affairs of the people as long as the public did not question the communist system. This agreement created disunity between the family and the school as modes of socialization. Ildikó Szabó, in her 1989 monograph on political socialization in Hungary, points out the tendency of families "to safeguard autonomy in their private lives by trying to evade politics" (cited in Zsigo 2003, 135). Families erased politics from private life. Passive political roles were transmitted to the young. The communist regime of Hungary instilled a tradition of nonparticipation and disinterest in state affairs.

Disinterest in politics and distrust in the government survived the transformation of the Hungarian regime. The current low levels of trust and participation stem from misunderstanding the responsibilities of a democratic government. Poll data show that an overwhelming 90% of the population supported democracy in 1990. Research reveals that half of all voters considered the role of a democratic government to include safeguarding jobs and the economy, providing welfare benefits, and decreasing the socio-economic gap. In 1995, a study concluded that over 85% of Hungarians considered the reduction of the socio-economic gap to be a basic responsibility of the government. It is clear that Hungarians have not grasped democratic concepts.

A misunderstanding about the nature of democracy, coupled with the harsh economic and social blows that hit Hungary after the political transformation, led to the popular view that the transition from communism to democracy was a transition from moderate prosperity to economic hardship. Democracy did not meet the expectations of the people. A country that was deemed the merriest barrack transitioned to one of high unemployment rates, high suicide rates, and periods of recession. The primary projects of the new democratic government in Hungary were to modernize the economy and dismantle the welfare state that grew under socialism. By 1994, prices of food, medicine, energy, and transportation services rose due to the elimination of consumer subsidies and increased price liberalization. Reduced export to the Soviet bloc and declining industrial output led to a sharp decline in GDP. By 1994, the GDP had a growth rate of negative 2%, and unemployment hit 12%. At this time, the external debt burden was one of the highest in Europe, reaching 250% of annual export earnings. Current budget account deficits reached 10% of the GDP. The economic stress in the region led to one of the highest substance abuse and suicide rates in the world. An immense increase in organized crime, corruption, and the socio-economic gap made democracy seem disastrous compared to the communist days.

At home, not only are Hungarian youth offered negative messages about democracy and political leaders, but they are also given the message that politics belongs to the corrupt and warring political elite. The home acculturates Hungarian youth with information and ideals that lead to an apathetic and passive view of civic participation. The Joint Center of Eastern Europe for

Democratic Education and Governance reported in 1995 that most Hungarians were experiencing increased apathy, corruption, and alienation. Hungarians believed that politics was a battleground for warring political parties. Voter turnout in many elections began to decline at an alarming rate. In the CivEd study, there were 164 questions relating to civic attitude. Answers by Hungarian students indicated that their beliefs closely matched their parents. Students believed that democracy denotes a welfare state and that social rights outweigh political rights. It is easy to see the influence of parental attitudes in Hungary.

New theories about voter-turnout decline in the United States point toward a sense of apathy resulting from the fact that political elites have found a way to achieve their policy goals without mobilizing the public. Americans no longer believe in the efficacy of deliberation. The role of politics in the American family unit is marked by a tacit agreement between ordinary citizens and the political elite: voters are chess pieces rather than decision makers. The political elite achieve their policy goals by "mobilizing revelations, investigations, litigation, administrative processes, institutions, and targeted niche voters" rather than by mobilizing a collective public spirit toward a cause (Heclo 2003, 493).

It is clear to citizens that the political elite can achieve policy goals without the collective engagement of the public. This is evident in both historical and current events. The Vietnam and Iraq wars share the fact that the government had the ability to fight a war, raise funds, and create security directives without approval from citizens. It is no surprise that the decline of voter turnout started in the 1970s, in the throes of an unpopular war, which raged for years without the consent of the governed. Party elites, union leaders, corporations, and interest groups understand that they are more likely to get what they want through the judicial process, bureaucracies, and lobbying than mobilizing voters. Even when political parties appeal to citizens, they do so in a way that treats citizens as potential buyers with money in their pockets, rather than decision makers. For example, in 2004, political leaders limited their campaign activities to so-called show-down states like Ohio and Colorado. The decline of civic participation is a reaction to the message that collective deliberation among citizens is not important to lawmakers.

Youth are influenced by negative messages from their parents about democratic principles. Studies show that students will rarely hear positive messages about the government or officials in the home (Baldi et al. 2001, 71). Surveys about trust in government institutions in both the youth and adult populations have shown similar results: 65.1% of youth report confidence in the national government while adults report confidence at 60% (Baldi et al. 2001, 71). Negative messages about politics, coupled with the image of parents that do not vote, create an American household that acculturates youth with values that demean democratic participation. The impact of parental attitudes is very clear in the United States.

Although the United States and Hungary have different political histories, the status of the home as a socialization institution is the same in both countries. Children learn moral, cultural, and political ideals in the household. The household defines political roles by assessing the values espoused by the system. In Hungary, political roles of citizens are passive and apathetic due to historical emphasis on nonengagement, the current view among citizens that warring political factions use Parliament as a battleground, and the fact that citizens incorrectly equate democracy with a welfare state. Citizens of the United States take on a passive view because politicians have found a way to exclude them from the highest decision-making processes. It is clear that if the United States and Hungary want to reverse trends of nonparticipation, the youth must hear positive opinions about democracy.

The School

There are many aspects of school life that influence political socialization. In the United States and Hungary, schools are the formal way that the government acculturates youth with civic virtue. Schooling is universal and required. Teachers, school curriculum, and classroom culture are three features of education that have the biggest impact on political socialization. The teacher is one of the major authorities in a child's life. Not only are teachers respected people in the community, but they are also the source of both consensus and partisan values. The teacher establishes both a social and a learning culture in the classroom through pedagogy. Classroom culture itself is a socializer. Critical thinking, competitiveness, obedience, cooperation, and independence are all stressed by the environment in which learning takes place. Various studies have found that democratic school environments are necessary to inculcate democratic ideals. For example, a classroom culture can instill democratic values if students have the ability to share opinions and exercise power over day-to-day life. The classroom can also disseminate a culture of authoritarianism if hierarchies of power are maintained and students are taught to defer to authority. Curriculum influences both the classroom culture and content. If there are expressed objectives in citizenship and politics, teachers are more likely to manipulate pedagogies around a curriculum that promotes democracy. Curriculum is a large factor in civic virtue; in fact, the level of literacy and the development of critical thinking skills have been directly linked to civic virtue. Results from the National Assessment of Education Progress and CivEd studies have shown that higher levels of literacy lead to higher civic achievement.

Historically, schools in Hungary had no responsibility when it came to acculturating youth with political values. After 1956, the communist regime shifted away from forceful communist education policies and eliminated communist ideologies from the curriculum. Curriculum about communist citizenship was eventually phased out of primary, secondary, and university levels of education. For example, the once-a-week Social and Citizenship Knowledge lesson mandated by the regime for the primary and secondary levels faded into an extra history course. The communist regime of Hungary erased politics from education in exchange for unquestioned power.

As political ideologies changed in Hungary, the curriculum quickly followed suit. The first democratic parliamentary elections occurred in 1990. The same year, the newly installed democratic government began work on a new National Core Curriculum. Due to political skirmishes among the political elite, the Public Education Act was not signed until 1993. This act created a National Core Curriculum (NCC) that outlined compulsory requirements for primary and secondary education. The NCC, a democratic approach to education, was innovative from both a pedagogical and curricular standpoint. Not only did the document introduce liberal and democratic principles that were banned during the regime, but it also gave more academic freedom to the schools and teachers to decide how to teach the new curriculum. For example, the NCC mandated only half of a school program; the teachers and principals had control of the other half. The NCC merged common disciplines like mathematics, history, and literature into multidisciplinary "cultural domains." Civic education is included in the Man and Society domain. There are goals related to understanding the election system, local government, Parliament, rights and responsibilities of citizens, and human rights. Under the Man and Society domain, students are taught objectives in social studies in grades 1 through 6. The objectives of civic and social studies are taught in grades 7 and 8. Grades 9 and 10 delve into the complexities of civics and economics. The NCC tries to take a democratic and multidisciplinary approach to civic education.

Although teachers have freedom to include civic education in their learning plans, it is clear that most have not taken that path. Lack of understanding about civic rights and responsibilities can be tied to how citizenship and democracy are handled in the basic curriculum. Analysis of the civic subjects encountered in Hungarian textbooks shows that civic topics are a small element of the average classroom lesson plan. It is appropriate to analyze the content of textbooks to study the curriculum since the CivEd study confirms that textbooks are the preferred method of teaching civic education. Investigation of the composition of popular textbooks gives insight into what teachers are actually teaching. In the civics textbook for 14 and 15 year olds, out of 170 pages, only 27 pages directly address civic rights and responsibilities. Eighty-four pages explain national institutions. This means students are not learning about democracy in a way that dispels popular myths about the responsibilities of citizenship. In the 234-page textbook used in the final year of secondary schooling, the topic of democracy appears only in historical and international contexts. Only 24 pages are devoted to democracy. Although the primary history textbook for 18 year olds has a whole chapter dedicated to Hungarian institutions, it is clear that democracy studies should be a larger part of the curriculum at this time: age 18 marks the time when Hungarians are allowed to participate in elections. Analysis of the civic subjects encountered in Hungarian textbooks shows that topics that relate to civic responsibility are a small portion of the curriculum.

Although the NCC has made large strides in creating a democratic education system, the pedagogies of teachers have not changed along with the curriculum, and school environments remain largely authoritarian instead of democratic. There are many root causes of this problem. Historically, Hungarian schools have focused on textbooks, lectures, and rote memorization as learning tools because of the large volume of information students must learn to pass examinations in the final year. Since there are no state examinations that assess civic knowledge, civic education takes a backseat to other subjects. Classroom environments where lectures and textbooks guide learning, instead of debate and discussion, do not promote the principles of democracy. History provides a reason why Hungarians do not embrace deliberative learning. Discussion about politics and the government outside of the home is viewed as threatening to personal autonomy.

There are many reasons why Hungarian schools have not used deliberation in the classroom. Lack of emphasis in the curriculum and an authoritarian classroom environment, combined with the traditional pedagogies used by teachers, mean that students do not have a chance to experience democratic and citizenship principles during the school years. Students cannot fully grasp concepts of citizenship and democracy through textbook learning alone, especially if those textbooks do not have a large emphasis on democratic concepts. Although the NCC presented teachers with curricular freedom, it is clear that teachers do not know how to exercise this freedom and create democratic classroom environments. Civic education is not a part of most teacher certification programs. There is pressure put on teachers to focus on subjects other than social studies. Debate and discussion techniques are avoided in schools due to the ongoing belief that public debate is dangerous to private autonomy.

Historically, schools in the United States have had the responsibility to inculcate civic competence and responsibility. During the early days of the nation, the founding fathers realized the importance of an educated citizenry. Thomas Jefferson said, "Information is the currency of democracy." Although there is no National Core Curriculum in the United States, voluntary national standards have been developed by professional societies for all content taught in public and private K–12 schools. State departments of education, teacher training institutions, school accreditation societies, and school districts use voluntary national standards to ensure uniform skill development and learning across the country.

Social studies became part of the curriculum in the 1890s. The National Council for the Social Studies says that the primary purpose of social studies is to help students develop the skills necessary to make informed and reasoned decisions as citizens of a diverse and democratic society. In 1994, the Center for Civic Education created the National Standards on Civics and Government. These standards have been integrated into K–12 curricula by most local and state governments. The standards create benchmarks for what students should know as they leave the 4th, 8th, and 12th grades. Benchmarks include intellectual skills related to understanding, evaluating, and defending positions, and participatory skills of understanding the role of civic participation at the local, state, and national level.

The United States also has problem relating to the lack of focus on civic education in the curriculum. Textbook learning dominates classrooms. The CivEd assessment indicates that American students are more likely to report reading a textbook or filling out worksheets than engaging in activities such as having visits from leaders or writing letters of opinion to representatives. The National Center for Educational Statistics reports that 37% of 4th grade students spend 1–2 hours a week on social studies and 31% spend 2–3 hours, but only 19% spend more than 3 hours. Subjects such as reading and mathematics get a higher priority than civic education for many reasons. Standardized tests assess mathematics and reading to determine levels of funding and enforce school accountability. Civic education is given a backseat in most schools due to pressure put on teachers to succeed in standardized testing and other endeavors that do not include civics.

Although social studies educators have supported democratic pedagogies for decades, no research supports the idea that American teachers create democratic environments in classrooms. As noted above, lecture and textbooks dominate classroom learning. The CivEd assessment reports that only 45% of students engage in debates and discussions about issues. Since emphasis is placed on subjects assessed in standardized testing, teachers do not learn democratic pedagogies in teacher-training programs. Teachers of 4th and 8th grade civics rated themselves as unprepared to use the voluntary national standards for civics and government (Pepper et al. 2003, 39). American schools do not embrace deliberation in the classroom.

It is interesting to note the similar issues that Hungary and the United States face when it comes to the socialization process that occurs in schools. Clearly, the weak socialization process does not occur because of flawed objectives, but from neglect in creating a classroom atmosphere that helps meet those objectives. Education in both countries undermines ideas related to democracy and collective deliberation. Teachers in both countries are not trained in democratic pedagogies and do not create democratic learning environments. The curriculum of both countries gives low priority to civic education because of pressures put on teachers and schools to teach other subjects and perform well on standardized tests.

Political Socialization and the Lack of Deliberative Institutions

Innovative solutions for the decline of democratic participation in Hungary and the United States must take into account that schools are not deliberative institutions. Examination of how children are being politically socialized at home shows that the older generations of both countries do not believe in the efficacy of collective decision making. In Hungary, history has instilled the idea that public discourse is dangerous and that decision making should be left to the political elite. In the United States, citizens are apathetic because the elite are sending messages that the government can run without the collective choices of citizens. The younger generations of both countries are receiving negative opinions about deliberation and civic participation.

Schools also affect civic knowledge and civic participation. An investigation of common pedagogies, classroom atmosphere, and the relationship between civic education and other subjects shows that schools are not teaching the students the importance of collective decision making. Education runs on an authoritarian model in both countries. School districts, teachers, and students make choices based on fear. For example, schools and teachers create curriculum based on the knowledge that if enough students fail a standardized test, funding will be cut, and teachers will be fired. In the classroom, decision making is a function of the teacher and the school, and students make decisions based on fear of punishment instead of collective understanding of the social contract. The fact that lectures and textbooks are the most popular teaching tools explains how students are taught that governance comes from authorities instead of from deliberation in the public sphere.

Both countries have failed to structure schools as deliberative institutions. If students are taught in an environment that stresses the importance of choices, they will be more willing to learn democratic principles, and they will understand the efficacy of democracy. If school districts and teachers are not induced by fear to rig classrooms to create students that score well on tests, they will have the chance to incorporate ideologies that teach mathematics, reading, and science through a democratic framework. Teachers cannot innovate under the immense pressure put on them to succeed in creating good test-takers. They rely on traditional and outdated pedagogies instead of innovating classroom culture.

INNOVATIVE SOLUTIONS

The education system must realize that a democratic classroom environment can teach critical subjects (such as reading and mathematics) while inculcating civic virtue at the same time. The education system must work to re-acculturate students with ideals that stress the importance of deliberative institutions. Schools must realize that there is no competition between civics and other subjects. Possession of critical thinking skills and knowledge about common school subjects is necessary to learn civics. For example, literacy levels have a positive correlation with civic education. Administrators and teachers must find ways to use civic education to fulfill goals related to literacy, reasoning, and critical thinking. At the national level, the best way to move toward democratic pedagogies is to expand teacher training to include the study of democratic classroom models. Teachers, administrators, and the government, must work together to create a system of district and teacher accountability that still allows for freedom and innovation in the classroom. Since that goal may take decades to achieve, the best thing for teachers to do now is to integrate activities into the curriculum that help students meet state learning goals in critical subjects as well as increase civic competency, heighten appreciation for the deliberative process, and instill the belief that the decision-making process of each individual is important.

Competition-based student programs that focus on subjects such as current events, politics, social policy, citizenship, and democracy are nontraditional tools that teachers can use to inculcate civic virtue. Examples include debate programs and civic competitions. *Project Citizen* in Hungary and *We the People* in the United States are two civic competitions that focus on local issues. For example, *Project Citizen* has students research the causes of a local issue, develop solutions, and use local government to try to change existing policy. Students gain valuable civic interaction skills, critical thinking skills, knowledge about current events, and the understanding that they can use local infrastructure to change their world. In a debate, students must study historical and current events, analyze material, and learn to argue sides of an issue. Programs like these inculcate civic virtue because participation in extracurricular activities increases civic participation, a competitive program places value and worth on civic competency, and skills from other domains can be incorporated into preparing for the competition. Student participation in extracurricular activities has a positive effect on civic education. The CivEd study found a positive correlation between student participation in student associations and civic participation. Students who were involved in extra-curricular activities were most likely to say that they would vote as adults. Competition also helps students see the value in civic learning. For example, if students participate in a debate program in which the level of civic skills and knowledge determines the winner, students attribute worth and values to civic competency.

Competition creates an environment in which students will push themselves to acquire civic virtue. Preparing for a debate tournament or a civic competition requires that students read and analyze materials, work together in teams, use critical thinking skills, and learn specific information about public policy topics. A sample Middle School Public Debate Program topic from a previous season, "American involvement in Iraq has done more harm than good," called on students to understand public policy concepts, international relations, and economic concepts. Another topic, "Governor Schwarzenegger has been good for California," had students learn about issues affecting the local government. Debaters of the topic "The United States should ratify the Kyoto accord" had to master political as well as scientific concepts to win their rounds. This shows that students apply information from critical subjects that they learn in the classroom. If students want to win the national *Project Citizen* competition, they must have the volition to work hard on their policy projects, study current events, learn about government infrastructure, and create a plan of action to influence local politics. Competitive civic associations increase knowledge and skills that help children succeed as citizens and as students.

Conclusion

It is clear that citizens in both the United States and Hungary do not completely understand the power or the necessity of their roles as decision makers. Citizens of both countries have rejected the efficacy of deliberative institutions. New pedagogies must create a democratic environment in the classroom, with principles regarding citizenship, deliberation, and collective bargaining. Schools must provide students with the ability to practice and apply citizenship concepts. The curriculum must incorporate learning related to critical subjects and critical thinking into civic lessons. Competitive civic associations and programs provide a model for how these ideas can be integrated into student life. Further research, and decision making by policymakers and the public, must focus on creating schools that are an innovative model for democracy.

Bibliography

Baldi, Stephane, Marianne Perie, Dan Skidmore, Elizabeth Greenberg, Carole Hahn, and Dawn Nelson. What Democracy Means to Ninth-Graders: U.S. Results from the International IEA Civic Education Study. NCES 2001-096, Washington, DC: United States Department of Education, National Center for Education Statistics, 2001.

Heclo, H. "Is the Body Politic Dying? A Review Essay." Political Science Quarterly 118, 3 (Fall 2003): 491–496.

Johnson, Carol. Civics: What Do 4th-Graders Know, and What Can They Do? NCES-2001-460, Washington, DC: United States Department of Education, National Center for Education Statistics, 2001.

———. Civics: What Do 8th-Graders Know, and What Can They Do? NCES-2001-460, Washington, DC: United States Department of Education, National Center for Education Statistics, 2001.

———. Civics: What Do 12th-Graders Know, and What Can They Do? NCES-2001-460, Washington, DC: United States Department of Education, National Center for Education Statistics, 2001.

Kim, Simon, et al. "Effects of Participatory Learning Programs in Middle and High School Civic Education." Social Studies 87, 4 (1996): 171–176.

Kubow, Patricia K., and Mark B. Kinney. "Fostering Democracy in Middle School Classrooms: Insights from a Democratic Institute in Hungary." Social Studies 91, 6 (2000): 265–271.

Pepper, K. "Strategies for Teaching Civic Education: An International Perspective." Kappa Delta Pi Record 40, 2 (Winter 2004): 83–85.

Pepper, K., et al. "Teaching Civic Education in a Democratic Society: A Comparison of Civic Education in Hungary and the United States." Educational Foundations 17, 2 (Spring 2003): 29–51.

Ridley, Helen S., Balazs Hidveghi, and Annette Pitts. "Civic Education for Democracy in Hungary." International Journal of Social Education 12, 2 (1997): 62–72.

Torney-Purta, Judith, Jo-Ann Amadeo, and Rainer Lehmann. "Civic Knowledge and Engagement at Age 14 in 28 Countries: Results from the IEA Civic Education Study." ERIC Digest. Office of Educational Research and Improvement (ED), Washington, DC. Vol. EDOSO20013. Indiana: ERIC Clearinghouse for Social Studies/Social Science Education, 2001.

Torney-Purta, Judith, et al. Citizenship and Education in Twenty-Eight Countries: Civic Knowledge and Engagement at Age Fourteen. Executive Summary. Netherlands: IEA Secretariat, 2001.

Zsigo, Frank Thomas. "Democratic Ideas, Understandings, Practices and Attitudes among Students in Post-Communist Hungary, 1989–2001." Ph.D. Diss., Syracuse University, 2003. Ann Arbor: UMI, 2003. 3081635.

Candace Williams is a philosophy, politics, and economics major at Claremont McKenna College in Claremont, California. Her work in education policy includes interning at the Claremont Colleges Debate Union, the Middle School Public Debate Program, the Pierce County Juvenile Court, and the Commonwealth Human Rights Initiative in Delhi, India.

The Role of Debate Activism for Civil Societies*

Joseph P. Zompetti

INTRODUCTION

The 1960s witnessed renewed vibrancy in American civil society when gains in civil rights occurred, citizens engaged in sustained activism, and public discourse about the state of affairs was rich and lively. In the 1990s, post-Communist countries in Eastern Europe began actively pursuing non-Communist versions of contemporary civil society with the hope of ushering in meaningful participatory democracy (Bryant, 1993, p. 397; Kumar, 1993, p. 375; Seligman, 1992, p. 4). Despite its recent popularity, the concept of civil society is still ambiguous, unmanageable, complicated, and even in some ways unreachable. Given its varied history and ambiguous meanings, recent scholars have suggested that civil society is under-theorized and lacks, as it currently stands, a cohesive framework for sustainability (Katz, 2002; Lenzen, 2002). Yet, most Americans believe that civil society is an important component to democracy. In fact, with voter registration drives, reports from national commissions, increasing levels of volunteerism, and higher political contributions from average citizens (Ladd, 1996; Schudson, 1996), one would think that civil society is not only a mainstay of American society, but flourishing.

However, we also know that there is growing political apathy, declining membership in civic organizations, and a burgeoning, albeit elaborate, network of market and government forces that largely influence major societal decisions (Brint and Levy, 1999; Council on Civil Society, 1998; National

*Presented at the annual IDEA conference, Istanbul, Turkey, November, 2004. Dr. Zompetti wishes to thank Kubo Macak for his helpful comments on an earlier draft of this paper. This paper is an earlier version of the article "The Role of Advocacy in Civil Society," published in *Argumentation: An International Journal on Reasoning*.

Commission on Civic Renewal, 1998; Putnam, 1995, 1996; Skocpol and Fiorina, 1999). While activists and leaders in government, business, and education have been clamoring for a renewed civil society since the 1960s, very little has been done to achieve a more vibrant sense of public space and discourse. In short, cynicism, apathy, lack of access, seduction of television, economic inequality, and other social pressures have caused deterioration in American civil society. Even in areas of the United States where civil society seems to be thriving, we would do well to notice how it is sustained, how it is improved, and perhaps how it can be emulated elsewhere.

In this paper I acknowledge the reformist ideas to reinvigorate civil society. However, an essential component of many strategies to sustain civil society appears lacking. What is missing is a strategy for training or encouraging citizens to participate more fully in civil society. Given this, I propose that skills of debate and advocacy can, at least in part, help renew civic activism. In what follows, I sketch the value of civil society and how debate and advocacy can help revitalize civil society.

The Importance of Civil Society

According to some recent scholars, none of the ancient or classical civil society models are sufficient to either explain contemporary understandings of civil society, nor are they able to functionally address previous criticisms of the sometimes subtle but often overtly discriminatory practices of governing and market forces. This is especially true when we look at societies where the state and market forces act in collusion with one another. What has resulted is a number of reformist ideas aimed at trying to preserve civil society. Perhaps most important is the idea that civil society can and should exist as a third space separate from both the state and the market (Bryant, 1993; Cohen and Arato, 1992; Hauser and Benoit-Barne, 2002). Christopher Bryant suggests that this is a *"space or arena between household and state,* other than the market, which affords possibilities of concerted action and social self-organisation" (1993, p. 399). In effect, society is defined as having three components: the political, the economic, and the civic. Thus, civil society can be defined as non-state and non-economic entities that influence, shape, and participate in society at large.

Over the centuries, civil society has morphed into different concepts, but the underlying principle of a *societas civilis* has generally been considered worth the struggle. Despite some rather compelling criticisms of civil society (see Ehrenberg, 1999; Encarnacion, 2000; Foley & Edwards, 1996; Gellner, 1994; Kumar, 1993, 1994; Noumoff, 2000; Pateman, 1988; Scholte, 2002; Skocpol, 1999), civil society is not only a valuable concept to discuss the roles of participating citizens as they relate to the state, the market, or other societal domains, but civil society is also an important ideal for us to construct, maintain, and preserve. As John Ehrenberg declares:

> Civil society's dense networks of associations increase citizens' political influence on the state, make them less vulnerable to mass demagoguery, and reduce the importance of politics by spreading interests over a wide public space.
>
> ... Civil society makes possible the sort of moderate political activity that reconciles Tocquevillean localism with the large institutions of contemporary political life. (1999, p. 205)

And, Alvin Gouldner suggests: "No emancipation is possible in the modern world ... without a strong civil society that can strengthen the public sphere and can provide a haven from and a center of resistance to the Behemoth state" (1980, p. 371). In these ways, civil society is an important check against excessive political and economic power.

Of course, if we take a more contemporary definition of civil society as the "realm of society, lying outside the institutionalized political and administrative mechanisms of the state and the state-regulated part of the economy, where people carry on their publicly oriented social and economic activities" (Ehrenberg, 1999, p. 197), then we can begin to see the transformative potential of civil society. Indeed, what all of the critiques of civil society have in common is a pessimism of will, or a reliance on a flawed conception of what civil society entails. Both themes can be addressed if citizens become more engaged in civic affairs—what I will argue is the meaning of advocacy. And, according to Richard Price (2003), there are empirical examples of successful pressure from civil society on both the state and the market to change. Or, if the criticisms are correct, then there is very little hope for deliberative democracy in general. In either case, reinvigorating civil society seems to be the better course to take. Indeed, as Bryant declares, "civil society ... refers to a cluster of phenomena of contemporary social and political significance more sensitively than any of the familiar components of liberal democratic theory" (1993, p. 399). In short, civil society is our only hope of fostering citizen activism and preserving liberties.

The Importance of Advocacy

It is rather common knowledge that American civil society has waned (Brint & Levy, 1999; Council on Civil Society, 1998; National Commission on Civic Renewal, 1998; Putnam, 1995, 1996; Skocpol & Fiorina, 1999). With the transition to democracy in post-Communist societies, particularly in Central and Eastern Europe, the fragmentation of civil society in America should pose some concern. After all, once democracy begins to flourish, what does that mean for a sustained, politically active citizenry? When we look at some of the reasons why American civil society has waned, we realize they are premised on the possibility that Americans simply don't know how to be engaged in a civil society (Dewey, 2003; Putnam, 1995). Robert Putnam (1995) adamantly proposes that the popularity of television is directly proportional to the decline of civil society. But, Ehrenberg (1999) convincingly argues that television is not enough to explain this social phenomenon. Instead, Ehrenberg declares, civil society is constructed and threatened by a number of factors, including political, economic, and social forces. What we need, then, is a concept that helps transcend the different factors to enable us to revive and sustain civil society.

One possible element that transcends the different problems plaguing civil society is advocacy. Generally speaking, advocacy is the ability to argue a compelling position that relates to an issue of controversy. More specifically in this context, advocacy can be understood as a process of thinking, as well as speaking, in that advocacy requires the critical thinking of societal issues to be synthesized into a particular argument position. Thus, the one engaging in advocacy, the advocate, must be able to process the main issues of the day in order to speak intelligently and compellingly regarding his or her position. It is not surprising that previous scholars have not picked up on the importance of advocacy in its relation to civil society, since, as Cairns (1998) declares, advocacy "has never been a subject for scholarly consideration" (p. 445). Americans, in general, do not know how to discuss, much less research, items of importance concerning contemporary America (Dewey, 2003). This may not be unique to the United States. What we see, then, is a correlative relationship between the inability to advocate and the collapse of civil society. I am not so naïve as to suggest that this relationship is causal or that advocacy is the only factor involved in the very complex civil society phenomenon. Nevertheless, the *role* of advocacy could play an important part in resuscitating American civil society.

A Brief Sketch on the History of Advocacy

It is perhaps no coincidence that advocacy, as a concept, has similar origins as does civil society. Both concepts related to the *polis* as well as to the *res publica*. The ancient Greeks and Romans were fond of discussing advocacy as a means of speaking on someone else's behalf (Dunne, 1999; Grace, 2001; Whalen, 2003). For the Greeks, the sophists initiated the importance of advocacy as they taught the skills of switch-side advocacy to students. In Rome, there were two types of advocates: the *advocatus*, the advocate for civic engagement and improvement of society, and the *jurisconsult*, or the advocate for someone else (Cohen, 2000). The role of *advocatus* was highly respected; it was seen as a special gift and eventually became a frequently sought-after profession, particularly with the development of Roman law. The *jurisconsult* was precisely that—a counsel to the court. The *jurisconsult* was less respectable than the *advocatus*, since the *jurisconsult* was an "advocate for hire" and lacked the passion to change society for the better, as opposed to the *advocatus*.

With Cicero (1949), we have the five canons that are key to advocacy as it primarily pertains to the *advocatus*—Invention, Arrangement, Style, Memory, and Delivery. In fact, it is with Cicero that we see the importance of civic engagement *qua* advocacy, as opposed to simple legal persuasion with the *jurisconsults* (Cicero, 1949; Hanrahan, 2003). Accordingly, Cicero emphasized the value of "expressing civic virtue and political stability as well as providing intellectual structure," in order to advance the cause of a "good society" (Hanrahan, 2003, pp. 313–314). Of course, it is Quintilian, after Cicero, who emphasized the ethical and moral element to advocacy. By highlighting that the "good person speaking well" is the keystone of a good society, Quintilian was advancing his conception of the valuable society. What's more, Quintilian offered the idea that the "good man [sic]" who speaks well was a model for society, and that his speech should reflect his own personal advocacy (Scallen & Wiethoff, 1998, p. 1143).

While we often think of the Roman *advocatus* as the origin of advocacy, we should not forget the importance of Aristotle. For Aristotle, the advocate was more about civic improvement than it was about individual improvement or financial gain. Aristotle, in *The Politics* (1968), described the *polis* as an entity of civic associations. In fact, Aristotle referred to the *polis* as the "association of associations" (Hodgkinson & Foley, 2003, p. ix). It was in the *polis* that individual citizens could interact and discuss matters, including those central to politics and law. Regarding legal matters,

Aristotle was careful to explain the role of the orator, as they studied the *logos*, *pathos*, and *ethos* of their advocacy. In *The Rhetoric*, Aristotle advanced that "the speaker," when discussing legal affairs, "must appeal to the universal law, and to the principles of equity as representing a higher order of justice" (1932, p. 80). Advocacy, then, for Aristotle, was premised on an ethical-political notion of justice. We might say that an Aristotelian advocacy is geared toward an ethical civic engagement.

After Aristotle, Cicero, and Quintilian, very little is written that discusses advocacy. We know that during the Medieval and Renaissance eras disputes were settled through means of advocacy that followed the traditions of the ancient Romans and Greeks. One may even chart the word "advocate" to 14th century France to mean the "pleading for or supporting" (Grace, 2001, p. 154). The lack of material describing advocacy since Greece and Rome is telling of the durability of the concept. Advocacy, simply put, is the passionate plea for a particular position. What's more, the concept of "advocacy" has essentially meant this for over 2,000 years.

The Skills of Advocacy

Contemporary training in advocacy directly corresponds to the ancient teachings of Aristotle, Quintilian, and Cicero (Jamail, 1995). David S. Coale, a former law clerk in the Fifth Circuit of the U.S. Court of Appeals and currently a private attorney in Dallas, convincingly argues that Aristotle's formula for effective advocacy—*ethos*, *pathos*, and *logos*—is the key to successful legal advocacy today (2001, p. 734). Additionally, James S. Gifford, who is an attorney in Hawaii, defends Aristotle's description of advocacy in laying the groundwork for modern American constitutional law (1999, p. 490).

Aristotle, as we know, was not the only one to expound about the nature of advocacy in the ancient period. In Rome, Quintilian and Cicero borrowed the Greek idea that advocacy was persuasion. As far as that would go, Cicero, in particular, was not satisfied. For him, specific elements such as style, arrangement, delivery, and so on were vital for effective speeches, especially oratory concerning legal or political affairs. Like Aristotle, we know that the Ciceronian "canon"— particularly of delivery, style, and memory—is vital for contemporary lessons of advocacy (Hanrahan, 2003). In fact, Jennifer Hanrahan helps explain that Cicero's "five canons" are used "to appeal to a jury's sense of ethos, pathos, and logos," thereby bridging the contributions of both Aristotle and Cicero (2003, p. 308).

Finally, at its core, advocacy means persuasion. Aristotle includes advocacy as a form of rhetoric, which he defines as "discovering in the particular case what are the available means of persuasion" (1932, p. 7). More contemporary argument and persuasion scholars also view advocacy as tied to persuasion:

> It is the advocate's job to persuade others as to the se-
> riousness of a problem, i.e., to get others to recognize the
> existence of a problem, as well as persuade others that the
> advocate's solution to the problem is a wise and workable
> one which should be adopted. The advocate, accordingly, is
> concerned with influence and power: he [sic] wants to be ef-
> fective, to be able to influence person A to accept solution X
> when otherwise A might accept solution Y or no solution at
> all. (Windes & Hastings, 1965, p. 24)

We may say that persuasion is to convince someone else of some item or belief. Advocacy, however, is a unique form of persuasion. Aside from arguing a problem and a solution, as Russell Windes and Arthur Hastings differentiate, what makes advocacy a special form of persuasion is its purpose to avoid coercion. According to current legal scholars (Hanrahan, 2003; Jamail, 1995), advocacy is the impassioned making of one's case. Its delivery and content are prepared and presented in ways that are integrally tied to the advocate's identity, ensuring that the onus is on the advocate, not the audience. This form of rhetoric minimizes the degree of coercion since the advocacy is, by definition, offered, rather than forced upon its listeners.

The skills of advocacy, then, relate to the ability to persuade, including the skills of *ethos, pathos, logos,* and the Ciceronian five canons. We may specify this by saying that advocacy also relates to persuasion by means other than coercion. In other words, the advocacy is premised on the advocate's passion for the content. While the goal of persuading the audience is always evident, the actual meaning underlying the content of advocacy is centered on the advocate's subjectivity, not the audience's. Finally, we can say that advocacy relates to a problem and a solution, as described by Windes and Hastings (1965). This emphasis requires us to learn basic skills of research, argument composition and construction, delivery, style, and evidentiary proof. Of course, if the advocacy generates discussion, particularly in the public realm, then skills of refutation must also be acquired (Windes and Hastings, 1965).

Advocacy's Role for Civil Society

In the spirit of Alexis de Tocqueville, Thomas Jefferson referred to the new American democracy as a "free marketplace," not as capitalism run amuck, but rather as a free-flow of open possibilities for citizens to discuss political affairs (Windes & Hastings, 1965, p. 9). This "freedom" occurs on two levels, both inquiry and advocacy, where inquiry refers to the ability of individuals to make rational judgments and advocacy as a form of persuasion. Indeed, as Windes and Hastings suggest, the freedom of "advocacy" develops as "people attempt to influence the belief of others *through* advocacy and are, in turn, influenced *by* advocacy, by the forceful presentation of the beliefs of other citizens" (1965, p. 11). In essence, advocacy enables the citizen to perform their role as a citizen—citizen *qua* citizen.

Fundamentally, if civil society is meant to provide a space of civic engagement separate from political or economic interference, then discussions should emerge about political and economic affairs that avoid the coercive, albeit hegemonic, influence of both the state and the market. What does advocacy bring to the table? By definition, a citizenry trained in the skills of advocacy would do the following:

1. Learn to recognize and avoid arguments of coercion (Quintilian),

2. Learn to research and reflect on civic issues of importance (Cicero),

3. Learn to be impassioned by means of reason to issues at hand (Cicero and Aristotle),

4. Learn to prepare and deliver effective arguments about the issue (Cicero and Aristotle),

5. Learn to refute oppositional claims and sustain credibility (Cicero and Aristotle).

Skills, not just ideals, can help propel citizens to become better citizens. Some of the greatest philosophers of all time (Aristotle, Tocqueville, Jefferson, Antonio Gramsci, etc.) have clamored for individual subjects to take a more active role in areas of governance that affect them personally. Advocacy skills can reinvigorate civic participation and deliberative democracy (Hanrahan,

2003; Jewell, 1998). Learning how to engage in advocacy can also help citizens understand the importance of civic engagement, thereby curtailing some of the distracting societal forces that have to date discouraged civic participation (Ehrenberg, 1999; Putnam 1995, 1996). These skills must be taught; unlike rights, they are not self-evident (Hanrahan, 2003). Classes in school that discuss citizenship and civic participation are a good start. Somewhere along the line, however, we have forgotten that civic engagement is a process; a process that requires sustained influence, especially when considering the number of distractions and impediments to participating in civil society (Putnam, 1995).

Educating the public about their responsibilities and duties to civic engagement is also a start (Dewey, 2003). Where John Dewey and others fall short, however, is their neglect of advocacy as an important process to give value to civil society. Advocacy, while not a cure-all, can help jumpstart the civil society process in many areas of the country. Where civil society is already taking root, the ability to advocate salient public issues can galvanize additional support and help maintain the spirit of civic engagement that is so critical to a functioning democracy (Hauser & Benoit-Barne, 2002, p. 271).

Perhaps the most important question to ask is: How can advocacy help civil society? The skills associated with advocacy should already appear significant when drawing a connection between advocacy and civil society. In addition, there are a number of events and opportunities that can use advocacy skills to maintain or construct notions of civil society. Besides training students and citizens about the skills of advocacy, public forums and/or public debates could help with reviving civil society. Gordon Mitchell (1998, 2000) has already argued that public debates can help foster a sense of community and inclusion. The idea here is that we can utilize the infrastructure that already exists within collegiate debate and speech programs to facilitate planned public debates about issues regarding our communities. Aimed at encouraging student and citizen participation, these debates could help foster additional discussions and possibly even generate additional public *fora* where deliberative, civic discussions take place.

Venues for a civil society can all be improved through the process of advocacy. Universities are a natural fit with this conception since advocacy skills can be easily disseminated in course curricula and student organizations. A university scene can also play an important part in the development and maintenance of civil society since, according to Gerard Delanty, "[t]he university is an institution of the public sphere; it is not above civil society but a part of its cultural tradition, in particular it is a part of the public sphere and its tradition of debate and reflection" (1988, p. 22). Universities can simultaneously instruct students in advocacy skills while also offering community outreach programs and public discussions about issues pertaining to civil society.

Perhaps a couple of examples will illustrate these points. First, academic debate can be a very useful project for training and exercising advocacy skills. With its focus on research and critical thinking skills, academic debate requires students to process multiple perspectives of contemporary social issues in order to develop coherent positions of advocacy. A process of refutation then occurs when two teams argue back and forth about the merits and drawbacks to the advocacy positions at hand. In the end, debaters learn more about their society and political systems, as well as gain valuable skills to become more active citizens. A terrific example of how debate can impact civil society is the Albanian debate organization of MJAFT! (Albanian for enough [from the government]). In recent elections, the MJAFT! debaters, highly-trained in the skills of advocacy, recorded promises made by politicians, then required the candidates, along with members of the audience, to sign a form indicating that such promises were made (Mitchell, 2004). Not only do such techniques make the candidates accountable for the promises (if elected), but they also demonstrate how individual citizens can take an active role in their civil society.

Another example of how the skills of advocacy can help civil society is with the recent youth conflict mediation and arbitration project sponsored by the International Debate Education Association (IDEA). According to IDEA, the program helps young students throughout Europe to engage in conflict resolution techniques. The program emphasizes "fine-tuned communication patterns targeted at specific audiences aimed at conflict resolution and democracy promotion" (IDEA Website). The program teaches advocacy skills in order to mediate conflict, which include analyzing the problem, discussing the issues with interested and relevant parties, assessing a target audience for the potential resolution of issues, brainstorming of conflict resolution issues, and ideas for implementation (IDEA Website). Overall, the project enables youth to utilize the skills they acquire to make productive changes in their society. Advocacy, then, becomes the framework for not only encouraging participation in civil society, but also to address some potential conflict areas that exist within civil society.

Finally, I have touched on the importance of civil society for deliberative democracy. Many scholars point to civil society's contribution to democracy, some even arguing that civil society is the *sine qua non* for democracy (Bryant, 1993; Cohen and Arato, 1992; Ehrenberg, 1999; Hodgkinson and Foley, 2003). But what is the role of advocacy in securing a functioning and prospering democracy? Advocacy is the lynchpin for preparing and delivering arguments. For a functioning democracy, public discussions about the merits and disadvantages of different courses of action are vital. Only through thorough research and development of arguments can this occur. Advocacy, then, is essential for both civil society and democracy. Theda Skocpol, borrowing from de Tocqueville, argues that "[u]nderstanding the causes and consequences of civic America's recent transition from membership to advocacy is vital if we are to reflect wisely on prospects for our democracy" (1999, p. 462). In a society where cynicism and apathy run rampant, learning how to advocate might just be the anecdote for a disease of despair.

Conclusions

Civil society for contemporary society should embrace the concept of the *third space*, as discussed by Bryant (1993), Jean Cohen and Andrew Arato (1992), and Gerard Hauser and Chantal Benoit-Barne (2002). The third space envisions civil society as an autonomous sphere, separate from governmental or economic influence. The third space minimizes the amount of undue influence that can emanate from the state or the market. As Cohen and Arato suggest, "the insistence that without public spaces for the active participation of the citizenry in ruling and being ruled, without a decisive narrowing of the gap between rulers and ruled, to the point of its abolition, politics are democratic in name only" (1992, p. 7). Venues for a civil society conceived as a third space, such as churches, synagogues, unions, voluntary organizations, schools, women's groups, and other arenas can all be improved through the process of advocacy. These groups and organizations, according to Skocpol, are "sites where citizens learn—and practice—the 'knowledge of how to combine' so vital to democracy" (1999, p. 462). As we have seen, advocacy skills are important for citizens not only to appreciate their role in civil society, but also to advance and refute positions regarding civic involvement and efforts at improving society. As I have discussed, incorporating advocacy into civil society, one can hope, will foster more meaningful discussion, less coercion, and more productive civic engagement.

I have wrestled with the concept of civil society—what does it mean, how does it function, is it important? Civil society is not without its flaws, one of which is it is not sustainable on its own. Something else must also be present for civil society to flourish. Its existence may depend on multiple factors, but one that seems most evident is a citizenry who is capable of using the skills of advocacy. Quite simply, this relationship between civil society and advocacy seems particularly salient to me since civil society requires civil engagement, and advocacy generates the ability and skill sets necessary to engage in discussions affecting the populace. Again, I am not suggesting that advocacy is a panacea. Civil society is struggling over other factors as well, such as the distraction of sports and television, the collusion between politicians and their constituents, economic demands preventing civic participation, and so on. However, assuming there are enough citizens who have the ability and willingness to engage in civil society, how could their participation be improved? How could civil society be more influential in its relationship to the state and market? How can citizens feel more secure and enthusiastic about their participation? I believe that the skills of advocacy can help answer these questions.

Some of the greatest thinkers in history have discussed civil society. Most agree that it is a concept worth keeping. Indeed, if democracy intends on listening to the voice of the people, then the people need to have a voice. Civil society serves as a tool for citizens to engage each other as well as the affairs of society. Only through a process of civic discourse, respect, and argument can this discourse serve any purpose. The ancient principles of advocacy are a reminder of how each individual has a part to play in civic engagement. Advocacy, not acrimony, can improve and resuscitate our civil society. And, in turn, perhaps it can improve our democracy.

BIBLIOGRAPHY

Aristotle. (1932). The Rhetoric of Aristotle (Lane Cooper, Trans.). Englewood Cliffs, NJ: Prentice-Hall.

Aristotle. (1968). The Politics (Steven Emerson, Ed.). Cambridge, UK: Cambridge University Press.

Brint, Steven, and Levy, Charles S. (1999). "Professions and Civic Engagement: Trends in Rhetoric and Practice, 1875–1995." In Theda Skocpol and Morris P.

Fiorina (Eds.), Civic Engagement in American Democracy (pp. 163–210). Washington, DC: Brookings Institution Press.

Bryant, Christopher G. A. (1993). "Social Self-Organisation, Civility and Sociology: A Comment on Kumar's 'Civil Society.'" The British Journal of Sociology, 44, 397–401.

Cairns, David J. A. (1998). Advocacy and the Making of the Adversarial Criminal Trial, 1800–1865. Oxford: Clarendon Press.

Calhoun, Craig. (2002). "Imagining Solidarity: Cosmopolitanism, Constitutional Patriotism, and the Public Sphere." Public Culture, 14, 147–171.

Cicero, Marcus Tullius. (1949). De inventione; De optimo genere oratorum (H. M. Hubbell, Trans.). Cambridge, MA.: Harvard University Press.

Coale, David S. (2001, Fall). "Developments and Practice Notes: Classical Citation." The Journal of Appellate Practice and Process, 3, 733–742.

Cohen, James A. (2000). "Lawyer Role, Agency Law, and the Characterization 'Officer of the Court.'" Buffalo Law Review, 48. Available from Lexis-Nexis.

Cohen, Jean L., and Arato, Andrew. (1992). Civil Society and Political Theory. Cambridge, MA: MIT Press.

Council on Civil Society. (1998). Why Democracy Needs Moral Truths. New York: Council on Civil Society.

de Tocqueville, Alexis. (1966). Democracy in America (J. P. Mayer and Max Lerner, Eds.). New York: Harper and Row.

Dean, Jodi. (2001). "Cybersalons and Civil Society: Rethinking the Public Sphere in Transnational Technoculture." Public Culture, 13, 243–265.

Delanty, Gerard. (1988). "The Idea of the University in the Global Era: From Knowledge as an End to the End of Knowledge?" Social Epistemology, 12, 3–25.

Dewey, John. (2003). "The Public and Its Problems." In Virginia A. Hodgkinson and Michael W. Foley (Eds.), The Civil Society Reader (pp. 133–153). Hanover, NH: Tufts University Press.

Dunne, Peter J. (1999, July). "The Origins of Advocacy." Historical Perspectives. Bar Association of Metropolitan St. Louis Website. Accessed January 22, 2004. Available at www.bamsl.org/stlawyer/archive/99/July99/Dunne.html

Ehrenberg, John. (1999). Civil Society: The Critical History of an Idea. New York: New York University Press.

Encarnacion, Omar G. (2000). "Tocqueville's Missionaries: Civil Society Advocacy and the Promotion of Democracy." World Policy Journal, 17, 9–18.

Foley, Michael W., and Edwards, Bob. (1996). "The Paradox of Civil Society." Journal of Democracy, 7, 38–52.

Gellner, Ernest. (1994). Conditions of Liberty: Civil Society and Its Rivals. New York: Allen Lane.

Gifford, James S. (1999). "Jus Cogens and Fourteenth Amendment Privileges or Immunities." Arizona Journal of International and Comparative Law, 16, 481–498.

Gouldner, Alvin. (1980). The Two Marxisms. London: Macmillan.

Grace, Pamela J. (2001). "Professional Advocacy: Widening the Scope of Accountability." Nursing Philosophy, 2, 151–163.

Gramsci, Antonio. (1971). Selections from the Prison Notebooks (Quintin Hoare and Geoffrey Nowell Smith, Eds. and Trans.). New York: International Publishers.

Hanrahan, Jennifer Kruse. (2003). "Truth in Action: Revitalizing Classical Rhetoric as a Tool for Teaching Oral Advocacy in American Law Schools." Brigham Young University Education and Law Journal, 299–338.

Hauser, Gerard A., and Benoit-Barne, Chantal. (2002). "Reflections on Rhetoric, Deliberative Democracy, Civil Society, and Trust." Rhetoric & Public Affairs, 5, 261–275.

Hegel, G. W. F. (1967). Philosophy of Right (T. M. Knox, Trans.). London: Oxford University Press.

Hodgkinson, Virginia A., and Foley, Michael W. (Eds.). (2003). The Civil Society Reader. Hanover, NH: Tufts University Press.

Holst, John D. (2002). Social Movements, Civil Society, and Radical Adult Education. Westport, CT: Bergin and Garvey.

IDEA Web site (no date). Available at www.idebate.org.

Jamail, Joseph D. (1995). "Advocacy and Lawyers and Their Role." Baylor Law Review, 47, 1157–1158.

Jewell, Elizabeth A. (1998). "Exploring the Role of Advocacy in the Arts Community." Thesis Abstract, Ohio State University. Accessed March 8, 2004. Available at http://arts.osu.edu/ArtEducation/APA/abstracts/jewell.html.

Katz, Stanley N. (2002). "Constitutionalism, Contestation, and Civil Society." Common Knowledge, 8, 287–303.

Kumar, Krishan. (1993). "Civil Society: An Inquiry into the Usefulness of an Historical Term." The British Journal of Sociology, 44, 375–395.

Kumar, Krishan. (1994). "Civil Society Again: A Reply to Christopher Bryant's 'Social Self-Organization, Civility and Sociology.'" The British Journal of Sociology, 45, 127–131.

Ladd, Everett C. (1996, June/July). "Civic Participation and American Democracy: The Data Just Don't Show Erosion of America's Social Capital." The Public Perspective, 7, 1 and 5–6.

Lenzen, Marcus H. (2002). "The Use and Abuse of 'Civil Society' in Development." Transnational Associations, 3, 170–187.

Mitchell, Gordon. (1998). "Pedagogical Possibilities for Argumentative Agency in Academic Debate." Argumentation & Advocacy, 35, 41–61.

Mitchell, Gordon. (2000). "Simulated Public Argument as a Pedagogical Play on Worlds." Argumentation & Advocacy, 36, 134–151.

Mitchell, Gordon. (2004, September 9). "re: [eDebate] Top Gun for Dorks . . . ahem Geeks." eDebate. Available at www.ndtceda.com.

National Commission on Civic Renewal. (1998). America's Civic and Moral Beliefs. College Park: University of Maryland Press.

Neocleous, Mark. (1995). "From Civil Society to the Social." The British Journal of Sociology, 46, 395–408.

Noumoff, S. J. (2000, September 21). "Civil Society: Does It Have Meaning?" Paper Presented at Development: The Need for Reflection, Centre for Developing Area Studies, McGill University, Montreal, Quebec. Accessed January 27, 2004. Available at ww2.mcgill.ca/cdas/conf2000e/noumoff.pdf.

Pateman, Carol. (1988). The Sexual Contract. Cambridge, MA: Polity.

Price, Richard. (2003). "Transnational Civil Society and Advocacy in World Politics." World Politics, 55, 579–606.

Putnam, Robert D. (1995). "Bowling Alone: America's Declining Social Capital." Journal of Democracy, 6, 65–78.

Putnam, Robert D. (1996, Winter). "The Strange Disappearance of Civic America." The American Prospect, 34–48.

Scallen, Eileen A., and Wiethoff, William E. (1998, April). "The Ethos of Expert Witnesses: Confusing the Admissibility, Sufficiency and Credibility of Expert Testimony." Hastings Law Journal, 49. Available from Lexis-Nexis.

Scholte, Jan Aart. (2002, July 1). "Civil Society and Democracy in Global Governance." Global Governance, 8, 281–304.

Schudson, Michael. (1996, March–April). "What If Civic Life Didn't Die?" The American Prospect, 7, 17–20.

Seligman, Adam B. (1992). The Idea of Civil Society. New York: The Free Press.

Skocpol, Theda. (1999). "Advocates without Members: Recent Transformations of Civic Life." In Theda Skocpol and Morris P. Fiorina (Eds.), Civic Engagement in American Democracy (pp. 461–510). Washington, DC: Brookings Institution Press.

Skocpol, Theda, and Fiorina, Morris P. (1999). "Making Sense of the Civic Engagement Debate." In Theda Skocpol and Morris P. Fiorina (Eds.), Civic Engagement in American Democracy (pp. 1–24). Washington, DC: Brookings Institution Press.

Whalen, Wayne W. (2003, February). "The Lawyer That Was Rome." The American Lawyer. Available from Lexis-Nexis.

Windes, Russell, and Hastings, Arthur. (1965). Argumentation and Advocacy. New York: Random House.

Joseph P. Zompetti is assistant professor of communications at Illinois State University. Dr. Zompetti's research interests include rhetoric, social movements, and argumentation theory. He has published in both rhetoric and argumentation journals.

Combining Parliament and Public: Open Parliamentary Debate

Michael Hoppmann

When one is looking for reasons why debating is so popular among high school and especially university students and still spreading further in most parts of the world, it is not hard to find a variety of answers: Debating develops arguing skills, trains you to work in a small team, teaches you presentation skills, gives you opportunities to research interesting political and social topics, and is even an excellent reason to travel to various cities and to meet other people with similar interests. But most importantly, it gives a great setting for rhetorical training under competitive conditions. This is the core quality of academic debating: providing a setting for training in the art of persuasion that is not only as realistic as possible but also greatly motivates the student by means of competitions that make one strive for the best.

Unfortunately, these two elements, realism and agonality, are partly in opposition to each other. While some debate formats put their focus on maximizing the realism provided in the setting, others care more about providing rules for fair and balanced competitions. The most eminent example of debate formats that supply a very realistic setting for the young orator is Floor Debates, with a large audience and participation in the debate generally open to a wider public. The best example of the latter, more tournament-oriented debate format is Parliamentary Debating, which generally works without any meaningful participation by an audience. It strongly motivates students to give their best in competitions and to strive for successes against teams from other clubs, schools, or states.

Both groups of debate formats show particular strengths and weaknesses, and appeal to different students depending on their prime interests.

Academic Floor Debates, like those held according to the "Oxford rules", are an excellent opportunity to train individuals for speaking in front of large audiences. Participating in Floor Debates exposes the speaker to audiences that at times might react in a very hostile manner to arguments that he himself believes to be very persuasive, and at other times audiences will happily applaud rather weak points. Speaking in this format will also quickly teach anyone that a clear and strong voice is sometimes essential to even be heard, and that a single interjection from the back row can destroy a fancy induction chain within seconds. And last but not least, Floor Debates provide a brutally honest mirror to the persuasiveness of a debater by means of open, closed, or "practical" votes. Having an impressive structure, beautiful metaphors, and nicely selected quotes in your speech is not going to make you content if the majority of the audience moves away from you from the beginning to the end or if all speakers from the floor argue against you. Thus, modern Floor Debates provide what classical declamation schools failed to provide, a reality check for the speaker which tells him if he is being persuasive and convincing his audience or if he is becoming more of an actor than an orator and is entertaining himself and others rather than learning how to speak effectively.

On the other hand, Floor Debates have severe limitations as well. They require a certain amount of work to be organized, they are limited to a frequency that attracts a sufficiently large audience, and they are generally unfit for major competitions since it seems very unlikely that any convener of a tournament could provide interested audiences for dozens of debates that are held parallel in different rooms and a number of rounds. That way the price for the high amount of realism of Floor Debates is an absence of agonal motivation by tournaments that limits the amount of competitiveness between debaters and the enthusiasm of students that is common in major sports events and other competitive activities.

This agonal motivation, competitiveness, and enthusiasm are precisely the main strengths of Parliamentary Debating. Parliamentary Debate formats like the British Parliamentary Style or the rules used by the National Parliamentary Debate Association and the American Parliamentary Debate Association are in some aspects quite the opposite of Floor Debating formats. Instead of a large audience that provides the rhetorical inhibition that is so crucial to a realistic setting, Parliamentary Debating is limited to usually two, three, or four debaters on each side whose positions are fixed and who speak in a preassigned order. This very simple setting, while being rhetorically quite deficient, has the great virtue of allowing very large competitions between hundreds of debaters. Since all debates can be held behind closed doors and require only two or four teams plus an adjudication board, dozens of debates can be held parallel and rounds can follow quickly after each other.

This big virtue, however, is offset by a number of serious vices. Since all debaters are fixed to one side or the other and the adjudicators have to remain neutral, all speeches are bound to be ineffective. A debater can be very persuasive, provide very good arguments, and be exceptionally eloquent, but still he knows that his speech cannot move one single vote. Every single participant in the debate will remain in his position: the affirmative side will present pro arguments and the opposing side will express negative standpoints. And not only will brilliant speeches have no positive effect, but very weak speeches will also do no harm. A debater knows from the moment he enters the room who will support and who will oppose him and the best persuasion in the world will not change this. As a logical consequence of this setting, Parliamentary Debaters no longer train to persuade and move an audience but to please adjudicators. And while persuading real audiences and fulfilling adjudication criteria can coincide, most of the time they don't. An explicit speech disposition usually impresses an average adjudicator but bores real audiences. Fancy metaphors and original examples might score on adjudication sheets but are very likely to arouse skepticism in everyday speeches. And while witty quotations and sophisticated argument structures win a lot of Parliamentary Debates, they can have very negative persuasive effects. In short: Parliamentary Debating teaches the student to permanently violate one of the most important elements of classical rhetorical teachings, the *dissimulatio artis*—if you want to persuade, hide your rhetorical art!

Thus, Parliamentary Debating falls a step behind Floor Debating and opens itself up fully to criticism that the latter has successfully overcome: to produce debaters that might develop an impressive ability to present pleasant speech structures (*divisiones*), to introduce moving narrations (*colores*), and to deliver clever punch lines (*sententiae*), but who are entirely useless at realistic persuading in everyday life. The parallels to Seneca's well-known criticisms of declamation schools are more than evident to anybody who has ever glanced at his very entertaining work.

So, apparently both major strengths of debating and the corresponding debate formats are closely linked to serious weaknesses. What then is the best option for the debater who wants to pick the best format? One possible solution, of course, would be to train in both kinds of debating and so be able to enjoy the competitive motivation of Parliamentary Debating at times while still making sure not to become detached from real persuasion training with the help of Floor Debates.

A group of lecturers and students at the University of Tübingen believe they have found a viable alternative; they analyzed the particular strengths of a number of debate formats and combined them to create a hybrid of Parliamentary Debates and Floor Debating: Open Parliamentary Debate (OPD).

The basic structure of OPD is rather simple. A debate consists of three groups of debaters: a team of three affirmative debaters (government), a team of three negative debaters (opposition), and a group of three to six faction-free speakers who are not bound to either position at the beginning of the debate. The members of the thus reduced floor have the task of listening to the opening and complementary pleas of the factions and then making up their minds whom to support based on their judgment of the exact proposition and the presented reasons. They receive half of the time of the faction speakers for their speeches and will use it to widen the range of arguments, give a more precise analysis, or present a different point of view. Same as the faction speakers, they are also allowed to offer points of information and to use interjections of no longer then seven words to create a realistic setting of rhetorical resistance for the speakers at the rostra.

At a club debate, OPD basically looks like a small Floor Debate with all its advantages. But other than usual Floor Debates, OPD is fully usable for tournaments as well. At tournaments the debate will be held with nine debaters from five different teams. While the affirmative and negative teams remain intact, of course, the three faction-free speakers are members of three other teams that are split into different rooms. In a sequence of three preliminary debates, each team will in turn speak once as government and once as opposition and will once be split into faction-free speakers, whose individual speaker points will add up to the scores of their team in that round.

To give a better overview of the way Open Parliamentary Debates are held, a short version of the rules is given below. The full rules and commentary can be found in Hoppmann, Michael and Bernd Rex (Ed.), *Handbuch der Offenen*

Parlamentarischen Debatte. 3rd ed. (Göttingen: Cuvillier, 2004) and Bartsch, Tim et al, *Trainingsbuch Rhetorik.* (Paderborn, 2005).

Brief Rules of Open Parliamentary Debate

Open Parliamentary Debate is a tournaments-suitable academic debate format, which combines the competitiveness of Parliamentary Debating with the realism of Floor Debates. OPD seeks to create the basis for development and training of constructive rhetoric under the condition of productive agonality.

The Topic of the Debate

The topic of a debate is a question of practical value. This question will be made available to all debaters at least three days before the debate takes place. The speakers of the government answer the question by means of their application in the affirmative; the opposition forces the denial of the question. Neither side of the debate simulates any real body.

The Speakers

Participants in a debate are: three faction-speakers (opening speaker, complement speaker, closing speaker) for the government and correspondingly for the opposition. At least three faction-free speakers take part in a debate; they represent the public and are (together with the audience) the target group of persuasion.

The opening speaker of the government puts the question of the debate into concrete terms, by expressing a precise application. By the use of the opening plea and the responding speeches, he tries to convince the faction-free speakers to support the government's application.

The opening speaker of the opposition responds to the opening speaker of the government's plea. He presents the counterarguments of the opposition and tries to convince the faction-free speakers to decline the government's application by the use of the responding speeches.

The complement speakers of government and opposition add new arguments to the opening pleas and consolidate already mentioned arguments. They offer points of information to the opposing side and disprove their argumentation. They may hold responding speeches instead of their colleagues.

The faction-free speakers examine the arguments and refutations of the faction speakers. They are allowed to offer points of information. After the pleas of the first four faction speakers, they speak according to a prearranged order to the application of the government. The faction-free speakers have to declare which side they are supporting within the first minute of their speech. They should disprove the argumentation of the opposing side and add new arguments to the side they decided to support. The new arguments may not contradict the argumentation of the chosen side. In the rare case that a faction-free speaker is firmly convinced that in opposing the application of the government he also has to contradict the opposition, he may pronounce a speech in general opposition. In this case he is liable to neither side.

The closing speaker of the government examines the argumentation of the opposing side and their supporting faction-free speakers by means of points of information. He summarizes the arguments of the government and their faction-free speakers, and pleads for consent to the application. He is not allowed to introduce new arguments to the debate.

The task of the **opposition's closing speaker** is analogous to the task of the government's closing speaker. He has the last word on the debate.

Chairmanship and Procedure

The chairman is the head of the debate. He ensures that the rules of the debate are carried out. He decides on the interpretation of the rules. Points of order and points of personal privilege are inadmissible.

If at any time during the debate the chairman leaves his chair, the debate is immediately suspended. It will only be continued by order of the chairman.

The chairman opens and closes the debate with a stroke of the bell. Prior to the debate, he announces its topic. After that, he submits the topic to an anonymous vote. The faction-free speakers and the audience are entitled to vote. The debate starts after the vote.

The chairman opens the negotiation and calls the speakers to the rostra. The time of the speech starts with the first word of the speaker. During the speech, the chairman marks the beginning and the end of the time in which points of information are allowed by the use of one gavel blow. The end of the first speeches is marked by a double blow of the gavel. If a speaker exceeds the time limit for his speech or his responding speech by more than fifteen seconds, he will be interrupted by the bell. If the time limit of a point of information is exceeded, the speaker will be immediately interrupted by the bell.

Each of the faction speakers gets seven minutes for his speech. The first and the last minute of his time are protected against points of information. Faction-free speakers get three-and-a-half minutes each. Of these, the first minute and the last thirty seconds are protected against points of information. During the remaining time, all opposing faction speakers are entitled to offer points of information.

Every speech of a faction-free speaker is followed by the responding speech of the opposing opening or complement speaker of at most one minute protected time. After this, response follows the next faction-free speaker. After the last responding speech follow the pleas of the closing speakers of the government and the opposition, during which every opposing speaker has the right to offer points of information.

At the end of the debate the chairman takes the application of the government to an open vote. Only persons who took part in the anonymous vote at the beginning have the right to vote openly. In both votes abstentions are inadmissible. The results of both votes are announced by the chairman.

Responding Speeches, Points of Information, Interjections

Responding speeches are obligatory, points of information are welcome, interjections are permitted.

(1) **Responding speeches** are the device of the opening speakers to react immediately to the speeches of opposing faction-free speakers. Responding speeches have a maximum of one minute duration, during which points of information are prohibited.

(2) **Points of information** are the device of the opposing side to force the speaker to clarify his arguments and his position. The permission to ask points of information is held by:

+ all faction-free speakers and the opposing side during the unprotected time (core time) of the opening pleas and the extension pleas;

- the opposing faction speakers during the core time of the faction-free speaker's speech.

Points of information have a maximal duration of fifteen seconds. They are announced by standing up and pointing with one arm toward the speaker. This gesture can be emphasized by the exclamation "point of information" or "point of information concerning [key word]." Points of information have to be expressly accepted or declined by the speaker. If more than one point of information is offered at any time and one is accepted, the others are automatically declined. Faction speakers should accept at least two points of information. Faction-free speakers are held to permit at least one.

(3) **Interjections** are a device of all debaters and the audience to point out weaknesses, contradictions, or absurdities in the argumentation of a speaker. Interjections have a maximal length of seven words. Dialogues are prohibited. A speaker has the right to prohibit interjections for one minute. During this minute, all interjections are prohibited. The chairman has the right to reduce the number of interjections if they disturb the speaker excessively. [Streitkultur e.V.]

For use in tournaments these rules are complemented by a set of adjudication criteria and principles and a full commentary to avoid any lack of clarity in the rules. The adjudication is based on five individual criteria and three team criteria that are added up and form the total score of a team. Teams are thus not judged relatively to each other but on an absolute scale. Power pairing and similar procedures can be avoided that way, and each team will see a variety of different debaters with different strengths.

This combination of the strengths of Floor Debates and Parliamentary Debates with some very clear and fair tournament rules and adjudication principles made Open Parliamentary Debate very popular in German-speaking areas. After its first use at a national tournament in 2001, it quickly spread among universities and became the most used rule set at German university debating competitions, including the annual German debating championships. The majority of university clubs in the quickly developing German debating scene use it at their weekly meetings as well. This great popularity of the comparatively young format surprised even the authors of the OPD rules.

The following list of the advantages of OPD for club debates and for tournaments is an attempt to provide an understanding of its great popularity and to highlight the purpose of this paper: to introduce Open Parliamentary Debate and to explain its main features.

Some strengths of OPD in *club debates*:

a) Realism

Open Parliamentary Debate provides a setting for the debater in the club to optimally train his rhetorical skills. In contrast to most Parliamentary Debate formats, it not only allows points of information but also interjections from all debaters and the audience that can be uttered at any time in the speech. Speakers in OPD are confronted with a very active audience that will clearly signal support or opposition, depending on the persuasiveness of a speech, by means of interaction and by the positioning of the faction-free speakers. To succeed as a debater in an Open Parliamentary Debate is a more complex task than in most other Parliamentary Debate formats, but the successful debater will more closely resemble a good speaker who will also be able to convince an audience in real life situations.

b) Variety

Open Parliamentary Debate offers debaters different positions and allows them to develop different abilities. This is not only evident in the variety of different aims among constructive opening speakers, analytical extension speakers, moving closing speakers, and relatively flexible faction-free speakers, but it is also reflected in the different lengths of speeches. Speeches in everyday life are not limited to exactly seven minutes at all times, and so it will be very useful to train to different lengths in a debate as well. Open Parliamentary Debate requires participants to speak for seven minutes (faction speakers), three and a half minutes (faction-free speakers), and one minute (responding speeches). This feature is also very helpful to beginners in debate, who can start with shorter speeches and later progress to other positions with longer speeches.

c) Flexibility

Debate clubs usually do not work with the same group of people but have to adapt to different numbers of participants and audiences at every meeting. In order to let as many debaters as possible participate, it is very helpful if the debate is not firmly fixed to four, six, or eight people but allows a certain amount of flexibility in size. Open Parliamentary Debates can be held with between nine and twelve debaters, which considerably reduces the gap between the number of people that can debate in one debate and the situation when two or more debates are held simultaneously. It thus allows a maximum of participants to take part in the debate independent of the total number of parallel debates.

d) Feedback

Open Parliamentary Debate features three votes during a debate: a secret vote at the beginning, a "practical vote" from the faction-free speakers who choose their side during the debate, and an open vote at the end. These votes give very valuable feedback to the debaters about whether their speeches and proposals have been effective and their argumentation consistent in the eyes of the audience or not. Additional judgments by adjudicators and trainers always have a certain value as well, but at the end of the day, what really matters is not the number of points one has received but whether one gets his audiences support or not.

Advantages of OPD for *tournament use:*

a) Fairness

Every position in a debate confronts competitors with different challenges and demands slightly different tactics and abilities. This necessarily leads to the fact that in some roles in a debate it is easier to win than in others for some or the majority of debaters. In order for a competition to be fair, it is therefore very important that all positions (government, opposition, others) are equally assigned to all teams. The rules of OPD make sure that during preliminary rounds each team will be assigned to each role equally often. That means that every debater will be once a speaker for the government (with his team), once a speaker for the opposition (with his team), and once a faction-free speaker (without his team) in a turn of three preliminary rounds. This setting, which cannot be overruled by any other priorities such as power matching of teams, guarantees a maximally fair starting point for a balanced competition.

b) Break selection

Another of the key strengths of Open Parliamentary Debate is a direct result of having faction-free speakers in all debates. As mentioned above, the positions of faction-free speakers are equally divided among all teams in the preliminary rounds. While this works very well in the preliminary stage, the break rounds require a different mode of selection. In each break round the position of faction-free speakers will be assigned to the best individuals of those teams that did not make the break. This leads to two very positive effects: Firstly, each break round will consist of an optimal selection of good debaters, because not only good teams but also good individual debaters will be selected. And secondly, this double selection motivates more experienced debaters to team up with beginners and form heterogeneous teams. That way the tension in uneven teams can be greatly reduced because every debater knows that if his team misses a break he can still make it to the finals by himself. No good debater will be left behind.

c) Motions

Another strength of OPD for fair debating competitions is its use of closed and precisely worded questions rather than open motions. While this might at first sight look like reducing the potential for creativity and originality on the government's side, it actually helps create fair and balanced debates. Having a closed question allows both teams to equally prepare their arguments prior to the debate, instead of one team preparing a neat case and the other team being restrained to some general ideas. And even more important, it prevents "prep cases." The teams in a round have to debate the actual question being posed and not some question they would have liked to hear. Debating should train the individual to analyze and understand any question that he is confronted with and not to somehow find a link from the question he is confronted with to a topic where he feels at home and that he would like to talk about. A victory should reward one's ability to prepare a case, argue it, and speak, rather than reward debating experience and the ability to remember how the same type of debate was won last time. In order to achieve this goal, sacrificing a bit of creativity is a worthwhile investment.

d) Absolute adjudication

In contrast to most Parliamentary Debate formats, OPD adjudication system is not based on relative rankings between teams in the preliminary rounds but on absolute scores that teams and individual speakers receive. This system requires a bit of training for inexperienced adjudicators, who need to do some scaling debates before being fully prepared for tournaments, but once they learn the system, it has some very convincing advantages. When the results of a team depend only on the performances of the team members and not on the luck of the draw or tabbing systems, some major problems of debate tournaments are automatically solved. Systems that try to reduce the effect of luck of the draw, such as power matching of teams, but that have serious side effects, are entirely unnecessary. Each team will be able to meet any other team and thus be confronted with a variety of different skill levels. That helps to improve debating, makes it more interesting, and does not create discriminating groups of the "experienced" and the "beginners." Debating should be a tool to meet as many different people as possible inside and out of debates. Being able to debate with anybody in tournaments is a good start for that aim.

This paper tried to give a short introduction to Open Parliamentary Debate and to point out some of its strengths. Due to the paper's limited length, it can, of course, only very briefly address most points that are treated in much greater detail in other publications. The most important sources of information about anything concerning German debating in general and Open Parliamentary Debate in particular are the Website of Streitkultur e.V. at the University of Tübingen (www.streitkultur.net) and the publications mentioned in the text.

Michael Hoppmann received his M.A. in rhetoric and philosophy at the University of Tübingen in 2003 and is currently working on questions of classical rhetoric and modern argumentation theory while teaching at the Universities of Tübingen and Furtwangen. He has worked as a debate coordinator and coach since 2001 and co-authored three German textbooks on debating as well as numerous articles on the topic.

Public Debates in Macedonia

Boyan Maricic

My presentation will examine the reasons that public debate has become a very important activity for our organization and for Macedonia in general. Several years ago, after considerable academic research on the theory and practice of public debates, we started organizing public debates to recruit new participants from the high schools. The range of debate was expanded to include many public events in order to increase the popularity of public debate and of our program, and in the process we attracted some donors and commercial sponsors. Public debate has now assumed an important role in promoting debate as an educational and intellectual concept.

I will describe how we used public debates to examine issues that appealed to private enterprise without promoting specific businesses, and how the program gained new members and supporters. More importantly, however, I will try to explain the underlying rationale for this format and its social and educational importance, which provides its real and unique value.

PRACTICAL EXPERIENCE

The integration of public debates into the everyday life of the debate clubs and program in Macedonia started six years ago when every club was obliged to hold these debates in order to add new members to the debate program. The concept of the public debate was actually first introduced as an option for our organization in 2002 when a group of our members participated in the OSI (Open Society Institute) and US State Department program SEEYLI (South East European Youth Leadership Institute) at Towson University, Maryland. In that program. public debate was one of the areas used to help participants gain and sharpen debating skills.

After that training, our organization decided to use the public debate format as a way to get people involved in the debate process. Holding public debates for new members and potential members proved to be a good way of introducing this format. The local debate coordinator would propose a topic that was considered appropriate to the local conditions. Basically, the topics were subjects of interest and concern to the young people in Macedonia (the right to education in your own language, the mandatory wearing of uniforms in high school, etc.). Although the topics and debates were simple, the local young people found them very compelling and were willing to research the issues and speak publicly on them.

A few years later we started holding debates in association with NGOs that were willing to raise some questions or at least have a discussion on a certain general topic, particularly situation in 2001 in Macedonia, which was very near to civil war. So our program was included in several NGO campaigns aimed at raising peacekeeping awareness. Members of our organization travelled around the country organizing public debates on such issues as building civil society, ethnic tolerance, and disarmament of the civil population in the post-conflict areas, a campaign we are especially proud of. This task was really difficult but it showed the power of the debate in the field.

In the meantime the debate program generated interest among members of the business community once they realized that it was a means of raising business-related issues publicly. They then sought to engage the debate program in their public relations work, and told us, "We would like to organize a public discussion on a certain topic, but we don't know how." As a result, we have been working on organizing public discussions about issues that some enterprises were interested in, for example, the government of Macedonia should sign a strategic partnership agreement with Microsoft, or Macedonia should sell all state-owned companies. This process helped us to increase the popularity of our program and resulted in an offer for a series of TV debates.

Because of their popularity, public debates have become an integral part of all our projects, especially those meant to raise public awareness. Public institutions and large foundations have included our program in some national efforts such as educational and social reforms, euro-integration, the building of European awareness, and the campaign against corruption in higher education.Moreover, in the last two years all our projects have incorporated public debates, inevitably raising public awareness.

List of debates and supporters of the debate (project):

+ Debates on the Skopje Film Festival 2000

+ Debate on "The state of civil society in Macedonia after the conflict" 2001 (Open Society Institute)

+ The public debate caravan on the basic topic "Disarmament of the civil population after the conflict." 2001 and 2002 set of 10 debates in different cities in Macedonia (Organization for Security and Cooperation in Europe)

+ Spring day in Europe 2003, 2004, 2005. Public debates on European awareness in Macedonia, topics: "The Macedonian youth deserves to be part of Europe" and "The Macedonian driver will be able to drive in the EU when he learns to stop at a red light" (European Commission and President of Macedonia)

+ "The government of Macedonia should sign a strategic agreement with Microsoft"—supported by Metamorphosis (electronic publishing), 2003

+ Several public debates on euro-integration and youth involvement in this process, sponsored by the Sector for Euro-integration of Macedonian Government, 2004, 2005

+ TV debate show "May I Have a Word?" 2004

+ Public discussion with the two candidates for rector of Sts. Cyril and Methodius University, Skopje, 2004

+ Three public debates on the topic "Anticorruption in Higher Education" (considering different aspects of the same topic), 2004, 2005 (OSI Budapest Higher Education Support Program])

+ Public debate on youth activism in Macedonia, 2006

- Public debates on U.S. role in the Balkans, 2006, 2007
- Public debates on the introduction of student parliament as a democratic body to represent students in their relationship with university administrations and faculties

General Conclusion

The debate program should monitor social trends and treat the most important issues of the day. Moreover, the debates should take place publicly to attract as large an audience as possible. Eventually, the practical value of debate will become obvious to sponsors and donors and to an increasingly broader and more attentive public audience.

Theoretic Support

From the official literature that our members received at training seminars and from our own experience with public debate, we have established several important principles:

1. Having the rules in advance for public debates allows you to create your own debate format. The teams can be firmly opposed to each other or be supplemental and complementary with different positions and approaches.

2. The number of speakers per team is usually two or three; increasing or varying the number of speakers creates problems.

3. The role of the moderator is crucial for the direction and development of the debate, especially in facilitating the entire process of public discussion among a large number of people with differing opinions.

4. The inclusion of an expert as a source of information provides authority and credibility to the debate and makes it different from a simple theatrical performance.

5. The order of the speeches is not strictly prescribed, although it is customary to schedule the expert speech between the first and second constructive speeches of the debate.

6. There is no prescribed way of judging the debate. Moreover,

staging a large event as a competitive debate is of questionable value.

7. The role of the audience, in effect, constitutes another element in the debate.

8. All of debaters aim to deliver their arguments and presentations to impress and convince the audience.

9. The interaction between participants and the audience makes public debate free and open, yet responsible, grounded, and serious.

The purpose of introducing debate as a tool for developing public discussion is to promote critical thinking and focus on any problem that interests or affects the people of Macedonia. The audience is an important factor in shaping the debate and its quality. Their and concern about the issue and their participation is critical to the success of the event. Audience members will be either supporters or opponents and may have questions for members of either teams or the expert. The questioning actually gives a magical spontaneity to the public discussion.

Social Importance in a Narrow Sense

Opening debate on public issues to numerous participants with different roles is a clever way of involving the audience, and it demystifies debate as a privilege of the intellectual elite. At the same time it enables the audience to apply logic and critical thinking to the presentations of experts, and gives the audience an opportunity to ask questions, make comments, and even judge who won the debate.

Social Importance in a Wider Sense

When our organization started this program, nothing seemed impossible. Now, every important issue (poverty, corruption, discrimination, marginalization of Roma people, nationalism, you name it) is a potential topic for a public debate. Everything is open for discussion and everyone can be included. It is no longer an academic exercise or a privilege of university students and professors, but an opportunity for anyone who is interested. Believe me, the last point is extremely important for transitional countries poisoned by prejudices and nationalism because it sheds an entirely new light on the notion of democratic inclusion through a different manner of public expression.

Educational Importance

The public debate format can be a good way for beginners to overcome their initial inhibitions and for experienced debaters to perfect their ability to respond and think quickly in front of an audience. It also provides an excellent opportunity for coaches to help debaters develop different skills, and gives an extraordinary chance for debaters to put academic skills into practice. To sum up, public debate is an excellent tool for learning and practicing debate.

Bojan Maricic is a project assistant in the Ministry of Interior of the Republic of Macedonia, working on coordinating Macedonian law to EU standards. He is also secretary general of the Youth Educational Forum—Macedonia, founded to develop leadership skills and encourage active participation by youth in solving Macedonia's problems. He received his law degree from the University of Sts. Cyril and Methodius, Skopje, in 2006.

Persuasion in the Prison

Danielle Stevens

Currently, debate communities in the US are confronted with a shift of parliamentary debate style from a more public-sphere oriented activity to a more technical and specialized activity. The conflict is very perceptible at Willamette University due to the way our program operates. Professor Robert Trapp, the director of the program, is an advocate of debate as a public-sphere activity, while the assistant director, Robert Layne, and a majority of students are swaying much more toward the technical arena. In order to provide an alternative for students who are interested in something more than technical debate, we have created an additional focus for our program. We call it "public track," and it is a small group of students who create venues where non-debaters can discuss issues that are important on campus, in the Salem, Oregon, area, and around the nation and the globe.

One facet of the program involves debating and doing speaking contests in the Oregon State Penitentiary. We have had six events in the past year—three debates, two poetry contests, and one speech contest. All went very well, and the entire team has been pleased with the outcome.

I have taken part in two of the events that we have done at the prison. The very first event we did was a debate on Bush vs. Kerry, and I was one of the lucky four who got to share ideas with the inmates. The second event that I did was the most recent one, a poetry contest. Most of the prisoners read poems they had written themselves, and a few used outside material. Sharing such personal thoughts with people so different from myself was an amazing experience.

I believe that this program of entering the prison has been very beneficial for both debaters and inmates. I am basing this conclusion on my personal experiences of going into the prison and participating in speaking events with them. In this essay, I will present narratives about the two events in which I participated and will follow those narratives with my conclusions about the advantages for both debaters and inmates.

THE NARRATIVES

The following are two of my personal stories about participating in persuasive events in the Oregon State Penitentiary. The first is a story about a debate on the Bush–Kerry presidential election and the second is a story about a poetry contest.

Debating in the Oregon State Penitentiary

Some random Tuesday in September my coach, Rob Layne, was prattling on about something random and debatery. Just as my attention span was stretched to its limit and my interest waning, I perked up to hear something about prisons. *Prisons?* I wondered. *Was this a new felony voter case?* With difficulty, I pulled myself out of my haze and paid full attention long enough to hear that we as a team were going into the state penitentiary to debate some prisoners. The rules of entering the prison were explained to us: (1) no tight or revealing clothing, (2) no blue jeans, (3) no blue shirts, and (4) no under wire bras. The fourth rule provoked laughter (and even misunderstanding as one of our debaters thought Rob had said "no underwear"), but the importance of that rule would become clear to us later.

Well, as it all turned out, this talk about prisons had little to do with the type of debate I was accustomed to. First, the teams were to consist of five people, four competitors (each giving one speech) and a "team captain." American Parli consists of two teams of two that debate one another, with the "leaders" speaking twice—introducing the case and rebutting for it. Secondly, the resolution was such that there was to be no sneaking out of its true intentions and coming away with a canned win—the Willamette team, a group of largely liberal students at a liberal arts university were opposing, thus put on the wrong side of a tough resolution—Vote Kerry.

Interestingly enough, the resolution was intended to discuss US–UN relations on foreign policy, with the focus centered on the differences in Bush and Kerry's policies. Mr. Trapp (our team's advisor) gave the inmates the choice of either supporting Kerry or Bush, and Kyle (the president of the Capitol Gavel Toastmasters club) replied, "Well, nobody in here really likes Bush, so I guess we'd better go with Kerry." I guess!

The weeks passed and The People Speaks events ensued, the election debates dragged on, and the fact that I was to be supporting Bush (even if only for seven minutes) and trying to persuade people to do the same (even if only to play this game we call debate) loomed ominously in my future.

On the night of the debate we drove to the prison and were directed to a waiting room. As I entered the room where we all were to wait for nearly a half-hour, I fidgeted nervously with my clothes, hoping that what I was wearing would be appropriate and wouldn't elicit inappropriate remarks or actions. Were my pants too tight? Would my shoes work? Upon noticing a couple from the community who looked kind and a little haggard, I quit fidgeting and watched them and their reactions. They seemed fine, so I decided that I was fine too. I was fine because I noticed that everyone else was fidgeting just as much as I was, and no one could keep his or her eyes or attention focused in one place. We shifted nervously, making silly jokes and talking about neutral topics until the guards called us up to check IDs and brief us on the situation. I stopped being completely fine when I was told that it was possible that we could be used as hostages if any problems were to arise. Then I stopped being fine at all when the guard read the following warning: "We must warn you that being taken hostage is always a possibility. We do not negotiate for hostages but we will come in to get you." My tummy flipped up and down and my eyes rounded, but other than that the nervousness quieted down.

Then the prison guards sent us through the metal detection devices, led us through a light gray, sloped hallway, and directed us to stay in one line, single file, moving ten at a time. I hid, childlike, behind my advisor and hoped that the "boogeyman" wouldn't decide to take me hostage. I handed my ID to a security guard behind a barred counter, and in return, he gave me a red clip-on badge that said VISITOR and an invisible stamp that said something silly. I giggled, hoping that, as usual, my goofiness would ease the tension in the room. Well, no such luck. At least the stern faced guards smiled. I can only try so hard, right?

After being carded, badged, and stamped, we were moved into another room that had tables and chairs and a fake wood paneled wall. We were greeted by yet another guard and the president of the Capitol Gavel Toastmasters Club. He eagerly shook our hands and welcomed us, ushering us to refreshments and seats. There were a few others in the room, and we moved around to talk to them. A few minutes later, the rest of the group came into the room.

The couple from the community looked happy to see some people whom they obviously had met before, but I could no longer pay attention to this couple. There were happy smiling faces everywhere! They all wanted to shake hands, laugh, play, and joke. I wished I had enough time to meet them all and concrete names in my mind. One man made the comment that he was pleased to be able to exchange ideas with a woman, because, he wisecracked with a wink, "There ain't a whole lotta them in here."

I was struck by the idea that this person was cut off from members of the opposite sex—I had never experienced that. I was also interested in the idea that he said "*in* here." They were in an enclosed space, with boundaries and walls—no thoughts of being *at* a place, ever. Only *IN* a place. Wow.

A large African-American man called Bear was a baker in the prison and had made a huge tray of pastries. I complimented Bear on his delicious cinnamon rolls. He beamed like a child praised for his effort. (That is, if a 6 ft.-plus burly black man with a voice comparable to Barry White's can be likened to a child in any way.) A few more snatches of conversations, and the debate began.

Fortunately for me and unfortunately for you, I don't recall much of what was said between the groups except for some good-natured trash talk egging the other on. The reason I say that my memory failure is fortunate is because through its absence, I was able to focus mainly on my reactions and [the reactions] of those around me. I remember nervous shuffles and throat clearings (coming from both sides), intense needs to please and prove, and anxious movements that showed me that hours of research had been spent on the issue. One man's face reminded me of my father, and so I remember his expressions most of all. He approached his speech logically, trying to use the facts he had to present something cohesive. The structure was not great, but the passion was there, and that is most likely what won the debate for them (in addition to the fact that they were lucky enough not to have to argue in favor of anyone named Bush).

Afterward, we again were allowed to mingle and partake in the glorious cinnamon rolls for just a little while longer. Again and again I was asked why I supported Bush, and I giggled and said that I didn't, "I was just doin' my job." The prisoners seemed awestruck at the idea that we could still be persuasive even when supporting someone (or something) that we abhorred. I liked the idea that I had been a part of helping someone learn a new valuable skill. It made the butterflies in my tummy turn into a warm fuzzy feeling in my chest.

The room was filled with smiles—every Willamette person looked to be glad that they had come, and every prisoner was ecstatic to have had some outside intellectual stimulation. Some of us (including prisoners) just looked plain relived to see that all had gone well.

Then the time came for the event to end. We helped rearrange the chairs, then they shook hands with us and were led into a hallway while we waited and watched, imagining—only imagining—the kind of life to which they were returning. We returned to our beautiful college campus and our comfortable rooms, having been changed by our interaction [with] people who we knew had done horrible things but who we now understood were people just like us.

But debating was not our only prison experience. Twice we were invited to present poetry interpretations.

Poetry in the Oregon State Penitentiary

"Hey, Rob! Will you cut this for me?" I ask my coach across the hall. I had about an hour to get something ready to read for this year's Poetry Slam in the Oregon State Penitentiary. I had been playing around with oddball pieces all day and had finally settled on "How to Write a Political Poem" and "Voice of an American Voiceover" by Taylor Mali. Both were energetic, politically charged, and most of all, fun to perform. As I practiced the piece, timing it and perfecting gestures and rhythms, it dawned on me that tonight I was going to jail.

It had been a while since I had gone on a prison trip, and I was ready to see everyone again. I smoothed my hair and thought about them. Nice folks, all with big smiles and hopes to please. I liked going there, even if it took a lot of energy.

My advisor, Robert Trapp, and a fellow teammate Alexandra (participating as a spectator) and I piled into the van and headed off. I was more comfortable this time than I had been the last two times. Debate is always so formal, and I was excited to be able to escape the adversarial atmosphere and just play with words.

This time the wait in the holding room wasn't so long. We walked in, showed IDs, and were briefed about warnings and cautions. Then it was time for the metal detector. Mr. Trapp went first, then Alex, and then me. Well, it was supposed to have been me. To my horror, I had just realized that I was wearing an underwire bra, something strictly prohibited. I informed the guard, and he asked me to try to pass through anyway. No such luck. Thankfully, I also happened to be wearing a camisole with a built in bra, which I showed to the guard as modestly as I could. We discussed my options for about three minutes, and eventually he allowed me to remove the under wire strapless and pass with only the built-in on. I buttoned my jacket as high as it could go, and called it good.

Next we were off the hallway, easing ourselves down the slope. A man with a thick leather jacket and the suspicious air of a biker was accompanying us, along with his Bible. We were ushered to the room with bars, and the security guard behind the barred counter again gave us badges and silly invisible stamps in exchange for our IDs. Not hearing nervous chatter was pleasant—the three of us knew what we were doing, and that was good.

The room we were put into was interesting. Both sides were lined with square "offices" made out of chain-link fence. On the back wall, starting at about three-quarters of the way up, was a large, intricate mural of a large mountain and surrounding forest. I'm told some of the prisoners themselves painted it. In random places there were silly things—like old broken pickups, caves that resembled skulls, and deer that looked like Bambi.

We had to wait a bit for the main group to arrive, so we passed the ten minutes or so with the three or four club members who had been brought in to help with setup. One man talked to me about Bend [Oregon] and his life as a basketball player for the local community college. Another came up and asked Alex if she would like to read some of his poetry. She agreed, and the plans to print it were made.

The others shuffled in, and we enjoyed some refreshments. I saw some familiar faces, and greeted them with smiles. I felt awkward because they *all* seemed to remember me by name. I wished I knew theirs, but there were so many! We joked around, and I challenged them all to try to win the contest, because, I said playfully, my poetry was unbeatable. They answered back with silly things, and a good time was had by all. I think for them being able to trash talk with someone new and in a safe way was refreshing.

We were called to order, and the contest began. The first speaker was a smallish man, who had the look of having seen and done some tough things. He had written two of the poems himself. These two were about his experiences with drugs and how grateful he was to be in the penitentiary. For him, it was the only way of cleaning up his act enough to see the sunset through sober eyes. His last poem had been sent to him by his mother, and as he introduced it, tears welled up in his eyes. The poem was about fallen angels, and it obviously hit home to everyone in the room.

The next speaker was an older man who definitely had been here a while. There was a sort of respect given him as he passed or spoke. His poetry recital was from the Book of Job in the Holy Bible. He did the entire thing from memory, using the space to bend and kneel as a servant would. It was an interesting speech, and I'm sure he did it to give a message to the younger men in the crowd, but I don't know how effective it was.

I was the third speaker, and as I was called up, an amused hush fell over the room. I could tell that they wanted to see what the little girl with the big voice had brought them. I smiled as I centered myself to speak.

The performance went wonderfully—and it was made particularly sweet by the last part. At the beginning, I get to beat a box a little bit, and the only four black men in the place happened to be sitting right in front, very close to me. As I started the beat, the men giggled and whispered taunts. At the end, as I accepted the first place trophy, I continued the game by teasing them for not helping me. Another man came from the back and said, "Go white girl!"

The fourth speaker was a man I had met before. He had debated the No Child Left Behind topic last year. I remembered that his speech, while not very organized, was very passionate. I liked that. He stood at the podium and cleared his throat. Then he began one of the most interesting poems I had heard in a while. He called it "Time." It was a commentary on how Time is different for someone in jail. He mixed rhythms with deep inner thoughts, and I really enjoyed the performance.

The fifth speaker was a very young man—he seemed no more than a few years older than me. He was also very well spoken, and his normal talk had an enviable rhythm and eloquence. His poems were all about different aspects of prison life, but from the view of birds and poets. All in all, a very good performance. I couldn't help wondering what had happened to get a man like that in a place like this.

Alex ended the show by reading one of the inmate's poems. She wasn't comfortable, but I know that she did it to be sweet and to try to make the inmate feel good by doing a good job with his poetry. The man was certainly touched.

The master of ceremonies awarded the winners and everyone laughed and joked one last time. The last cookie was eaten, and I congratulated the men sitting up front near me on their amazing poetry. I asked them if they would allow me to perform it on the competitive circuit, and they told me they would. I am still very excited to do that.

Then they were called away to the "pill line." The man that had given Alex his poetry complained, "They ain't gonna make me take my pills if I don't wanna." I felt sorry for him, but I also wondered if not taking the pills was what had landed him here in the first place.

At the night's close, I reflected again on how fulfilling it was to go to the prison and see those people and treat them like people, not criminals. I wished that life didn't have to be so hard, and hoped that by going in there again we had made someone's day. I think we did, and that is why I will continue to go back.

Speaking at the prison is much more than just speaking and hoping to win the ballot and go home. It provides a release for the inmates, a way for them to get back a little bit of humanity. I think it is also a way for debaters and speechies to fully understand that communications skills are developed for more important uses than tournaments.

Advantages of the Prison Persuasion Program

Advantages for Inmates

The persuasion and poetry programs offer certain advantages for inmates in general and others that are specific to those who will be released and to those who will not. The overarching advantages for all prisoners include:

- In many cases, inmates have had the problems they have had because of an inability to communicate. The unique opportunity provided to both students and inmates gives the inmates a chance to build interpersonal and professional communication skills in a non-threatening environment. While interacting with the team, inmates have a chance to playfully interact with people who do not want to intimidate them or spread a mission to them. This really allows them to relax and enjoy speaking.

+ Prison life is not exactly conducive to diversity. There are not many opportunities to interact with people from "the outside" who can provide prisoners with different points of view. Speaking with the team helps fill in the gap. It is also a way for inmates to interact with people "of the day" (people who are current with the outside world—for example, know all the current slang) to help them feel more connected to the world in which they live.

+ The program gives inmates more contacts in the outside world who can help them while they are on the inside. Oregon's funding for the prison system is so under-budgeted that, in some cases, education is beyond the reach of the inmates. The problem has become so bad that for one inmate, the only thing standing between him and his degree is a few exams that need proctoring. Our advisor has offered to help him, and plans are in the works. Meeting people who want to help and have the resources to do so can give inmates an opportunity to advance of which they cannot otherwise make full use.

Advantages for Inmates Who Will Eventually Be Released

+ Participating in debates with college students gives inmates an opportunity to learn in a relaxed atmosphere with people in whom they have confidence. Consistently their speeches improve as they hear more of our speeches, see more of the style that is most effective persuasively, and have more opportunities to do research. Although we have yet to contact anyone who has gone from the inside to the outside, we have seen that membership has increased since we have started our program.

Advantages for "Lifers"

- When a person is convicted, their life and their attitude toward life change dramatically out of necessity. Once they are sentenced for life without parole, they must reorient their dreams and ambitions. For some of the inmates, involvement in the Capitol Gavel Club has become a life's dream and ambition. This is what they have to look forward to from time to time.

Advantages for University Students

- Practice makes perfect, and that philosophy is really applicable to debate in that using words to be persuasive and articulate requires constant refinement and thought. Every debate a debater sees or participates in makes them better. Also, due to the conflict on the American circuit between public and technical spheres, this setting really helps debaters tailor their skills to the public sphere (as opposed to competition which encourages technical skills).

- Community service is always a good idea, and this type is particularly rewarding because the group that we work with is, in most part, always the same and always there. We have a chance to make a lot of progress with limited amounts of time.

- Every time I tell someone that I debate with prisoners, they ask me if I am current with my medication. This is a problem—people need to realize that most prisoners are people too, and that they need to be treated as such even more than people who are not incarcerated. The stereotypes in the prison system are ugly, and no one really wants to talk about them, and so they don't change. This work that we are doing can help accomplish that.

Conclusion

Competitive debate and speech are excellent activities that provide students with enormous skills. However, there are drawbacks to participating in a primarily competitive atmosphere. This situation allows students to work on being people who have debate skills instead of debaters. Many public debate programs, and this prison program is just one, can provide tremendous supplements to the traditional competitive debate and speech programs. They fill in the gaps that competitive speaking leaves in many programs (e.g., apathy to the issues and concern only for competitive success).

Additionally, it is also a great thing for inmates who are looking to improve their communication skills and have a good time.

Danielle Stevens graduated from Willamette University with a B.A. in Sociolinguistics in 2007. The program continues its work at the prison and it is growing every year.

Chapter 4
Debate as an Educational Method

Debating and Creating Our Future: Using Debate Pedagogy to Support Youth-Driven Urban Change

Mackay Miller

The use of academic debate methods outside of scholastic settings is an area that deserves more research and discussion. Practitioners of debate who cross institutional boundaries to apply their methods in the arena of community organizing and civic development will benefit from case studies of others who are working in settings to effect genuine changes in their communities. The Providence Youth Council is an example of an academic debate practitioner working outside of the typical setting, joining with non-profit directors from a variety of backgrounds to build a model of youth development that connects to relevant local issues, builds networks of knowledge, and strengthens capacity for youth-driven change.

From 2004 to 2006, a group of young people and youth organization directors designed and implemented a vehicle for youth civic engagement in Providence, Rhode Island. Hours of input from dozens of young people, as well as a scan of youth policy bodies nationwide, resulted in the concept outlined in this paper. Mayor David Cicilline actively promoted youth engagement as a critical piece of his vision for Providence. His invitation for youth organizations to rise to this challenge, to cooperate in support of meaningful youth participation in political culture, was a vital part of bringing this project to life.

The Rhode Island Urban Debate League was asked to convene the project and build a model of engaging youth in local policy issues. The author began by building a "Resource Coalition," a small network of organizations committed to civic engagement and youth empowerment. The Resource Coalition consisted of four organizations that provided strategic and pedagogical support for this work: Youth Pride, Inc. (an organization that pursues comprehensive strategies in support of gay and lesbian youth); New Urban Arts (a nationally recognized arts after school program); Youth in Action (a youth-driven after school organization); and the Rhode Island Urban Debate League (a policy debate league working with 9 schools in urban Rhode Island). Each organization brought unique skills and substantial experience to the project.

The Providence Youth Council (PYC) in its inaugural year (2005–2006) operated in close cooperation with policy leaders, community activists, and college students to educate 20 young people about important policy topics, and to encourage their participation in civic life. Specifically, PYC members successfully carried out 2 projects that they designed through a process of dialogue and research—a food drive for victims of Hurricane Katrina, and a panel discussion and public forum about the positive career opportunities for youth.

The Structure of the Youth Council

The Council consists of a core membership of 20 youths, ages 15 through 20. The initial core membership aims to equally represent affiliated youths (regular participants in existing programs) and "unaffiliated" youths (with the Youth Council being their first and primary community venture). A 1:1 ratio was the target of student outreach, and in the inaugural year it was a difficult target to reach, although 4 previously unaffiliated youth maintained good attendance at PYC meetings.

Following initial outreach to potential Council members, selection to the Council was based on an application process, reviewed by the director and Resource Coalition members. Membership lasted for one year, with an option to stay on for a second. Membership was restricted to students of high-school age, although they did not need to be enrolled. Working students were actively encouraged to apply, and stipends were available. Every attempt was made to ensure representation from all neighborhoods and high schools.

Initial orientation and community building within the Council membership was critical. The series of orientation events focused primarily on community building exercises and discussions of personal histories; the relating of personal situations to overarching policy discussions; and the creation of bylaws and dispute resolution processes for the internal management of the Council. Roles and responsibilities within the PYC have been assigned pragmatically, based on the requirements of specific projects, and drawing on particular skills of the membership. Roles that Council members have played in pursuit of their projects involve:

- Coordination of specific short-term projects,
- Coordination of outreach to unaffiliated students,
- Design and publishing media and logos for the PYC,
- Management of the agenda and research of the PYC, and
- Building relationships with policy-partners.

The Resource Coalition

The combined strengths of the four involved organizations are broad: queer advocacy and anti-discrimination training, arts and media creation, youth-led governance and health education, and policy analysis and public-speaking training. Year one focused intensively on combining the practices of the four organizations into a coherent pedagogy for youth policy engagement. It is a key challenge for debate practitioners to reach out to diverse partners in building vehicles for inclusive youth involvement. Effective trainings and meaningful policy-partner relationships depend on Coalition leadership to a significant degree.

PEDAGOGY: GENERATING AND SELECTING POLICY PROJECTS THROUGH DEBATE AND ARGUMENTATIVE INQUIRY

The PYC represents one of the first instances in the country in which an Urban Debate League has been invited to play a leading role in driving a city-supported policy change initiative. In describing the role that debate pedagogy played in this Council, as well as details of its design and pedagogical method, the author hopes that this example will be of use to others engaged in urban policy reform.

Building an inclusive process for brainstorming, discussing, refining, and pursuing specific plans is critical for the success of effective community planning and organizing. Such a process should be structured enough to ensure fairness and equal opportunity for input, while remaining flexible enough to encourage creativity and collaboration. Additionally, the model should have a low-entry barrier to new participants and participants with a variety of educational backgrounds. Traditional models of group decision making (e.g., focus groups, expert-facilitated round tables, and legislative bodies using *Robert's Rules of Order*) rarely meet all of these criteria. The methods of debate can be modified to create such a process. For this project, the modified version of debate is an alternative we called *argumentative inquiry*, a facilitation model combining debate, idea- and community-mapping, and empowerment pedagogy. This process has been used successfully on a large scale, most importantly to guide the 2001 redesign of the Indonesian national radio station from a propaganda instrument to a grassroots democratic communication forum. It is a proven method of democratic group decision making.

Perhaps most importantly, argumentative inquiry is designed to be carried out by non-experts. Where traditional focus-group processes require a skilled facilitator, argumentative inquiry allows people with no prior facilitation background to manage collective brainstorming, consensus building, issue prioritization, and project implementation. *Consensus building through argumentative inquiry replaces expert analysis.*

Argumentative inquiry is a four-step process: (1) Generating preferred-future scenarios; (2) Reaching consensus via reasoned debate; (3) Mapping policy suggestions; and (4) Developing implementation plans.[1] After a full-day orientation and community-building process established the groundwork for collaboration, Council members met weekly to develop their understanding of local issues. In designing the weekly seminars for the PYC, the author, together with Resource Coalition members and university student assistants, collected maps of the communities of Providence, as well as movies and policy papers about specific issues in Providence such as gentrification, immigration, and generational poverty.

After several weeks of seminars, PYC members began the process of generating individual propositions or claims about their hopes for Providence, e.g., "In the future, Providence will provide more opportunities for young people to hang out at night." Then, in groups of 5–6 students, these 1–2 sentence statements were debated and refined until at least 75% of the group considered the statement *complete, accurate,* and *relevant.* The facilitator suggested edits to the original propositions until this standard of consensus was reached. If needed, some members could have been designated as devil's advocates to achieve well-considered statements. (This was not necessary in the PYC case.) A note-taker recorded levels of consensus and all edits made to the statements.

This set of policy suggestions was then mapped out on axes of *difficulty of implementation* and *breadth of impact.*

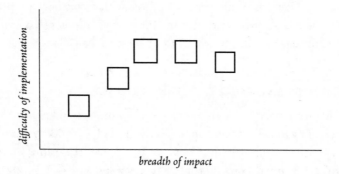

breadth of impact

For example, the suggestion to give every student an additional public transportation ticket occupied a position in the lower left of the map. A suggestion to add two voting positions for youth at both the City Council and the State Senate occupied a position somewhere toward the upper right of the map. It was out of this process that the Hurricane Katrina Food Drive and the Youth Jobs Forum were selected.

This process helps to visually represent and assess potential paths of action. Relative to other formats, it yields better coverage of issues, higher commitment to outcomes, better approaches to consensus building, and good sensitivity to a variety of viewpoints. Additionally, the promotion of reasoned argumentation in this process is historically proven as a non-violent method to challenge and construct ideologies:

> The dialectic, reasoned, rhetorical, or argumentation process is about the only nonviolent mechanism humans have to construct, refine, apply, or challenge diverse perspectives.

People who claim to have a new idea or perspective are asked to justify their claims by providing supporting evidence, while others are allocated the competitive task of thinking of ways to counter this evidence ... This process of organizational argument goes to the heart of democratization of community groups between and with government services.[2]

This policy-suggestion–mapping and community-mapping facet of the Youth Council model positions it at the intersection of two powerful pedagogical methods: debate pedagogy and power-analysis mapping. Combining visual representations of networks of power with a collaborative process to articulate details of advocacy tactics and policy suggestions, offers a vision and a method of how to cultivate critical thinking for urban change.

The Importance of Policy-Partners

Delivering real, manageable solutions to policy makers and policy advocates, and organizing to make them happen, is the goal of any effective youth council. The Youth Commission in Hampton, VA (one of the primary models for this project), regularly provides input to city planners. Conversely, the city Planning Department regularly provides information and background to the Commission. The Hampton Comprehensive Plan features a Youth Component that directly informs the focus of the Youth Commission. This level of access to policy, and this sort of integration into the institutional framework of the city, is critical to progressive youth involvement.

Policy-partners are those individuals and organizations who make and/or advocate for local policy change. They will be a critical link in any effort to construct meaningful youth councils. Representatives from City government, as well as community organizers and advocates, should be actively invited into partnership with the Council. The PYC targeted School Board and Rhode Island Department of Labor and Training officials to attend meetings and talk about their work. It was a key relationship with the Department of Labor and Training that made the Youth Jobs forum a reality.

Conclusion: Debate Pedagogy in the Struggle for Civil Society

In today's economic, social, and political climate, civil society organizations need to collaborate in order to thrive. Often individuals and smaller organizations find it difficult to navigate and influence public policy, but it is exactly this kind of participation that is at the heart of many current reform agendas.

Debate advocates must collaborate with diverse partner organizations, too. It is clear that debate instruction in its own right can help to cultivate leadership. One former Rhode Island urban debater has already proven her skills to influence Rhode Island policy. Ms. Evelyn Duran, a graduate of Hope High School, three-year member of the debate team, and current Brown undergraduate, sought out legislative allies, undertook extensive research, and subsequently co-authored state-level legislation, all within her first 2 years out of high school.

But translating debate models into more accessible vehicles of youth empowerment for non-debaters is more complicated, and demands debate practitioners to be networkers and conveners of partner organizations. The PYC demonstrated that complexity, but in the end also demonstrated that debate instruction is a vital tool in the toolbox of youth-driven activism.

Youth can change cities for the better through rigorous research and public speaking instruction, when that is coupled with effective adult leadership to connect policy ideas to the right people. The hope is that by effectively working as meaningful participants in civic life, debate practitioners will cultivate the concept that debate pedagogy can be a tool for systematic change.

NOTES

1. Dennis List and Michael Metcalfe, "Sourcing forecast knowledge through argumentative inquiry", *Technological Forecasting and Social Change*, vol. 71, no 5 (June 2004), 525–535. See also www.audiencedialogue.org/consensus. html for background on audience dialogue and argumentative inquiry. The *Argumentative Inquiry* model is attributed to Professors Dennis List and Michael Metcalfe at the University of South Australia, who provided helpful advice about the planning of the Providence Youth Council.

2. Ibid., p. 534.

Mackay Miller is the former Director of the Rhode Island Urban Debate League, Swearer Center for Public Service at Brown University. He is currently serving as High School Reform Facilitator for the Providence Public School Department in Providence, Rhode Island.

Introducing Debate into the Curriculum of *Gimnazija Franca Miklošiča Ljutomer*, Slovenia

Liana Miholič and Martina Domajnko

Debate in Slovenia is gathered under ZIP—*Zavod za kulturo dialoga Ljubljana* (Institution for the Culture of Dialogue). It works on the level of elementary schools, general secondary schools (*gimnazijas*), and universities. *Gimnazija Franca Miklošiča Ljutomer*, with students age 15 to 19, is a 4-year (upper) general secondary school preparing students for studies at the university level.

The Structure of the Education System in Slovenia

Pre-school Education

Pre-school education, offered by pre-school institutions, is not compulsory. It is designed for children between the ages of 1 and 6. The curriculum is divided in two cycles (from ages 1 to 3 and from ages 3 to 6). The new system offers different types of programs such as day, half-day, and short programs. There is also the option of pre-school education at home, or occasional care of children in their homes.

Until the school year 2001/2002, children between the ages of 6 and 7 had to attend compulsory one-year pre-primary classes (*priprava na osnovno šolo*) before entering elementary school. The pre-primary education curriculum was implemented in 1999/2000. The pre-primary classes are being gradually abolished. Children at the age of 6 enter the new 9-year compulsory education.

Basic Education

Legislation extends basic (compulsory) education from 8 years to 9 years. The new 9-year elementary school curriculum is being implemented gradually, and an optional 10th year will be introduced. A 10th year of education has been planned for pupils who fail or who wish to improve their results in the external knowledge assessment.

Nine-year basic education is divided into 3 three-year cycles. Elementary schools provide compulsory and extended curricula. The compulsory curriculum must be provided by the school and studied by all pupils. It consists of compulsory subjects, electives, homeroom periods, and activity days (culture, science, sports, technology). The optional elementary school curriculum must be provided by the school, but pupils are free to decide whether they will participate. It includes educational assistance for children with special needs, remedial classes, additional classes, after-school care, other forms of care for pupils and extracurricular activities.

Successful completion of basic education enables pupils to proceed to education in their choice of secondary school. Pupils who fulfill the legal compulsory education requirement and successfully complete at least six grades in the eight-year elementary school or at least seven grades in the nine-year elementary school can continue their education in a short-term vocational education program. Success at that level opens doors to other, more demanding secondary school programs.

Toward More Integrated Forms of Special Education

The new law on special education was adopted in 2000. Instead of a static placement scheme, placements based on children's development and a system enabling transfers of children from one program to another were introduced. The new law is based on contemporary principles of mainstreaming children, a gradual introduction of changes, equal opportunity (taking into account the differences in children), the right to choose the school and type of education, possibilities for parents to become involved in the educational process, differentiated and individualized programs, and co-operation of various professions.

Children with special needs enroll for special curricula provided by elementary schools specialized to accommodate such children. Secondary school courses can be adapted for pupils with special needs.

Changes in the 9-year Compulsory Education

The major debates currently taking place are focused on the follow up and the evaluation results of the new 9-year compulsory school. A group of parents, supported by opposing parties, initiated a great public debate on the supposed study overload of pupils (too many subjects in the last cycle, too much home work and too many out-of-school activities). Another argument was raised within the selected expert circles in connection with the external national examinations at the end of each cycle. The debate was about the existing system of final evaluation of pupils, the relation between the written and oral parts, and how the results obtained in final examinations should be expressed in the certificate awarded to pupils (combining it with the marks and the work over the final year).

As a response, the Amendments to the Elementary School Act were proposed and have just been passed into law by the Government. They are expected to bring some changes.

Pupils in the last cycle (grades 7–9) will be allowed to choose 2 or 3 optional compulsory subjects henceforth (as distinguished from the current situation of choosing 3 compulsory subjects). The final grade shall be based on the 2 highest marked subjects only, instead of 3 as at present. The second change refers to more appropriate standards of knowledge, assessed at the end of 3 cycles of compulsory education through the external national examinations.

(Upper) Secondary Education

Secondary education follows the compulsory general education. Secondary schools include vocational and technical schools that prepare students predominantly for labor, and general secondary schools (*gimnazijas*) that prepare students predominantly for further studies at the University. Programs in secondary education vary in content, duration, and goals.

General Secondary Education

A general secondary school preparing students for further studies is called a *gimnazija*. *Gimnazija* programs are divided into two groups: general and professionally oriented (technical *gimnazijas*). They last four years end with an external state examination (the same examination for all *gimnazijas* in Slovenia, taken at the same time and corrected by a panel of teachers) called a *matura* examination. Those *gimnazija* education students who for various reasons do not wish to continue their education have an option to enter the labor market by taking a vocational course and gaining a qualification in a selected occupation.

The aim of vocational courses is to provide a bridge between general and vocational and to make it possible for graduates from general, classical, and technical *gimnazijas* to obtain initial vocational qualifications at the level of corresponding secondary vocational and technical schools. Educational aims are the same as for vocational and technical education. The course leads to a vocational qualification needed in the labor market or for further studies at post-secondary vocational and professional colleges.

Secondary Vocational and Technical Education

The planning, programming, and provision of vocational and technical education are a joint responsibility of social partners (employers and trade unions) and the state.

Short-term vocational programs should last a year and a half for students and apprentices who have completed their basic education, and two and a half years for those without completed basic education, and finish with a final examination. The certificate of the final examination enables students to enter the labor market or to enter the first year at any other (upper) secondary vocational school.

Pupils who have successfully completed elementary school can enroll in 3-year secondary vocational programs. Vocational education programs are offered in the dual (apprenticeship) system and/or in the school-based system.

The certificate of the final examination enables students to enter the labor market or to continue education in two-year vocational–technical programs. Vocational–technical programs are designed as upgrades to vocational education. The aims of vocational–technical programs are the same as those of technical education programs and lead to educational qualifications at the level of secondary technical school, also called a technical qualification, in a specific field.

Technical education is designed primarily as preparation for vocational and professional colleges. Secondary technical programs last four years, ending with a *poklicna matura* (vocational final examination).

Post-Secondary Vocational Education

This type of education is a new feature in the system. Programs are markedly practical and tightly connected with the world of work. Post-secondary vocational education lasts for two years, ending with a diploma examination. A post-secondary vocational diploma enables students to start work in specific occupations. Vocational college graduates are able to enroll in the second year of professionally oriented higher education programs if the higher education institution providing this type of study allows such arrangements.

Further Development of Upper Secondary Education

The *gimnazija* program has undergone considerable modernization. Specialized *gimnazija* programs have been developed, focusing respectively on classical languages, economics, technology, and the arts (music, painting, theatre, dance). Technical programs and vocational education programs have been modernized, too, and adapted to students with special needs.

To further promote the development of a European dimension in upper secondary education, a group of experts has designed a special adaptation of the *gimnazija* program in which a sense of European awareness is evident throughout the curriculum. It is known as European Classes. Besides focusing on learning foreign languages, the European Classes curriculum aims at making students acquire a deeper understanding of European geography, European history, and the role of the European Union and its institutions, as well as a greater understanding of the daily lives of other Europeans and their cultural heritage. European awareness is also demonstrated in subjects such as music and art, but most of all through various international exchange projects. This adaptation of the *gimnazija* program is being implemented on a pilot basis, starting with the school year 2004/2005. *Gimnazija Franca Miklošiča Ljutomer* is one of twelve *gimnazijas* in Slovenia that began such a program in one of its first year classrooms.

The educational process is guided by official documents: the Framework Curriculum documents for each school subject (indicating the content areas that should be taught in schools and objectives to be achieved) and the *Matura* Catalogue and the Vocational *Matura* Catalogue (defining what is to be assessed). The *Matura* and the Vocational *Matura* Catalogues have been supplemented with new content and subjects. Major debates, which took place a year ago, resulted in the new guidelines for the development of vocational and technical education and changes in the financial system of schools, which were adopted in 2003. The first vocational education program based on the new guidelines document was adopted and will start in 2004/2005 as a pilot project. The open curriculum ensures that the school and its partners (businesses, kindergartens, factories, etc.) may decide on 20% of the curriculum content. The program aims at achieving competence in general and occupational-specific education. There is the recommendation for a minimum duration of 24 weeks of practical training in an enterprise. A lump sum model of financing the selected pilot schools will be introduced in the future.

Higher Education

Higher education includes academic university studies and professionally oriented studies. The former should prepare students for highly demanding professions and for more advanced academic studies and research, while the latter should prepare them primarily for highly demanding professions. Universities and single faculties established as private institutions offer both types of program, while professional colleges provide only professionally oriented programs. In addition to teaching, higher education institutions also carry out research and fine arts programs. Study is organized at two levels. At the undergraduate level, students obtain a diploma and the first of the degree titles. At the post-graduate level, students are awarded either a second degree title, the title of specialist, or the academic title of either *magister znanosti* (*magister umetnosti* in artistic fields)—the title is comparable to a master's degree—or *doktor znanosti*, which is a doctoral degree.

Next Steps in the Development of Higher Education

Moves to bring the higher education system in Slovenia into line with the principles of the Bologna Process began in 2002, when the National Assembly adopted the Master Plan for Higher Education. Two years later, the Government adopted the amendments to the Higher Education Act (2004), which will form the basis of further development of the Slovenian higher education system by incorporating the aims of the Bologna Declaration. The act anticipates a three-stage structure, consisting of undergraduate programs (3–4 years, 180–240 CP [credit points]), followed by post-graduate programs (1–2 years, 60–120 CP). The variations of 3+2 and 4 +1 will be possible. The professional titles will be preserved (graduate, university graduate, *magister*, *doktor*), with the exception of specialist, which will be abolished. The substance of the actual research based academic qualification of *magister* will be redefined so that it will represent a qualification known as "master" in Bologna terms. The third stage—doctoral level—will require 3 years of study (180 CP).

The new structure of study programs, including joint degree programs, will be gradually implemented. The last enrollment of students under the old system will be in 2007/2008.

The Council for Higher Education will preserve the responsibilities of counseling, planning, and managing the accreditation system; however, its membership will be complemented by representatives of employers and students. A quality assurance system will be provided by the new National Agency and the new Council for the Evaluation of Tertiary Education.

IMPLEMENTATION OF DEBATE INTO THE CURRICULUM OF *GIMNAZIJA FRANCA MIKLOŠIČA LJUTOMER*, SLOVENIA

As already mentioned, *gimnazija* is a 4-year upper secondary education program that prepares students age 15–19 for studies at the university. At *Gimnazija Franca Miklošiča Ljutomer*, Slovenia debate is being implemented into the curriculum in three different ways.

Debate Club

Since 1997, when debating started at *Gimnazija Franca Miklošiča Ljutomer*, there have been two debate clubs (Slovenian and English) and two coaches. The clubs have been an optional extracurricular activity that meet after lessons in the afternoon and they attend and organize tournaments on weekends. The students liked the idea of debating and thought they might use it in classes as well. They suggested having one-to-one debate in classes instead of individual oral examinations that are usually carried out by teachers at the beginning of the lesson.

The classes that first introduced debate were the classes that the coaches— Mrs. Martina Domajnko and Mrs. Liana Miholič—teach: sociology, English, and German. In the beginning it was possible only in classes with some experienced debate club members.

As it proved successful, the coaches suggested using debate as a learning (teaching) method in classrooms and gave advice on how to do it to other members of the staff at *Gimnazija Franca Miklošiča Ljutomer*. Teachers of geography, history, biology, and Slovene were asked to try it and give feedback. Additional information and encouragement was provided by Dr. Alfred Snider's lectures in January 2003. In addition, the teachers experimented in classrooms with some experienced debaters. All these made the experiment of implementing debate into the curriculum of *Gimnazija Franca Miklošiča Ljutomer* easier.

The headmaster's support for debate, which was already present when both school debate clubs organized numerous international debate tournaments, increased when, in January 2003, Dr. Snider visited *Gimnazija Franca Miklošiča Ljutomer* and gave a lectures on introducing debate into classrooms. The lecture was attended by elementary and secondary school teachers from the whole region. They liked the idea of introducing debate into their classes, and in a discussion after the lecture, they considered ways to do it "officially" and for the whole of Slovenia. ZIP director Mrs. Bojana Skrt felt that the conditions to do this were best at *Gimnazija Franca Miklošiča Ljutomer* and encouraged the coaches Domajnko and Miholič to start activities to reach the final goal, which was to make it possible to implement debate into this *gimnazija's* curriculum and maybe in the near future also into the Slovenian curriculum.

Implementations and Teachers' Reactions

Debate has been used this way with experienced debaters in the following classes: Slovene, German, English, sociology, environmental studies, geography, and biology.

In **environmental studies**, topics debated included:

+ Producing genetically modified food is justified.

+ Improvement of rivers and brooks in the Pomurje area is justified.

+ Wind power should be used in the Kras region of Slovenia.

In **sociology**, debating was used as a way of introducing new topics (students' own research before the lesson), as preparation for the essay on the final exam, and as an oral examination. Topics included:

+ The workload in the gimnazija program should be diminished.
+ The minorities in Slovenia enjoy too many rights.
+ The traditional family is the only form of family that enables proper personal development of a child.
+ Slovenia is a welfare state.
+ Zois scholarships are a way of recruiting the elite in Slovene society.

In **English** classes debates were conducted on obligatory topics in the curriculum. Topics included:

+ Cloning
+ Professional sports
+ Addiction
+ The right to die
+ Big brother is watching.

Debating was used as:

A) group work during the lessons when it came to discussing issues

B) a way of introducing new topics (students did the research at home and debated one to one at the beginning of the lesson as an introduction to teaching)

C) preparation for the essay on the final exam

D) a way of oral examination

In other subject areas, the topics included:

Slovene:

+ Preseren is the greatest Slovene poet.

German:

+ Brand names guarantee good quality.

+ German sauerkraut is better than *kislo zelje*.

Geography:

+ Being neutral is an advantage for Swiss people.

+ The Netherlands should be a role model in legislation concerning drugs and prostitution.

Biology:

+ Diabetes is the result of inappropriate eating habits.

+ HIV testing should be free of charge and anonymous.

To find out what advantages and disadvantages using debate in class had, all teachers were interviewed by the debate coaches. Some teachers were surprised by the fact that the students could learn in this way. Others liked the idea but were not too enthusiastic about the extra preparation such a lesson required. They all agreed that debating develops critical thinking and makes lessons more interesting.

The final result was that most teachers support the idea of introducing debate into the curriculum and they will use it in their classes after they have attended a course and workshop on how to do it, given by ZIP—*Zavod za kulturo dialoga Ljubljana, Slovenija* (explained in more detail below). None of the teachers completely refused to use debate techniques in classrooms.

Compulsory Extracurricular Activities

As another way of introducing debate into the curriculum, debate coaches Mrs. Miholič and Mrs. Domajnko suggested to the headmaster of *Gimnazija Franca Miklošiča Ljutomer* that debating should be offered as one of the compulsory extracurricular activities. These are a part of the *gimnazija* curriculum, and each of the students has to accumulate 90 hours in the year—extracurricular activities are meant to develop the students' personal growth but are not graded as are other compulsory subjects. They are divided into a compulsory common part, offered by the school, and an optional individual part. The compulsory common part is meant for all students and is given as a course. Debate at *Gimnazija Franca Miklošiča Ljutomer* was put into the compulsory common part, and in the school year 2003/2004 debate coaches Liana Miholič and Martina Domajnko taught 150 first graders the elements of debate.

The aims were:

+ to teach children not only the format of the debate but also how to apply it in real life (e.g., critical thinking, looking at things from different viewpoints, using arguments and evidence, team work, confidence in public speaking, etc.).

+ to enable students to use debate in the classroom.

The special aim was to introduce formal debate into classes of different subjects and maybe serve as a model for other Slovenian upper secondary schools.

In co-operation with ZIP—*Zavod za kulturo dialoga Ljubljana*, it was decided that each first grader should have 18 45-minute classes of debate as a compulsory extracurricular activity.

The Structure of the Classes

In the first two lessons, students were encouraged to give their own views on an actual topic that touches them (wearing slippers in school). They came up with different ideas, tried to convince each other, and became louder and louder. At this stage they were stopped and were told that what they were doing could be called debate, although not debate that is really acceptable. This way they were shown that they already possess some of the skills relevant to debate, but they need training to learn how to do it properly. They were taught about the roots and history of debate, different debate formats, debating principles, etc.

The next two lessons included training for concentration (telling the story with distractions), playing different roles (mirror in our bathroom, my schoolbag), giving two-minute spontaneous speeches (school system in Slovenia), and discussing interesting topics (violating school rules, etc.).

Demonstration debate, performed by older debaters took **two hours.** The audience was encouraged to actively follow the debate by writing down the arguments and to recognize the roles of the speakers. In addition they had to pay attention to style.

The fourth meeting (7th and 8th lessons) was dedicated to analyzing their work and teaching the format and the aims of the debate (Karl Popper format, roles of the speakers, etc.). They started learning argumentation. Their homework was to flow the news, which was good practice for flowing and learning about current events.

The fifth meeting was meant for learning and practicing basic skills for the debate: brainstorming, preparing the argument, problem solving, building the case, refuting, rebutting, critical analysis of the opponents' views. Exercises were: Baron, Balloon, and a few exercises taken from *Discovering the World through Debate* (resolutional analyses, resolutional analyses worksheet, etc.).

As one of the aims of introducing debate into the Slovenian curriculum was to teach the students how to perform in public, they were expected to debate each other. This is where the experienced debate club members joined in again and helped prepare the first graders for debates. They also helped with judging and giving feedback at debates. Each first grade student was expected to go through all stages of the debate from brainstorming to debating. This took six hours. Students debated resolutions, which they suggested themselves (e.g., Today's parents are too permissive; Religious education should be introduced in schools; Teenagers should be allowed to drive at the age of 16; Soft drugs should be legalized; There should be censorship of TV programs, etc.).

They debated using the Karl Popper format in groups, which they formed themselves. There are 32–34 students in each class, so to save time, the debates were performed at the same time in different rooms. Older debaters were timekeepers and judges, and the coaches moved from one room to another and gave additional advice.

The last two hours were for filling out a questionnaire and evaluation. The questions they were asked were very simple:

a) What was good about this course?

b) What was bad about it?

c) What did you learn from it?

d) What would you suggest?

Their answers were more or less expected:

a) They liked the idea of debating, they learned how to speak in public, some of them recognized the importance of team work.

b) Some didn't like the fact that the course was compulsory and some found it exhausting.

c) They learned how to react quickly to arguments; they experienced teamwork.

d) There were no new suggestions proposed.

As a result, *Gimnazija Franca Miklošiča Ljutomer* will continue offering debate as a compulsory extra curricular activity in the future.

Institutionalization Through the Slovenian Ministry of Education, Research and Sport

In May 2004 the Slovenian Ministry of Education, Research and Sport called for applications for innovative projects in the field of education. *Gimnazija Franca Miklošiča Ljutomer* applied with the innovative project called Debating and Implementing Debate Techniques into Classes.

> *The suggested field was*: Ways to qualitative learning/ knowledge.
>
> *The research question was*: Does using formal debating and debate techniques in classes contribute to more qualitative learning?
>
> *The aim was*: To change the attitude toward gaining knowledge and to develop the role of students and teachers in the process of learning/teaching.
>
> The project was prepared on the basis of experiences of debate work at *Gimnazija Franca Miklošiča Ljutomer*. It was started in school year 2004/2005 and is aimed at implementing debate into Slovenian curriculum.

The project, under supervision and support of the Ministry of Education, Research and Sport, is going on at the moment and will last until the end of the current school year (2004/2005). During this period most of the teachers at *Gimnazija Franca Miklošiča Ljutomer* will be educated on how to use debate and debate techniques for teaching. The 16-hour course and workshop has already been given by ZIP—*Zavod za kulturo dialoga Ljubljana, Slovenija*.

The aim of this workshop is to:

+ Educate teachers in new teaching methods;
+ Show teachers the techniques of debate and how to use them in classes;

- Enable teachers to form resolutions for their subjects;
- Spread the idea of using debate in classes among colleague teachers at other *gimnazijas* in Slovenia.

During the workshop, teachers tried debating each other, but the most important outcome was that all participants decided to use debate as a teaching tool in their classes. Some of the suggested resolutions, which will be used in classes during the school year 2004/2005, are the following:

History:

- Napoleon and Hitler made the same mistakes.
- When spreading their religion, Islam was more tolerant than Christianity.

Geography:

- Child labor in developing countries should be punished.
- The floods in Asia bring more good than bad.

Mathematics:

- Logarithm and exponent function are important in life.
- Square function is more useful than linear function.

Psychology:

- Learning in a group takes less time than learning individually.

German:

- Using the passive is essential for fluent German.
- Werther's decision for suicide is justified.

English:

- American English is more applicable than British English.

Physics:

- Power stations on the Mura River are justified.
- Alternative energy sources can substitute for fossil fuels.

Chemistry:

- Iron is more applicable than aluminum.

Art:

+ Abstract art is of higher quality than figurative art.

Physical Education:

+ Doping in sport is essential for achieving top results.

In the end, the evaluation of the project will be made by the teachers of *Gimnazija Franca Miklošiča Ljutomer* with the help of the Slovenian Ministry of Education, Research and Sport. If the results prove to be positive, there is a high possibility that debate will in some way be introduced into the Slovenian curriculum.

BIBLIOGRAPHY

Driscol W., Zompetti P. (2003). Discovering the World through Debate. New York: The International Debate Education Association.

Snider A., Schnurer M. (2002). Many Sides, Debate across the Curriculum. New York: The International Debate Education Association.

Slovenia Ministry of Education and Sport. Available at www.mss.gov.si/.

Zavod za kulturo dialoga Slovenija. (2004) Material from the courses for debate coaches by ZIP.

Liana Miholič teaches English and German at *Gimnazija Franca Miklošiča Ljutomer*, Slovenia and implements debate as a learning/teaching method into her classes. She also coaches the English Debate Club, organizes international debate tournaments, and judges at the national and international levels as well as at the World Schools Debating Championships.

Martina Domajnko has been a teacher of pedagogy and sociology, a counselor, and a debate coach at *Gimnazija Franca Miklošiča Ljutomer*, Slovenia since 1997. She works on integrating debate into the curriculum as a learning/teaching method in classrooms through the Ministry of Education, Slovenia.

Debating Toward Dialogue and Educational Transformation

Frank Duffin

INTRODUCTION

The United States public education system is embroiled in one of the most intense transformations in its history. Regardless of public policy, such as the No Child Left Behind Act or other federal and state legislation, public education is facing a post-postmodern public with little appetite for what education has been over the course of 150 years. As an institution, an organization, or a system, education looked radically different after industrialization. Compulsory education introduced many more people into the educational system, a system that found, surprisingly, the efficacy of the factory model to create a population to work in a factory setting. As society and the marketplace are changing, education is trying to adaptively change with them, but public education is struggling to meet societal expectations. Adaptive change is not transferring to educational practice.

Higher education and private industry have conducted research on the public school system and have made many suggestions on how to adaptively change it to meet societal expectations. Yet many of the recommendations, theories, and "best practices" for improvement don't make it from the page into practice (Zemelman, Daniels, and Hyde, 1998). Given the current challenges of public education, where all students and their educators are being held more accountable for their education, there is a growing realization among public education institutions that they cannot do it alone. They need to interact with other institutions and have a fluid exchange of ideas and knowledge. The factory model of isolation, where educators closed the classroom door and did their own thing, is a thing of the past. Schoolteachers in elementary and secondary settings are encouraged, if not mandated, to interact with businesses, higher education institutions, and other educators within the same building.[1]

A key idea behind educational institutions' collaboration with outside organizations is to share information, share knowledge, make the learning more real for educators and students, and potentially produce better workers for a better society. According to Peter Senge and colleagues, "The industrial-age school puts the classroom at the center of the learning process. Yet genuine learning occurs in the context of our lives and the long-term impact of any new learning depends on its relationship to the world around us" (2000, 41). David Tyack and Larry Cuban suggest that "many of the best programs of instructional change involve close collaboration between practitioners who share common purposes but adapt them flexibly to their local circumstances" (1995, 139). They go on to list national organizations and institutions that promote collaboration on a large scale to advance a "broad-based social movement to improve learning and to promote greater equality in schooling" (139). Collaboration is also a driving force behind federal grants supporting school-to-work/career initiatives (Perkins Act, 2006). Howard Gardner even articulates a vision of education for all humans that "would yield individuals who feel a commitment to their community and to the larger world" (2000, 245).

The idea of collaboration is attractive to many people in contemporary learning organizations, but it also puts major constraints on organizations and on individuals: within the existing logistical confines of all organizations, it is difficult to schedule the time to bring business, secondary education, and higher education together without restructuring what school looks like and how businesses interact with education. In addition to commitments of time, there also has to be a willingness to collaborate by all parties. Given the institutional memory of educational systems, it may be difficult to relinquish classroom autonomy and isolation for a more open and social learning environment. On an even more local level, educators within the same building, in the same department, or even adjacent to one another don't create the time to collaboratively exchange ideas. In response to educational reform initiatives, institutions, and legislation (National School Reform Faculty

Program, Annenberg Institute for School Reform, New England Small Schools Network, Carnegie Foundation, MacArthur Foundation, Perkins Act, No Child Left Behind legislation, Southern Regional Collaborative, etc.), educators have had difficulty transferring these types of collaborative theories and mandates into practice. The major focus of collaboration in this paper is on teacher collaboration within the same building and the sustainable structures that support it.

In an attempt to develop a sustainable collaborative system, the Providence School District hired Diana Lam, former Superintendent of San Antonio, Texas, in the summer of 1999. Accompanying her to Providence was a reputation of shaking things up, of political confrontation, of very short tenures, and of educational reform. The city of Providence concluded it was time to shake up the educational status quo and thought Lam was the person to do it. In order to get the reform message out, Lam trained the principals of each school in a rigorous indoctrination of cognitive learning and theory. With the guidance of the Institute for Learning at the University of Pittsburgh, the principals were trained in the Principles of Learning and a constructivist approach to pedagogy. Yet at the end of the year, teachers didn't have a clear idea of the reform efforts, other than some rather meek attempts by administrators to use "accountable talk" as a tool to teach and to learn. With principals in various schools understanding the reform initiative at varying levels, the implementation was fragmented and inconsistent. Some principals gave the initiative lip service and presented the professional development on a superficial level. Other schools took the initiative seriously, but with the principals already having managerial and administrative responsibilities in addition to presenting the instructional and literacy strategies of the initiative, time was a sparse commodity and professional development was unsustainable. Some principals also had adversarial relationships with their faculties, while their faculties didn't intellectually respect them. The Principles of Learning, and other instructional frameworks put forward by the district, had sustainability issues in the system. In short, teachers saw minimal impact from the reform efforts in the first year and were distrustful of the district's direction.

The next stage of the reform effort was to hire literacy coaches for each school. It was the job of the coach to work with teachers in the classroom and to conduct after-school professional development to improve classroom instruction by opening up practice with embedded instructional professional development. Literacy coaches were trained in the Principles of Learning, reading strategies, and writing strategies. Yet, with the entrenched cultural memory of isolation, many teachers in Providence were distrusting of having anybody enter into their classrooms. In fact, instead of opening up practice and adaptively changing to a progressive pedagogy, many teachers became more entrenched in closing their doors and, as Paulo Freire would say, disseminating an oppressive pedagogy (1995). Despite the reform difficulties, one of the most influential and sustainable best practices was Debate Across the Curriculum (DAC) that grew at a grassroots level and spread throughout the entire Providence school system. Digging deeper into teacher collaboration and how sustainable models for school reform are developed and implemented, I will focus on one school in Providence, Rhode Island that took a different approach to educational reform.

EDUCATIONAL REFORMATION AT FRANKLYN HIGH SCHOOL

Franklyn High School in Providence, Rhode Island, first opened in 1995, was officially closed the last day of school, June 28, 2001, for poor academic performance and political infighting. It was reopened in September 2001 as the New Franklyn High School with the same students from the old school, but with a new staff, new administration, and a new vision. The Franklyn design team, in conjunction with the district, created a school that is performance-based and chants the mantra "excellence is the constant and time is the variable." In trying to fulfill this vision during its first year of operation, Franklyn grouped its students heterogeneously (9th graders through 12th graders in the same classroom) with the intent of having seniors mentor younger students. What the school discovered, however, was that the incoming 9th graders were better prepared to succeed academically than were the seniors. The seniors seemed to be afflicted with "senioritis" from the onset of the school year and were inhibitors of progress rather than contributors to the reform efforts. There was also a strong alliance to some of the old Franklyn teachers who were not hired back to the school, which probably encouraged some of the seniors' hostility and lack of performance. The school also started phasing out the traditional grading system (A, B, C, etc.) and adopted an assessment system based on a numeric continuum (0, 1, 2, 3, 4, 5, 6). This assessment system focused on what students could do rather than the time they put in their seats—performance tasks vs. seat time. This meant that students, upon demonstrating they could meet the standards, could graduate regardless of how much time it took them to do it. Likewise, those students who needed more time were afforded that luxury. This approach drew attention to the actual work instead of just time spent.

In Franklyn's second year it phased in a School One and School Two model, in which students who hadn't met the standards were in School One and students who had met the standards were in School Two. This division also helped scaffold the idea of heterogeneous grouping with a structure that would build on the academic foundation from School One to a more independent and individualized learning structure in School Two. The idea was to prepare School Two students for the post-high school experience, academically, socially, and emotionally. In School Two, students had the same academic subjects (English, science, social studies, and math) but at a more rigorous level, with the additional component of a one-month internship in a field they were thinking of studying or working in after high school. The school had students interested in education, nursing, business, architecture, journalism, etc. and provided them with internship opportunities in all of these areas. In addition, the School Two teachers were in the process of developing professional relationships with the organizations that provided the internships, with the expectation that the teachers would integrate the knowledge into their practice.

As Franklyn High School went through the process of trying to become a successful school, one of the most transformational "best practices" in the classroom was DAC. Of the four teams in the school [Red (School Two), Orange, Yellow, and Blue], the Blue team (one of the three teams in School One) initiated and implemented DAC into its practice across the disciplines. In 2001 the team, consisting of five teachers (English, social studies, math, science, and special education) implemented debate during the last quarter as the culminating research project. The collaboration between the English teacher, ML (the debate coach at Franklyn), and the social studies teacher, JJR, resulted in a debate format more akin to an informal assertion and rebuttal. They divided their combined classes in two; one side made an assertion and the other side had to respond with a rebuttal.

In the 2002–2003 school year, the team developed a DAC structure that modeled a format developed in the summer by the Providence Instructional Reform Facilitators, under my guidance and that of the Rhode Island Debate

League (RIDL), that was used for the Providence School District's curriculum scope and sequence. The team demanded more academic rigor from the students in backing up their assertions and rebuttals with evidence than they did the previous year. The team also invited the entire school to observe and judge the culminating debates during the fourth quarter.

In the 2003–2004 school year, the team developed an even more sophisticated and collaborative DAC structure that was integrated into its educational fabric throughout the school year, instead of just the fourth quarter. During the summer of 2003, the team worked with the RIDL to construct a DAC curriculum framework that could be used as a national model. The team decided to adopt the "oceans policy" theme developed by both the National Association of Urban Debate Leagues (NAUDL) and the National Forensics League (NFL) in order to tie into the extensive research already conducted on a national level and to integrate the classroom dialogue into a national dialogue with debate leagues across the nation. The teachers—CD (science), JJR (social studies), and ML (English)—worked throughout the summer on a values debate curriculum that they could use the first semester (the school had not yet hired the math teacher, who was to be part of the team). Planning for the second semester focused on a policy debate format that built on the debating skills that were taught in the first semester and increased the academic rigor substantially.

METHODOLOGY

Data Collection and Analysis

For the purposes of this study, I will analyze the quantitative data of the students' basic understanding and their analysis and interpretation skills in reading from the New Standards Reference Exam (NSRE). I will also analyze the qualitative data collected from the teachers and students on the effectiveness of DAC as a best practice to improve student performance, to transfer learning, to cultivate collegial dialogue, and to distribute cognition. The data process I will follow is a two-way interaction between School Processes and Student Learning.

I compiled state level data between 2001 and 2004 that included scores from the reading comprehension and reading analysis and interpretation sections of the NSRE. This is a criterion-based reference exam developed by the

Learning Research and Development Center (LRDC) at the University of Pittsburgh and the National Center on Education and the Economy (NCEE). Students are asked to read short passages and answer questions about their content. They are also asked to analyze and interpret longer passages and are instructed to write the answers in their examination booklet. According to the students' responses to the questions, they are awarded a score based on a national point of reference to national standards and a limited time frame that reflects standardized conditions.

I also conducted interviews using questions designed to ensure comparable data were collected from all of the teachers and students interviewed. Questions were constructed based on Adaptive Change, Collaboration, Dialogue, Distributed Cognition, and Transfer of Learning and were intended to elicit open responses from both the teachers and students who were interviewed.

Reading: Meeting the Standards for Basic Understanding

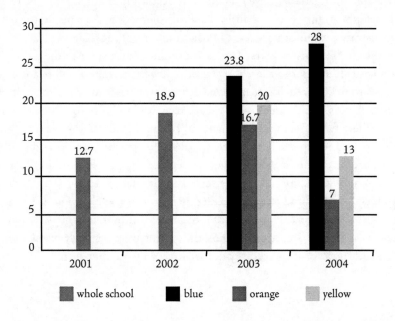

In the 2000–2001 (represented by the 2001 data) and the 2001–2002 school years (represented by the 2002 data), the data was not disaggregated. In the school year 2002–2003 (represented by the 2003 data), the school rearranged the teams into Orange, Yellow, Blue, and Red, based on teacher preference and on administrator discretion. In the school year 2003–2004 (represented by the 2004 data), the Blue team was fairly consistent: the English teacher, the science teacher, and the social studies teacher stayed with the team throughout the entire year. In 2003–2004 the Orange team lost its English teacher because she moved to a reading position in the school that was an elective position, thus taking her out of the team structure of English, social studies, science, and math. The science teacher on the Orange team was not actively involved in team planning and the English teacher was a substitute for the entire 2003–2004 school year. At the onset of the 2003–2004 school year, the Yellow team got a new English teacher and a new science teacher. In looking at the three teams, there is consistency in collaboration between the Blue team's English and social studies teachers over the course of three years; there is also collaborative consistency between the Yellow team's social studies teacher and the math teacher over the course of two years; and there is no collaborative consistency on the Orange team among personnel staying on that team, which may have influenced the data and the ability for the team to develop working processes and collaborative practices. As a result, the data demonstrate a significant increase in basic understanding from the Blue team over the course of three years. The data also illustrate a spike in the scores in 2003 with all teams, but the Orange and Yellow teams take a significant turn downward in 2004. As was mentioned before, the Blue team consistently used Debate Across the Curriculum as a mediating tool to unite the students and the teachers with a common pedagogical strategy. In 2002 the teaming was between the English teacher and the social studies teacher. In 2003–2004 the team introduced the science teacher to the debating process, and in the academic school year 2003–2004, the team fully implemented DAC with English, social studies, and science, leaving math out of the planning due to the lack of a full-time teacher and philosophical differences in pedagogy. The processes of reading instruction on the other teams were somewhat consistent, but not at the level of consistency demonstrated by the Blue team.

Reading: Meeting the Standards for Analysis and Interpretation

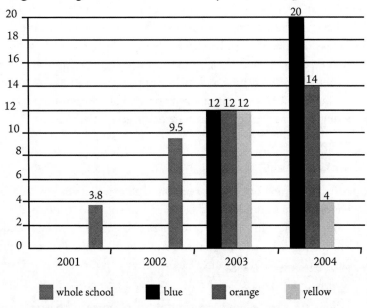

As we see, the scores for reading analysis and interpretation generally improved for all teams in 2003, but the Blue team significantly outperformed the Orange and Yellow teams in 2004. The data in the analysis and interpretation category are particularly interesting. It is assumed that analysis and interpretation are higher order thinking skills compared to basic understanding; yet in 2003, when all teams performed at the same level in this category, improving from the previous year in general, the 2004 data suggest that the Orange team gained ground by 2 percent and the Yellow team lost ground in analysis and interpretation by 8 percent, while the Blue team increased its performance by 8 percent from the 2003 data. Although the correlation between school processes on the Yellow team and the Orange team are consistent with the basic understanding data, the slight increase of 2 percent in analysis and interpretation on the Orange team, with its personnel turnover, could be an anomaly. If anything, a downturn in analysis and interpretation would have been anticipated. Although the data is encouraging and suggests the Blue team is on the right track, it does not establish a correlation between DAC and improved reading ability in the students. The best correlation comes from a qualitative analysis of teaching practice, teacher responses on both the Blue team and the Red team, and student responses to the use of Debate Across the Curriculum on their academic performance. As I conducted the qualitative research, a few prominent theories surfaced: activity theory, transfer of learning, dialogue, and distributed cognition. The importance of these theories, as well as the impact Debate Across the Curriculum had on student performance, were generative in nature. They promoted an open-ended approach to education that created dynamism between the teaching and the learning where the lines between the two were sometimes blurred in a generative process of creation and recreation. The following exegesis attempts to articulate the generative process.

Transfer of Learning

In the particular context of DAC in relation to all members of the Blue team, transfer happened on multiple levels: between students and students, between teachers and students, and between teachers and teachers. When students were asked how the debate strategy affected their academic abilities, specifically in reading, writing, speaking, and thinking, they had the following insights:

> **Student 1:** "When you debate you are ready for anything. There are people who are waiting to disagree with you. When I learned how to debate I learned to construct counter-arguments. I learned how to switch their facts into my facts. In School Two we are debating stem-cell research."

> **Student 2:** "When I saw debate I saw it as a lawyer thing. You know, in becoming a lawyer, but it's not about that. When you debate, I didn't know this until I started debating, I didn't know this—your speaking skills get better, you understanding of things get better. Like before, I used to read something and it used to be hard, but now when I read I make sense of it. So, I think debate is a good thing for that, like it helped me in a lot of ways. Like the reading, the understanding of things, it helped me—to speak my mind, not only in school, but outside of school. Even with my parents—I speak with them, like, in a different way."

> **Student 3:** "It just, like, if you keep practicing you get good at it. So, um, like at first I don't like to speak in front of people until I get used to them and stuff. Yeah, so like I just getting used to them and stuff."

Student 4: "It helped a lot by the way I think. Now when I debate I don't really come to one conclusion—now I think of the whole thing in how it really happened. I think of how it happened, why it happened. All of those questions come to mind … If I don't understanding something, I ask questions, I write it down, and I continue to read. If I don't find it I try to look back at the chapter."

When teachers were asked about the implications for transfer on the teacher level, the findings were also profound:

In using debate across the curriculum were you able to learn from your colleagues?

ML: We all have areas of expertise and we definitely learn from each other, but I think we learn more content than anything else. We also learn some skills. JJR and CD are doing more environmental work and I'm learning from them more of the social skills. The trip to Burlingame Park, we did work with different bunches of kids and were able to keep their interest, whereas I'm much better in the classroom. Between the three or four of us we figure out all the different types of kids. As a team, if the students don't gravitate to you they will gravitate to another teacher and that's how we reach all of them.

CD: How? Just work with them daily … a lot of great stuff. Uh, one of the members was keen on debate and I got a lot of great stuff from her … she was English … a lot of structure. And the paper was assessed by her for English, and the structure and the way she gets her … I'm losing the English speak…help me out here. Her paper, which was also mine, and they were assessed by me for the science content, and were also assessed for English. Just working on that collaboratively opens your eyes to a lot of strategies that were employed by …; you know reading strategies, reading for comprehension, summarization skills, higher order skills. When you pull out what makes the difference between a good argument and a great argument on a written page without reflection, without a written differentiation from them is not easy. Those arguments are made for the interests of science and for the rhetoric itself. So, in working with the English teacher, it helped me flesh it out, that's the way of approaching it, not only what I didn't think but didn't realize kind of thing. It's the same thing with everybody, but it's just one that I thought of.

JJR: Absolutely. It was exactly a parallel situation for us as it was for the kids. We brought what we brought to the table and we were able to learn from one another and share that knowledge.

FD: Could you give some examples of the things you learned from your colleagues?

JJR: In terms of content? In terms of my understanding of debate?

FD: It's open.

JJR: Um ... boy, there are a lot of examples. We would focus on debate and approach our own content areas individually in our classrooms, so having that stuff on the table, you're constantly looking at each others' work. You know, we would always be sharing "this is what I did." We would put on the board the method you would use without actually having the goal of teaching each other "this is how I approach ..." or "these are some of the methods we use ..." because we were sharing the unit with a focus on debate we were sharing how we taught in our classrooms, which we do anyway, but we did it more because of the structure of how we worked together. How teamed around debate a lot more: research methods— "this is what I do when I roll the computers out and I want the kids to research something"; note–taking—"this is what I do when I want to teach the kids strategies for comprehension"; group work —"this is how I structure, and these are some of the ways I work with different ways that I work with the groups, or even on an individual basis"—"When I work in the group, I would never put this kid with that kid"—which is something we would normally have anyway, but the same that we enjoy because of the teaming and at the same time we have more so because we're focused around debate. We learn how it happens. We see it happening right in front of us in our meetings and it transfers to our classroom practice. We see it happening with our kids. The kids see it happening with each other. They pick it up. It's how we learn, it's how they're learning and it works.

Aside from the quantitative test scores and qualitative evidence from the Blue Team in establishing a correlation between improved academic performance and DAC, a strong correlation can be established by School Two's analysis of the academic performance of students entering School Two from School One, as evidenced by the following School Two interview:

School Two Questionnaire

Explain the general characteristics of the students who entered School Two at the onset of the previous year (2003–2004).

Last year the School One students were very independent, strong-willed, and strong-minded. They were not necessarily clear on what the School Two academic expectations were. They were not as organized in their thoughts as they thought they were. They had very strong opinions but they couldn't necessarily support them; although they were very confident they were right, they didn't know why. They also had mixed amount of preparedness in their ability to write and speak clearly. Mathematically they were weak across the board, with a couple of individual exceptions. Perhaps they had a phobia to mathematics.

Were there any specific characteristics that distinguished students from one team as opposed to another?

Last year I started guessing that some kids were particularly strong in writing and they typically came from the Blue

Team. I didn't notice anything particularly strong in their reading skills from one team to the next. Organizationally, and in their ability to organize themselves, students from the Orange Team procrastinated more and the characteristics of students from the Yellow Team seemed to be lost without scaffolding. It seemed they were much more dependent on scaffolding than the students from the Blue Team. Problem solving and critical thinking skills seemed to be generally stronger from the Blue Team. The Blue Team students were definitely more logically organized and stronger academically both individually and in group work. Those students were definitely more prepared of all the other teams and it's the same this year.

Over the course of the year, did students from one team excel more than students from another team? In what ways and to what do you attribute the differences?

The Blue Team, especially since we've been doing a lot of informal debating, can get up and verbalize arguments, defend a position. We can even assign them a position and they will defend it. In terms of verbal skills, the Blue Team kids excel. In terms of writing we don't see as much of a difference between the teams, but in terms of thinking and reading, the Blue Team kids can find an argument from articles or by listening to others and can respond to it. Perhaps the reason why the Blue Team students didn't excel more in writing was because they were missing their English teacher for half the year who was out on maternity leave. The Yellow Team kids were schooled more in the basics and were boxed in with their thinking. The Orange Team seemed to be a bit more creative in their thinking, but weren't as strong academically.

Dialogical Learning

The word *dialogue* has been used in many ways for many purposes. One of the most noted authors on dialogue, David Bohm, identifies the meaning of dialogue as a way of collectively observing presuppositions, hidden values, intentions, motivations, patterns of incoherence, beliefs. Although he states that the primary purpose of dialogue is not to communicate, he also indicates its essence is learning. In the study "Towards a Practice of Critical Teaching About Teacher's Work," Robert Hattam and Geoffrey Shacklock call for a dialogic space: "we are attempting to develop what Shor calls the 'third idiom' or a 'third discourse'—that 'is a learning area between students' speech and understandings, and those of the teacher'" (1997, 203). Kris Gutierrez et al. refer to this "third space" "as the social space within which counter-hegemonic activity, or contestation of dominant discourses, can occur for both students and teachers" (1995, 451); and Hattam and Shacklock argue, "Dialogic space needs to be developed and sustained in which we can speak to each other" (1997, 7).

This "dialogic space" is somewhat apparent in the following excerpt from an interview I conducted for this research:

> **CD:** From my perspective coming in the first year (2002–2003), the team was set with two people who were already in the team the prior year. So, coming in new, you're at a disadvantage in this kind of thing. You really need to be in it all year. During the first semester of my first year I wasn't really involved. During the second semester it was more about the project, but not until the debate was I fully involved in the team. It was a daily event-by-event planning process during the day where we see a fourth of our kids during a single day and over four days we see all the kids. We separate it from our math, English, social studies, and science part of the day. So that was a skills-based time where we each would approach the same kind of skill they needed to have to debate in a different way, so over the course of four days the kids got one particular skill, touched on by three different people, not in the perspective of science, math, English, and social studies teachers, but in the perspectives of individuals that see and teach differently. So the first thing we did was A.R.E. [Assertion, Reason, and Evidence]. All of us approached that, even in talking in planning the day before, a different way. This was a revelation we didn't plan for, but soon learned, after talk-

ing to students, hey, it was different, hey it's different and it was interesting because if we are doing our A.R.E.s and talking about it in different contexts, if you will, and then move on to the next thing, which might be presentation skills, and then on to another thing that will extend that systematically, building up to debate which is included in the end of the semester. There are so many things to key in on, realizing that people teach things different way and students learn things in different ways. Eventually they understood they had never had the same four teachers doing the same thing but in different ways and heading toward the same goal. They realized through that skills-based part that the core was actually doing the same. And that core was science, social studies, English, and math. We were teaching a theme that was all around a book that was the same ... but in a different way.

FD: So, how did you deal with those differences, like with the A.R.E., so that you come in and teach it a different way; you get the feedback from your students who have heard it in another room in a different way. How did you deal with those differences in your teaching styles?

CD: With a smile. It was very nice. They're picking up on it, not all would. Some students would pick one teacher's way of teaching it while other students would stick to another way, and that's ok because aren't we doing the same thing? It really opened up this nice dialogue between student and teacher that was a little bit different than I had experienced prior, and they started picking up the differences. It really didn't matter which way you approached it. Not only didn't it matter, but also why not try it another way because there are many different ways to solve a problem or approach an issue in many different ways.

FD: So were those differences between how you taught versus the other teachers created a dialogue between you and the students, but also with the teachers? Tell me about the dialogue between the teachers.

CD: It was kind of funny with the teachers, because and it happens now. The first day of run through of something we talked about and four or two would want to change it up a bit. Each time we talked to one another about how to do it better, and it would get better and better. Because everybody was doing the same plan, the input was kind of fast and furious; it really created for an exciting year. I have never seen so many people involved. You get that immediate feedback and you really want to be involved in it. We were fortunate to have some of that time … to really refine it, because you're really refining something and you're realizing that maybe one more day, maybe one more rotation we really need to keep with the arguments. For instance deciphering, do animals have feelings? There's a lot out there. Is it just to kill? From the perspective of the animal and the human, we are trying to decipher that. That was more of a skills-based activity, but using some of the ideas, sometimes you end up spending more time to agree as a group. I think I'm diverging from the question.

FD: That's good. Do you think the dialogue between the students is similar to the dialogue with the teachers?

CD: Well, less so, but definitely an increase over something I've had from my four years in some traditional schools. I mean, you're funnier than the last teacher we had, but that was about it. It wasn't really any kind of interest in how your approach this differently. I mean, you guys are talking about totally different things, yet you get in the same place. How does that work? We just came upon it and sort of chuckle about it. It's leading by example. I mean, here's a problem. It might be better the way he did it or she did it. Use it!

FD: Open.

CD: Very open.

Discussion

Over the course of this study, I have combined many disciplines and theoretical frameworks to study the efficacy of Debate Across the Curriculum on classroom practice: activity theory, cognitive psychology, literary theory, hermeneutics, existentialism, Zen Buddhism, and transfer of learning theory, via the mediating tool of Debate Across the Curriculum. The combination of all of these fields and thinking, coupled with the DAC tool, resulted in an inspiring classroom practice at Franklyn High School and is generalizable to meaningful human activity. Paul Ricoeur, in his book *From Text to Action*, asks a seminal question, similar to the question I asked at the onset of this study: "Can the concept of imagination employed in a theory of metaphor centered on the notion of semantic innovation, be generalized beyond the sphere of discourse to which it originally belongs" (1991, 168). In other words, how does theory translate into practice? In answering this question, Ricoeur takes it to the realm of activity in the form of practice:

> This question itself belongs to a wider-ranging investigation, to which I earlier gave the ambitious name of poetics of the will. In the present essay, one step is taken in the direction of this poetics. But one step only: the step from theory to practice. Indeed, it seemed to me that, for a theory constructed within the sphere of language, the best test of its claim to universality lay in determining its capacity for extension to the sphere of practice. (1991, 168)

In analyzing the content of the interviews, coupled with the testing data, we can see a direct correlation between theory and practice with which we can make some conclusions about the DAC activity:

➢ The participants had buy-in to the activity at all levels
  ✦ The participants saw value in the activity
  ✦ It required the participants (both teachers and students) to engage one another at many levels of intellectual interaction
  ✦ There was prior experience with the activity
  ✦ The participants helped co-create the activity
  ✦ he participants agreed on a goal that was situated locally and nationally

- Topics were   chosen based on student, teacher, local, and national contexts
- Performance indicators were collaboratively established

> To facilitate the activity, structures were developed that were responsive and flexible based on an activity feedback loop whereby the activity informed the process and the process informed the activity:
  - DAC structures from the Providence scope and sequence
  - Common planning time for teachers
  - Feedback from student performance

> Transfer of learning was multidimensional and heterogeneous:
  - Supported through DAC structures
  - Facilitated by dialogue

Buy-In: A Goal-Directed Activity

In answer to the first question, why the team decided to use DAC in the first place, the origin was difficult to pinpoint. Nobody could actually place where the original idea came from, but with ML as the debate coach, combining her expertise and interest, and with the practice firmly etched in JJR's imagination, as a social studies teacher, the possibility of it being useful in his practice and for the students contributed to the formation of the idea. In fact, the idea somewhat originated when I traveled to Atlanta, GA in spring of 2002 for a national debate conference, and I promised to spearhead DAC in the Providence School District because I saw its value in my classroom and could see the practice transfer to other classrooms and other disciplines. I did not, however, impose the practice on anybody, but planted seeds of the practice in the imaginations of my colleagues across the school district and at Franklyn High School. When I first approached ML about using a DAC model, she was apprehensive with any "across the curriculum practice"—Writing Across the Curriculum, Reading Across the Curriculum, and Debate Across the Curriculum. If I or any other person had mandated the practice at Franklyn High School, it probably would not have been as effective as it was. Regardless of origination, the participants had buy-in.

There were also varying ideas or mental models of what the activity was. As JJR noted, he had an idea of debate across the curriculum that didn't quite match what he encountered and ML didn't know if the practice would transfer from the debate team to the classroom. CD, being new to the team and naturally willing to take risks, jumped headfirst into the practice, which, as he mentioned, really made him part of the team. CD even said, when I pressed him about disagreement, that because the team mutually agreed on a goal from the outset, major disagreement was virtually non-existent and the minor disagreements did not derail the team from making progress. In fact, one could argue that the minor disagreements that occurred improved the quality of the team's efforts as opposed to detracting from them. From these three diverse perspectives I could see a co-evolution of DAC that took the tool to another level. If there were a prescription for DAC that the teachers had to rigidly follow, the interaction would not have been as rich or as productive.

Responsive and Flexible Structures with a Recursive, Dialogical Feedback Loop

As the team became a team over the course of four years, they used existing structures for DAC to build new structures on, and used the feedback from one another and from the students' work to improve those structures. What was even more insightful was the dialogue during the team meetings that facilitated the improvement. The teachers also put their classroom practice on the table and talked about it through dialogue. Since the structures were in place to meet every day and to plan during the summer, the teachers were afforded a "dialogic-space" to inform their instruction. As indicated by all three teachers, trust was at the foundation of their relationships and at the core of allowing dialogue to occur.

Multidimensional and Heterogeneous Transfer of Learning

The transfer of learning occurred on all levels: between teachers and teachers, between students and students, and between teachers and students. This heterogeneous and multidimensional interaction created a learning environment that was open, fluid, and democratic, as opposed to closed, rigid, and hierarchical. The students' learning environment paralleled the teachers'—it was learner-centered knowledge-centered, assessment-centered, and community-centered (Bransford, et al., 2000, 190–199). This heterogeneity of DAC mental models paralleled a socio-cultural heterogeneity implicit in a Vygotskian model of distributed cognition. Even when a student assumed he philosophically and politically disagreed with the social studies teachers (JJR), that student was being pushed to think more deeply about his beliefs and was required to articulate them, hence the reason for him perceiving himself to be tongue-tied. As his ideas and thoughts became more complex, he had difficulty articulating them. I also saw diverse levels of teacher experience pulling together to use that diversity to get the job done. The teachers were practicing what they were teaching their students, or as JJR stated: "It was exactly a parallel situation for us as it was for the kids."

The DAC tool promoted an activity that the team found valuable in teaching both processes and content throughout the curriculum. The DAC structure directly addressed the persuasive writing standard, the research paper standard, and the speaking/listening/viewing standard. And ultimately, the DAC tool was pedagogically interesting to most members of the Blue team. Indirectly, the DAC structures the teachers developed also addressed a collaborative process Franklyn High School was in the process of developing collectively. In fact, in the academic year 2004–2005 the Yellow team participated in a summer workshop with the Rhode Island Debate League to implement DAC into their curriculum and processes for the school year. Given the parallels between the DAC tool and the educational needs, the value of DAC was explicit in satisfying those needs.

Nevertheless, the implicit ramifications of the DAC tool have the potential to be profound. It ultimately helped promote an open-ended approach to education that created dynamism between the teaching and learning environment in a generative process of creation and recreation. In listening to the interviews, watching the team work together for three years, and helping roll out the DAC framework in the district, I have seen firsthand how a tool-centered activity like Debate Across the Curriculum can transform educational practice, transform student performance, and transform education. We are not only debating toward transfer of learning, we are debating toward the transformation of the U.S. educational system.

Note

1. Just last year the Rhode Island Board of Regents Recommendations for High School Reform instituted a series of mandates that require high schools to collaborate with higher education, businesses, and non-profit organizations.

References

Bakhtin, M. 1992. The dialogic imagination: Four essays. Ed. Michael Holquist and trans. Caryl Emerson and Michael Holquist. Austin: University of Texas Press.

————. 1993. Toward a philosophy of the act. Ed. Michael Holquist and Vadim Liapunov and trans. Vadim Liapunov. Austin: University of Texas Press.

Bellon, J. 2000. A researched-based justification for debate across the curriculum. Argumentation & Advocacy 36 (3): 1051–1431. Retrieved July 24, 2004 from http://0-web11.epnet.com.helin.uri.edu/citation.

Blanck, G. 1990. Vygotsky: The man and his cause. In L. C. Moll (ed.), Vygotsky and education: Instructional implications and applications of sociohistorical psychology, ed. L. C. Moll, 31–58. Cambridge, MA: Harvard University Press.

Blumenthal, A. L. 1980. Wilhelm Wundt: Problems of interpretation. In Wundt studies: A centennial collection, W. G. Bringmann and R. D. Tweney, 435–445. Toronto: C. J. Hofgrefe,

Bohm, D. 1996. On dialogue. Ed. Lee Nichol. London: Routledge.

Bransford, J., et al. 2000. How people learn: Brain, mind, experience, and school. Washington, D.C.: National Academy Press.

————. 2003. MacArthur Foundation meeting notes. December 5.

Burbules, N., and B. Bertram. 2001. Theory and research on teaching as dialogue. In Handbook of research on teaching, 4th ed., ed. Virginia Richardson. Washington, DC: American Educational Research Association/University of Illinois, Urbana–Champaign. Retrieved February 1, 2004 from http://faculty.edu.uiuc.edu/burbules/ncb/papers/dialogue.html.

Carl D. Perkins Career and Technical Education Improvement Act of 2006. Retrieved January 3, 2007 from http://frwebgate.access.gpo.gov/cgi-bin/getdoc.cgi?dbname=109_cong_bills&docid=f:s250enr.txt.pdf.

Dewey, J. 1938. The determination of ultimate values or aims through antecedent or a priori speculation or through pragmatic or empirical inquiry. In The twenty-seventh yearbook of the National Society for the Study of Education,ed. G. Whipple. Bloomington: Public School Publishing.

Elmore, R. 2001. Building a new structure for school leadership. Albert Shanker Institute and the Center for Policy Research in Education. Winter.

Engestrom, Y., R. Miettinen, and R. L. Punamaki, eds. 2003. Perspectives on activity theory: Learning in doing: Social, cognitive, and computational perspectives. Cambridge: Cambridge University Press.

Farr, R. 1987. The science of mental life: A social psychological perspective. Bulletin of the British Psychological Society 40:1–17.

Freire, P. 1995. Pedagogy of the oppressed. New York: Continuum.

Gardner, H. 2000. The disciplined mind: Beyond facts and standardized tests: The k-12 education that every child deserves. New York: Penguin Books.

Gormley, B. 2004. Personal interview, October 21, 2004.

Gutierrez, K., B. Rymes, and J. Larson. 1995. Script, counterscripts, and underlife in the classroom: James Brown versus Board of Education. Harvard Educational Review 65:445–471.

Habermas, J. 1984. The theory of communicative action. Boston: Beacon.

———. 1987. An alternative way out of the philosophy of the subject: Communicative versus subject-centered reason." In From modernism to postmodernism: An anthology, ed. Frederick Lawrence, 589–616. Cambridge, MA: MIT Press, 1987.

Hattam, R., and G. Shacklock. 1997. Towards a practice of critical teaching about teachers' work. Teaching in Higher Education, 2 (3). Retrieved January 14, 2004 from http://o-web1.epnet.com.helin.uri.edu/citation.asp?tb=1&_ug=dbs +aph+sid+5F6A4FC1%

Heifetz, R., and D. Laurie. 1996. The work of leadership. Harvard Business Review. Jan.–Feb., 124–134.

Kaufmann, W. 1969. Existentialism: From Dostoevsky to Sartre. New York: World Publishing Company.

Kierkegaard, S. 1992. The concept of irony, with continual reference to Socrates/ Notes of Schelling's Berlin lectures. Trans. and ed. Howard V. Hong and Edna H. Hong. Princeton: Princeton University Press.

MacMaster, T. 2004. Personal interview, October 29, 2004.

Morrison, S. 2004. Personal interview, October 18, 2004.

Perkins, D., and G. Salomon. 1992. Transfer of learning. International Encyclopedia of Education. 2nd ed. Oxford, England: Pergamon Press. Retrieved February 7, 2004 from http://learnweb.harvard.edu/alps/thinking/docs/traencyn.htm).

Resnick, L. 2002. Making America smarter. National Center for Education and the Economy and the University of Pittsburgh.

Ricoeur, P. 1991. From text to action: Essays in hermeneutics, II. Trans. Kathleen Blarney and John B. Thompson. Evanston: Northwestern University Press.

Rosenblatt, L. M. 1978. The reader, the text, the poem: The transactional theory of the literary work. Carbondale, IL: Southern Illinois University Press.

Sartre, J.-P. 1953. Being and nothingness. Trans. Hazel E. Barnes. New York: Washington Square Press.

Senge, P. 1994. The fifth discipline: The art and practice of the learning organization. New York: Doubleday.

————, et al. 2000. Schools that learn: A fifth discipline fieldbook for educators, parents, and everyone who cares about education. New York: Doubleday.

Slavin, R. E. 1983. When does cooperative learning increase student achievement? Psychological Bulletin 94:429–445. Cambridge, MA: MIT Press.

Suzuki, D. T. 1949. Essays in Zen Buddhism. New York: Grove Press.

Toulmin, S. 1981. Toward reintegration: An agenda for psychology's second century. In Psychology's second century: enduring issues, ed. R. Kasschau and C. N. Coter, 264–86. New York: Praeger Special Studies.

Tyack, D. and L. Cuban. 1995. Tinkering toward utopia: A century of public school reform. Cambridge, MA: Harvard University Press.

Vygotsky, L. S. 1925. Consciousness as a problem of psychology of behavior. In Psychology and Marxism, I, 175–198. Moscow–Leningrad: Government Publishing House.

————. 1978. Mind in society. Ed. Michael Cole, et al. Cambridge, MA: Harvard University Press.

————.1987. Thinking and speech. New York: Plenum. (Originally published 1934)

————. 1988. The problem of the cultural development of the child, II. Journal of Genetic Psychology 36:415–434.

Wundt, W. 1921. Elements of folk psychology. London: Allen & Unwin.

Zemelman, S, H. Daniels, and A. Hyde. 1998. Best practice: New standards for teaching and learning in America's schools. 2nd ed. Portsmouth, NH: Heinemann.

Frank Duffin is a school improvement specialist at the Southern Regional Education Board, a nonprofit, nonpartisan organization that works with leaders and policy-makers in 16 states to improve pre–K through postsecondary education.

Chapter 5
Dangers of Debate Training

Debate and Demagoguery: A Civic Education?

Aaron Fishbone

We teachers of debate would do well to acknowledge what it is that we are teaching students. The ability to speak effectively and well in public is both a vital tool and a deadly weapon that can be used toward constructive or destructive ends. Those individuals who can muster their fellow men and women to action become the leaders of their communities, and whether they use their talents to drive their communities toward good or bad ends depends entirely on them. Some of the worst abuses in history, such as the Holocaust of 1936–1945 or the ethnic violence in the former Yugoslav republics in the late 1990s, have occurred because powerful orators convinced people to follow them down destructive paths. Likewise, some of the most notable humanitarian enterprises, such as the U.S. Peace Corps at its inception, came about because forceful and impassioned orators and leaders were able to convince their fellow country people that these were important enterprises to be a part of. Thus, given the power of public speaking, it is vital for us as educators to dwell on whom and what we are teaching.

Debate is one activity that we teach that has such a broad capacity. Through "debate"[1] students gain a wide variety of skills, such as the ability to construct, organize, analyze, and rebut arguments, and become effective public speakers. In a debate, an individual or team is paired up against another individual or team and they are given a topic to debate. Students are then each given a side—affirmative or negative—which they must defend and make arguments in favor of while simultaneously responding to the arguments made by their opponent. Debates occur in classes, in competitions, or in public, and in each setting they are a bit different, but all kinds of debate involve students doing primarily the same things.

Given the many ways that debate develops the ability of individuals to communicate, it is often regarded as a very effective form of civic education. Civic education is a type of education that teaches students about their government and the workings of society, their history, and identity. For example, in the U.S., civic education involves study of the history of the country, the Constitution, what a democracy is and why it is the system we have, the parts and workings of the government, and the role of the individual in society. According to the renowned political theorist William Galston, "informed engagement' should be the goal of civic education."[2] By this he means that citizens in the U.S. should be informed of the issues in and workings of their society, and engaged so that they put this knowledge to use; for example, being a part of an activist group or knowledgeably voting for the candidate of your choice.

Civic education is especially important in a democratic society because democracies encourage people to discuss ideas in public and hash out their differences peacefully. Democracies rely on their citizens to take an active part in the governing of society, to criticize government and propose alternative ways of doing things, and to make informed decisions about their elected officials. Democracies even encourage their citizens to run for elected office themselves, as both the highest form of public service and as a way to peacefully redress grievances and solve problems in society. Since people are not born with this knowledge, civic education is required in order to impart the values of the system, and to ensure that the citizenry is aware of the nature of the government and the many opportunities it provides for getting involved, both inside government and outside. Civic education also involves teaching skills that allow people to best utilize the system, such as debate and public speaking, which teach communication; role-playing activities, which teach how to stand in someone else's shoes and see the problem from their perspective; and trial advocacy, which teaches the mechanisms and workings of the trial system.

Yet even (and especially) within a democratic society there are opportunities for talented rhetoricians to abuse their skills:

> Democracy is based on the optimistic assumption that one's neighbor can be trusted to act reasonably and respon-

sibly. Yet we live in democratic polities deeply pessimistic about these better instincts prevailing. The majority commonly fears that elites will use their wealth, education, birth, or position to acquire power and administer the state for their own advantage. Elites commonly fear that an uneducated and deprived majority will fall prey to demagogues who promise advantages at their expense ([Eli] Sagan. To both sides, rhetoric appears to be the tool of those who would subvert democratic procedures for personal or class advantage. As [Wayne] Booth argued in response to Joyner, what we teach does not guarantee an informed moral awareness. Rhetoric at its best teaches students to practice trustworthy argumentation, but we know that it also produces, in Booth's memorable coinage, "rhetrickery." We need, therefore, to empower students to analyze the ethical dimensions of rhetorical situations. The test of rhetoric is not its ideological commitments, to reiterate Joyner's view, but its consequences.[3]

According to University of Colorado communications professor Gerard Hauser, rhetoric, as important as it is, has some potentially disastrous consequences, namely demagoguery. A demagogue is a leader who arouses the populace by making impassioned appeals to the emotions or prejudices of an audience. This typically involves simplifying problems so that an easy solution can be identified (all the populace must then do is to put the demagogue into power to implement that solution), scapegoating another group for the ills of society, and other such practices. It is quite easy to see how teaching rhetoric, and especially debate, with its premium on being able to think on your feet, turn the crowd against your opponent, survive cross-examination without really answering questions, and deliver convincing appeals, could enable the right person to become a demagogue. Of course, that person would have to already be thinking a certain way and have ambitions beyond the mere learning of rhetoric, so it is not like debate or rhetoric can be blamed for demagoguery, but they certainly teach skills that better enable someone to become a demagogue.

The issue of the role of debate in teaching demagoguery is not one that can be taken too lightly, especially as the activities of international non-governmental organizations (INGOs) like the International Debate Education Association (IDEA) involve teaching debate to people who come from societies in Southeast Europe that are newly emerging from demagogic rule and countries in Central Asia and Africa that are still run by authoritarian demagogues. While demagogues like Slobodan Milošević came to power prior to IDEA's teaching of debate in the former Yugoslav republics, the situation in the republics and elsewhere provided opportunities for a convincing demagogue to play an extremely destructive role. It is therefore especially important to look closely at the possibility that teaching debate could have very negative consequences.

However, just as there are two sides to a debate, there are two sides to this issue. Debate has been, and continues to be, a powerful form of civic education that does far more to benefit the members of society than it does to harm them. Even if a demagogue does emerge from a class of debate students, the other students will be that much more equipped to challenge the aspiring demagogue's authority and claims. On balance, teaching debate does more good than harm.

There are many benefits to teaching debate that weigh against the possible negatives. Demagoguery assumes that the demagogue manipulates the 'unwitting masses' with his/her smooth tongue, convincing manner, and oratorical prowess. Claims made by the demagogue are taken as true because they sound good, because they access some deeper emotions or prejudices in the community, or simply because the community does not critically or independently analyze the information. However, debate counteracts this by making the 'unwitting masses' much less unwitting. Debate teaches people to challenge and critically analyze everything, such as arguments, evidence, and authority, and not to simply take them for granted. Thus, a populace trained in debate would presumably not take the demagogue and his/her propaganda at face value, but would rather demand more proof. If the proof were not forthcoming or convincing, a debater would scoff at the claims and not give them credence.

A debate-trained audience would also realize that what the demagogue is doing is primarily play-acting and rousing emotions, as those would be skills that they would also be familiar with. Being familiar with those tricks of the trade would make the members of the community much less susceptible to them.

Debate is also the form of civic education that best strengthens the democratic fibers in society and in government. While it is entirely plausible for a demagogue to come to power in a democracy such as through "mob rule" or the "tyranny of the masses," it is much less likely in a society where vibrant discussion occurs on a variety of political and social issues. In such a society people would be less likely to simply follow one person's opinion blindly, but would be used to challenging and discussing the issues and candidates. Debate fosters this kind of culture in many ways.

Firstly, debate is an oral activity. Ideally, debaters do not argue or yell, but rather debate, which involves a healthy and constructive clash of arguments that challenge one another. Those who learn about debate or participate in it inevitably continue their discussions outside of the debate round or classroom, and become accustomed to discussing, seeing numerous sides of an issue, and arguing for the one they prefer. Once this culture permeates society, it will be the strongest bulwark against demagoguery because people talking among themselves will erode the simplicity of the demagogue's solution, which is central to the demagogue's appeal. Debating about policies and government also teaches people how complex most issues really are, "to be wisely averse to either/or solutions, tolerant of ambiguity"[4] and generally more critical. Thus, the "unwitting masses" that the demagogue needs to follow him/her do not exist, and in their place stands a communicative citizenry, used to discussing the issues and unwilling to blindly follow anyone. Among methods of civic education debate is especially effective at developing this type of citizen because it is participatory, communicative, and constant, and the topics to be debated often involve the government. Being participatory, it forces all students to be active and thereby ensures that they learn. Debate tournaments or events can and do occur regularly, developing a culture of public discussion, as opposed to being a one-time educational seminar or class. Debating the substance of the topics forces students to learn about government and how it operates, thereby increasing their knowledge of how it functions and how to avail themselves of it, if and when they need to.

Finally, the IDEA network is itself a bulwark against demagoguery. This international teaching of debate does not occur in a theoretical vacuum distinct from reality. Rather it occurs with real people in real places. IDEA sponsors a variety of events that involve bringing students and educators together to learn debate, discuss issues, and meet one another. In this way the participants transmit stories and histories, meet people whom their government demonizes, share values, and come to see those values and traits that are wide-spread. IDEA and its affiliates also have Websites and other forums that enable people from all over the world and from its myriad of programs to communicate regularly. In this way IDEA, as an INGO, has developed what has become in effect a human rights network, where the participants can be aware of what is happening in the countries of other IDEA members and where the members can advise each other and have discussions outside the realm of officialdom that allow them to arrive at constructive solutions to problems. If I, as an IDEA affiliate in the US, see that former students of mine in Zimbabwe are becoming victims of a demagogue, a network exists for me to transmit that information, along with my advice and my hopes for better times.

Thus, while teaching rhetoric is inherently risky and may result in negative consequences, the benefits to society and the individuals within it far outweigh those possibilities. What we, as teachers of rhetoric, need to do is to foster public discussion and critical awareness, and impress upon our students the moral responsibility which comes with becoming skilled public speakers. It is ultimately up to the students to make the right choices and challenge the ones they see as damaging to their societies.

NOTES

1. By "debate" here, I am not referring to any one specific form or type of debate, such as Karl Popper, policy, or parliamentary, but rather to the whole genre of oratorical activities in which people make arguments against each other on a given topic in an attempt to win.

2. Joel Westheimer and Joseph Kahne, "Reconnecting Education to Democracy: Democratic Dialogues," *Phi Delta Kappan*, Vol. 85, no.1. (September 2003).

3. **Gerard A. Hauser** "Teaching Rhetoric: Or Why Rhetoric Isn't Just Another Kind of Philosophy or Literary Criticism," *Rhetoric Society Quarterly*, Vol. 34. (Summer 2004).

4. **Westheimer** and **Kahne**, "Reconnecting Education to Democracy."

Aaron Fishbone has taught argumentation and debate in more than eight countries. He is accredited as an IDEA International Debate Trainer and has served on the curriculum committees of the 2006 and 2007 IDEA Youth Forums and the 2006 DC Debate Institute.

Are We Training Better Demagogues?*

Liza-Maria Curteanu

A "debate" on whether debate training produces responsible citizens or just more persuasive demagogues.

Responsible citizens are those who make informed decisions, are aware of their rights and the limits of their rights, respect the law, involve themselves in the life of the community and do their best to improve it. Demagoguery is generally associated with a public figure questing for power; being a demagogue implies deceiving the public through false promises and bombastic speeches, designed to attract popularity, according to the dictionary. Debate training opens development opportunities for both categories, as it forces people to think, research, and discuss current important issues and, at the same time, to support positions they don't necessarily believe in. Reducing the differences between the two categories to "the moral sense of a person," the question becomes: What role does debate have in training the moral sense? Does debate in itself encourage demagoguery? Will it encourage demagoguery in all debaters or only in certain people? Or what are the specific factors that make debate a demagoguery ramp or a source of model citizenship?

I believed for a long time that the influence of debate depends solely on the debater's natural, "genetic" predisposition and little could be done to change that stream. Now I believe that the way the trainers and judges shape a student's approach to debate can make the essential difference. I believe debate in

*This paper is a reviewed and modified version of the paper presented in Istanbul in 2004.

itself, at the ideal level, is a means of developing the moral sense and encourages the assimilation of a set of essential values, the values of democracy. However, we must confront the reality that debate is often misused and that it often degenerates beyond the boundaries of its rules. Frequently propagated by judges and coaches, this misuse alone may nurture and propagate demagoguery.

WHAT IS THE CONNECTION BETWEEN SPEECH AND CHARACTER?

Our relationship with the world is mediated through language. According to the "social construction of reality" thesis, knowledge is a social process and, therefore, argumentative, since it could always be otherwise. Our character finds its base on a point of a scale measuring the solidity, the *generality* of social values (the generality of social values refers to the relationship between individual and society, varying virtually between the utmost individualism to the values of perfect harmony in a community); it is also the point where the truth and logic problems of our inner construction are born. This point ultimately reflects the person's approach toward communication.

The type of relating that a person naturally establishes with other people reflects a certain communication availability constant, a ratio that can be established between the degree of simulating communication (and establishing a dominating ratio of power) and the degree of genuine communication. This constant marks the "radius" by which a person on average deviates from what is true and logical in order to adapt to the subjectivity of the listener. The communication availability indicates how much a person is open to deeper communication, how much a person exposes herself to the possible critics or rejection from the others.

Debate appeals to the very means in which our own reality is constructed, as it seems logical that we first use the type of arguments that seems convincing to us and we primarily evaluate our public according to our own self-perception. The way each student initially approaches debate reflects very accurately his/her character features, the manner in which his/her very personality is built, the way the person generally thinks and speaks, and the *values* he/she is guided by.

THE ROLE OF TRUTH IN DEBATE

Nick Turnbull states that rhetoric "deals with reality insofar as reality is useful in particular situations." But debate represents more than mere rhetoric.

Truth represents firstly a more or less accurate reference for setting the frame of a debate. In debate formats like Karl Popper or British or American Parliamentary, truth has a *conventional* role. In value debates, what is stated in the first speeches and is not contested by the opponents is established as true. In policy debates, the role of the status quo is essential, as it represents the starting point for change. The purpose of the discussion is to improve the common state of facts; therefore, debaters should refer to the ideal level, but within the limits of reality.

From this point on, logic should represent the means for constructing a new policy (in policy debates) or for establishing relations between needs and values (in value debates). The problems of truth and logic in argumentation are closely related. Just as the misuse of logic represents an obstruction of truth and reality, in debate "truth problems" represent only a particular case of intentional or non-intentional misuse of logic, because in debate certain facts cannot—and are not supposed to—be verified as true, but as logic according to the prerequisites set at the beginning of the game. Therefore the argumentation line has to be considered from the point of view of its truth-value.

What Are the Symptoms of Demagoguery?

When speaking, the debater is obliged to develop a proportion between building and delivering, explaining the arguments, the proportion between substance, complexity, accuracy, on one hand and impact, on the other. Debaters experience that what they gain in one direction, they lose in the other.

Building arguments and delivering them are two distinct processes that stimulate different directions of thinking and totally different abilities. Building argumentation is always a rational process that implies the use of *convergent thinking* (which uses synthesis for building notions, drawing conclusions, discovering general laws and principles) in order to generalize social, political, or economic phenomena. Delivering arguments implies the use of *divergent thinking* (which is explorative and creative, and possesses fluidity, flexibility, and originality) in order to particularize and illustrate the general arguments (and express them verbally). As a child develops, the development of the two opposed processes of analysis and synthesis (connected with divergent and convergent thinking) determines the proportion of shared energy and speed between the capacity to express an idea in a manner as loyal as possible in relationship with the system of which it is part and the capacity of finding the adequate words to express an idea to everybody's understanding.

An unbalanced development of the two types of thinking takes two forms: speaking at a too general level (the speaker's thinking is too rigid and he/she is incapable of expressing ideas in an intelligible and persuasive manner) and, on the other hand, delivering at a too particular level (when the speaker has little substance in his/her argumentation and consequently implies that his/her attitude is supported by righteous arguments that he/she simply illustrates); this is usually associated with an emotional appeal, which is used the more the speaker is aware of the weakness of his/her argumentation line.

So the difference between demagoguery (persuasion that lacks the base of argumentation) and argumentation is that in the case of the former, the process of delivering arguments has to hide the lack of the structure of arguments, of "the constellation of propositions" logically tied. In debate for itself, each debater naturally develops abilities of building arguments and presenting, each at the optimum level of the individual. Here, I believe the key factors are the general ones that determine a child's development, the genetic predispositions, the cultural and family environment. Beyond that, I believe every "debate environment"—as an interactive "net" of debaters, coaches, trainers, judges (in debate we learn significantly from one another and through one another) is an important factor in creating "the risk of demagogy."

Most frequent "obstructions of truth" are half-truths and speculations— something that cannot be determined as true or false, but is claimed to be true. In *The Demon-Haunted World*, Dr. Carl Sagan gives a few examples of invalid arguments that are based on ignoring the truth: "Statistics of Small Numbers" (considering something to be true because of a small number of examples); "Observational Selection" (the enumeration of favorable circumstances, presenting only facts that support the speaker's statements); "Suppressing Evidence or Half-Truths" (ignoring information that casts doubt on your position); "Appeal to Ignorance" (the claim that whatever has not been proven false must be true). Several logical flaws in argumentation that Dr. Sagan identifies are "false arguments," not supported by reasoning ("Ad Hominem," "Argument from Authority," etc.); ignoring parts of reasoning ("False Dichotomy," "Short Term vs. Long Term"); and problems related to causality ("Post Hoc, Ergo Prompter Hoc," "Slippery Slope," "Confusion of Correlation"). In debate, specific problems are related to topicality, reasonableness, or legitimacy.

Is "Compromising" the Truth Necessary in Debate?

The key points in evaluating the role of debate training in shaping a student's character is the context (competition context) and the nature of the speech (objective or at least apparently objective, persuasive, oral, public speech).

You Debate in Order to Win

Whereas in the scientific speech "to understand" represents a purpose in itself, in the speech orientating toward social action determining understanding is only a means. The desired following effect is "convincing"; the next steps are "accepting" and "taking action"; as argumentation or persuasion are the ways in which shifts in policy occur, the speech becomes "goal-oriented." But the fact that the debate speech is a *persuasive* speech *does not make it already prone to degenerate into demagoguery.*

Persuasion represents the power of convincing someone to believe, to think, or to do a certain thing. When using persuasion, the speaker (whether his/her speech is based on argumentation or not) has to adapt to the public, to explain his/her arguments so that the public fully understands them and is attracted to agreeing with the speaker. Argumentation is "a verbal, social and rational activity aimed at convincing a reasonable critic of the acceptability of a standpoint by putting forward a constellation of propositions justifying or refuting the proposition expressed in the standpoint (van Eemeren and Grootendorst 2004,1). Argumentation is a particular form of persuasion; the aimed result is the same, but the methods used differ. The debate speech in its ideal form should be, thus, a pure construction of arguments and the persuasion should have as means just the arguments and should only constitute presenting them in an intelligible form. With this goal in mind a debater develops his or her skills in the sense of increased preciseness, organization, coordination between meaning and word, speed of reaction.

Supporting a Half Truth

The debate speech is supposedly an *objective* discourse, as it operates within established social institutions; however, debaters must support only one side of a balanced resolution. They often have to put emphasis on one value rather than another in a hierarchy that is never certain, if not impossible, to establish (for example, when arguing which one of two basic human rights is more important: the right to information or the right of the public person to privacy). The question is does this type of speech necessarily presume supporting a half-truth or even the untruth or at least—from the point of view of the truth value—just probable statements? (Nick Turnbull [2003] believes that the key difference between rhetoric and logic is the construction of syllogisms that are only *probable*; rhetoric accepts disputable propositions as starting points, but, again, a debate case should be, in the sense of a system of arguments, more than rhetoric).

I believe that on a correctly thought and phrased resolution, there is always a reasonable and truthful interpretation of the resolution that must be found, one single way that allows you to build a case based on true arguments and not just probable syllogisms (the reverse of this "strategy of truth" is the risk of the arguments sounding like truisms, which must be avoided by sticking to the relevance of the case, to the impact).

In value resolutions, there is always "a line" that can be identified between the two opposed values and that line must not be crossed, because by crossing you step into the area of the value supported by the opponent. When defending a case, the point where the opponent crosses the line is the point where that person becomes vulnerable to the abstract attack. For policy resolutions, the lack of reasonability (though more relative and more difficult to identify) should also be the point of attack.

The "right perspective" on a resolution can be reached through debate practice; it is only through the method of debating in general that one can reach logical conclusions about an unknown problem. The conflict highlights the common base, outlines the subjective "deviation degree," and pinpoints the weaknesses of the divergent ideas.

Adapting to the Public

When delivering arguments, a speaker is obliged to adapt his/her speech to the cultural level and level of understanding of the *public* (and, implicitly, to its background, to the *context*), that is, the average level. May it be an undeniable reality that the average audience is most easily convinced through emotional means—but debaters do not/should not address the average audience! However, the fact that the emotional appeal functions quicker and sometimes more efficiently should be the warning for debaters that good ideas are worthless if they are not clearly explained and convincingly supported.

Adapting to the Opponent

As a basic efficiency principle, debate experience teaches every debater that adjusting to your *opponent's* point of view is more important than detailing your own. So the question arises: is it also more important than maintaining your own point of view intact? Is compromise with truth and logic required in order for the debate to take place?

Resolutions offer freedom of interpretation at each level one may choose to approach the problem, so a direct conflict of ideas is almost impossible; in debate practice, there is no such thing as perfect syllogisms and perfect argument-counterargument ping-pong. As any debate gets pretty messy, victory subsides within the clash between different styles of thinking. A risk appears when differences between the players' abstract levels are significant and one approach of the resolution is very profound while the other one is very shallow. Debaters supporting the first type of approach bear the risk of losing the game if they don't adjust in time.

What I believe to be essential is actually a trust in the ability of the others to understand and to be reasonable. Before debating "against" each other, we debate "together," and the interest of building a common ground and adjusting to the arguments of the opponent is a common one; there is no reason to fear the "unfairness" of the opponent, as it may always be turned against him/her. This is exactly what I believe to be the core of debate: identifying the clash between truth and untruth—may it be intentional or unintentional.

Is It More Difficult to Support the Truth?

All debaters know it: it is more difficult to support "the truth." This task narrows the path of thinking to necessary causal links and obliges the student to support a whole system of concepts, which may be puzzling. An important factor is also the *time limit*. The speaker does not have enough time to explain the system of concepts; this system is *implicit* in his/her speech. The speed and spontaneous organization of the speech in *oral language* add up to a frame that makes truth more difficult to be supported—in the first instance. But in the long term, the greater the effort, the greater the progress. And every negligence or deviation is a weak point that makes the case vulnerable to attack. For debaters to understand and assume this, the role of judges and coaches is essential.

KEEPING THE DEBATE SPEECH OBJECTIVE

Firstly, I believe there is a great need for thorough, almost "scientific" identification and explanation of the "false" arguments, in order to give the debaters a practical and theoretical education concerning the exact type of intentional or accidental errors of reasoning.

Secondly, the role of trainers, coaches, and adjudicators is to encourage students engaged in academic debate to support what they think is true, to explore and "up-grade" their own perception of a phenomenon they are about to debate. As coaches, trainers, or judges, we should concentrate our efforts on inspiring the students with trust in their own power of discerning and also trust in the power of the opponent to understand.

I believe the feedback the student receives is essential in encouraging his/her trust in the fact that building solid ideas (that through their power of generalization and/or reasonability contain "more truth") has greater winning potential than "speculation," "juggling" with ideas, and "empty" rhetoric.

Thirdly, the guidelines debate educators should promote among debaters is that a good debate speech contains good arguments presented in a persuasive manner. Strong arguments speak for themselves and have a power of their own. But deficiencies in explaining the arguments and presenting them persuasively, in adjusting to the opponent's attacks, and in making the clash between one's own arguments and the opponent's can make the best arguments useless—and correcting these deficiencies (mostly through practice) makes a debater's work twice as hard.

In the end, yes, I believe debate can influence decisively the way we construct our lives. We may be prone to "believe" that what we say and do doesn't make a difference; but I believe we can learn that truth is the ultimate advantage for winning, that we have a responsibility for our words and one of fairness toward the other person's, that debate should be more about "finding solutions" together than "fighting each other". In this respect, I believe coaches, judges, and trainers have an immense responsibility toward the young people they have the power to influence and toward society. That is why I believe they too should be trained carefully, as they have either the power to shape responsible citizens (and maybe even beautiful human beings), or to train or simply allow young people to become demagogues, by leaving in their hands the most powerful of weapons —THE WORD.

Bibliography

Sagan, Carl, and Ann Druyano. *The Demon-Haunted World: Science as a Candle in the Dark*. New York: Random House, 1996.

Turnbull, Nick. "The Implications of the Division of Logic and Argumentation for Policy Theory." 2nd ECPR Conference, Marburg, Germany, September 18–21, 2003.

van Eemeren, Frans H., and Rob Grootendorst. *A Systematic Theory of Argumentation: The Pragma-Dialectical Approach*. Cambridge: Cambridge University Press, 2004.

Liza-Marie Curteanu was born in 1984 in Iasi, Romania. She is a law student at the University of Trier, Germany.

Chapter 6
Debate Coaching and Commitments

The Dilemma of Dr. Dolittle's Pushmi-Pullyu: The Juxtapositional Tension Between Debate Coaching Duties and Marriage and Family Commitments

Jack E. Rogers and Arthur Rennels

Behold the Pushmi-Pullyu who only makes progress by carefully studying where it has been. I say, a rather ingenious animal!—**Dr. John Dolittle**

The Pushmi-Pullyu is a mythical beast that most closely resembles a llama with a head at each end facing, and therefore pulling, in opposite directions. A great deal of tension is created because each head is presented with equally attractive and yet equally competing directions for travel. Therefore, the only way to make progress in any one direction is through careful study and compromise. Ultimately, a great deal of balance is required to ensure survival. If both heads pull against the middle, the Pushmi-Pullyu will inevitably be torn asunder to its utter destruction.

He, she, or it, as the case may be, is illuminated for our consideration as a metaphor for juxtapositional tension in the children's classic *Dr. Dolittle*. Who would have thought that an absurdist children's adventure written in 1920 by Hugh Lofting would transcend the years to push the mythical Pushmi-Pullyu to the front of the line of possible metaphors? Even a somewhat cursory examination proves the utility of the Pushmi-Pullyu as a metaphor for such diverse applications as economic market theory (Nolte, 2005), physics (www.physics.brown.edu), automotive design (News.com), Internet management theory (Gleick, 1997), biology (Seigfried, 2002), communication technology (www.cordis.lu.euroabstracts), advertising (Tanner, 2005), and educational theory (McFarland, 2005). The central metaphor for each of these applications is that two forces pulling in nearly equal proportions against one another create a central tension. Without a careful balancing of these dynamic tensions, the object is likely either to accomplish nothing or to tear itself apart.

How does our Pushmi-Pullyu metaphor transpose itself into the world of competitive forensics? The answer is simple. Jensen and Jensen note that "a positive coexistence of forensic and family time requires a great deal of effort that may often frame family time and forensic participation as competing and not complimentary goals" (2003, 2). The academic forensics literature (Bartenan, 1996a, 1996b; Dickmeyer, 2002; Gill, 1990; Gilstrap and Gilstrap, 2003; Jensen, 1998; Jensen and Jensen, 2001, 2003; Jones, 1997; Littlefield and Sellnow, 1992; McDonald, 2001; Olson, 2000; Preston, 1995; Venette and Venette, 1997; Whitney and Johnson, 1996; Williams and Hughes, 2003) has long reported the tensions associated between balancing forensic coaching duties with marriage and family commitments. Too often, the long hours and extensive travel schedules take their toll not only "burning out" coaches but leaving dysfunctional or disarticulated family units in their wake.

The impetus for this study was provided by Jensen and Jensen (2004) in a paper presented at the 2004 Annual Meeting of the National Communication Association. Their study provided a statistical analysis from a national sample ($n = 44$) of forensic professionals designed to measure perceptions of difficulty between balancing forensics and personal/family relationships. Jensen and Jensen (2004) entered the study expecting to validate previous findings within the literature that "forensic professionals feel frustration at what they see as a difficulty in balancing forensics with family and personal relationships" (12). Their goal was to lend quantitative validity to the literature by providing statistical rather than anecdotal evidence. They were "surprised by the results of their study" (12). Jensen and Jensen reported:

> [W]hile the sample reports some agreement with the assumptions we brought into the study, respondents seem generally neutral to the idea that forensics and family/personal relationships compete with one another. While there is enough

agreement with our assumption to justify further investigation and effort to facilitate an activity that is more friendly to the personal and family relationships of its participants, this study also suggests that conclusions about forensics and an assumed negative impact on relationships should be accepted only with close scrutiny into the methodology leading to said conclusions. (2004, 12–13)

Needless to say, the authors were also surprised by the findings reported in Jensen and Jensen (2004). During subsequent discussions with the Jensens, it was discovered that they had included only respondents currently serving as forensic professionals. It could be argued that those forensic professionals still actively coaching had either not been coaching long enough to encounter relational pressure and subsequent burnout or had discovered a way to circumvent or alleviate the relational pressure effectively. In either case, the "further research" called for by Jensen and Jensen would seem justified. This study collected data from a national sample ($n = 60$) of forensic professionals who have left the active coaching ranks and compares that data set to the Jensen and Jensen sample for statistically significant differences that may provide insight into the relationship between coaching duties and personal/family relationship commitments.

Review of Literature

The literature juxtaposing forensics and family generally reports the perception of significant tensions between career and family. Given the state of marriage within the U.S. working force, this should not come as a surprise. Lauer and Lauer (1997) argue that divorce rates are closely tied to marital crises that result from job-related stress. Jones points out that "work related stress, pressure, tension and even travel are often displaced into the home creating a rift which erodes the marriage to the point of disintegration" (1997, 2). Individuals who work in high-stress career fields report higher than average divorces rates, including physicians (Sotile, 1997), police officers (Came, 1989), firefighters (Noran, 1995), and Wall Street employees (Kaplan, 1996).

While the life of a forensics coach may not be quite as "hazardous" as that of a police officer or firefighter and the hours not quite as long as those of a physician, the adverse effects of working non-standard schedules is worthy of examination. Staines and Pleck (1984) examined the effects of non-standard work schedules, defined as working other than a standard fixed day schedule, upon family, conflict, and quality of life. They concluded that non-standard work schedules do have adverse effects. According to Staines and Pleck, "not unexpectedly, workers on a variable schedule of days reported lower levels of family adjustment ... working non-standard days is associated with less time in family roles, higher levels of specific types of interference between work and family life, and, in one instance, lower family adjustment" (1984, 521). Researchers (Bast, 1960; Drenth et al., 1976; House, 1980; Jamal and Jamal, 1982; Mann and Hoffman, 1960; Maurice and Montiel, 1965; Shamir, 1982, 1983) all report a positive relationship between the number of weekends or holidays worked and the level of conflict between work and family life.

In more current work, Jamal (2004) studied employees who work weekends as a regular part of their job. His study concludes "employees involved with weekend work reported higher emotional exhaustion, job stress and health problems than employees not involved with weekend work" (2004, 117). "Finally, in a recent study involving 1992 data from the National Study of the Changing Workforce in the U.S.A. ($n = 2905$), it was found that employees on standard work schedules (Monday through Friday) reported less work-hour imbalance, and work-home conflict than employees working on weekends. Moreover, employees with non Monday through Friday schedules also reported higher levels of burnout" (Fenwick and Tausig, 2001, 118). Baba and Jamal (1991) found that "the majority of problems associated with non-standard work schedules may be due to these employees finding themselves out of line with society's established physiological and social rhythms (383)." In summary of the nonforensic literature, nonstandard work duties have been found to be strongly associated with personal, marital, social, health, and organizational consequences (Blau and Lunz, 1999: Bohle and Tilley, 1998; Fenwick and Tausig, 2001; Jamal and Baba, 1992, 1997; Krausz, Sagie, and Biderman, 2000; Presser, 1995).

There can be no argument that those professionals within the forensic community work non-standard schedules, which include numerous weekends and holidays. The stresses to self and family are further exacerbated by working, for most, Monday through Friday, juggling the teaching, research, and service commitments of a "regular" faculty member. How, then, do these deleterious impacts of non-standard work schedules manifest themselves within the lives and families of the professional forensics community?

In addition to the previous works cited (Bartenan, 1996a, 1996b; Dickmeyer, 2002; Gill, 1990; Gilstrap and Gilstrap, 2003; Jensen, 1998; Jensen and Jensen, 2001, 2003; Jones, 1997; Littlefield and Sellnow, 1992; McDonald, 2001; Olson, 2000; Preston, 1995; Venette and Venette, 1997; Whitney and Johnson, 1996; Williams and Hughes, 2003), the literature devoted to forensics has long reported the tensions associated between balancing forensic coaching duties with marriage and family commitments. Jones (1997) found a significantly higher incident of divorce among coaches involved in forensics, largely due to the time demands required to successfully coach debate students and the excessive travel schedules in a competitive season that stretches across nine months, not including summer debate camps and workshops. Of the twenty-three divorced respondents, almost half (45%) reported "that forensics had created a strain on their marriage or was responsible for numerous conflicts regarding the coaches absence from the home" and "claimed that forensics was directly involved in the break-up of their marriage" (Jones, 1997, 3). Bartenan, weighing in on the question of relational breakdowns for forensic educators, found that one in five reported that "work in forensics had contributed to the end of a marriage or significant relationship" (1996, 7). Olson noted "researchers have found significant negative consequences to psychological health as well. Forensics can easily become an all-consuming activity, leaving little time to devote to a successful family life" (2000, 7). Interestingly enough, a study by Cronn-Mills (1999) found that of the top ten debate programs in the United States all were coached by single coaches. Deaton, Glen, Milsap, and Milsap (1997) reported a negative impact on family life for those involved in debate. Bartenan (1996b), who conducted a comprehensive national survey, found that 74% of forensic professionals responded that forensics detracts from quality family or relationship time. In summary, perhaps Jensen put it best when he argued that "there are enough common characteristics of forensics at the end of the 20th Century that lead to a categorization of the director of forensics as an at-risk population" (1998, 28). Further, Jensen and Jensen argued that the "parallel relationship between increased value of forensics and increased value of family times creates a need for balance that must be addressed" (2003, 6).

Given the overwhelming negativity of the literature toward the impacts of a critical imbalance in work-style/life-style that forensics presents its participants, these researchers were just as surprised by the results reported by Jensen and Jensen (2004) as the authors of the study. In view of the methodological limitations noted by Jensen and Jensen (2004) and subsequent discussions, this study seeks to include respondents who have elected to leave forensic education as a comparison group to those who are currently engaged in the discipline. This study collected data from a national sample ($n = 60$) of forensic professionals who have left the active coaching ranks, and compares that data set to the Jensen and Jensen (2004) sample for statistically significant differences that may provide further insight into the relationship between coaching duties and personal/family relationship commitments. Toward that end

H1: Former forensic educators will perceive that their forensic activities negatively impacted their familial relationships.

H2: There are significant differences in perceptions between former and current forensic educators with regard to the impact of forensics activities and familial relationships.

RQ1: How will a heterogeneous sample perceive the challenge of balancing the duties of a career as a forensics educator and the commitments of marriage and family?

METHODOLOGY

Jensen and Jensen's (2004) survey instrument was replicated with minor wording changes. Since the target respondents were all former forensic educators, where appropriate, survey statements were modified to reflect a past relationship (e.g., "My forensic career negatively impacts my relationship with my children" was changed to "My forensic career negatively *impacted* my relationship with my children"). The survey instrument is designed to ask former forensic educators a variety of questions concerning the nature of the program they coached, the history of their non-platonic relationships, and their attitudes concerning a number of potential relationships between forensics and family. Analysis of the data set was conducted in two steps. Study One is directed toward Hypothesis 1. In Study One statistical analysis focused on the perceptions and attitudes of former forensic educators. Study Two uses statistical analysis to compare between groups (current and former forensic educators) to provide insight into Hypothesis 2.

Results and Discussion

Results—Study One

A sample of convenience (former coaches known to the researchers and referred to the researchers by former coaches) was identified, and 64 surveys were mailed. Sixty surveys were returned. Of the 60 respondents in the data pool, 45 had coached individual events, 53 had coached debate. Some had obviously coached both. Prior to exiting the discipline, the respondents had a mean of 4.83 years of coaching experience,[1] with 6 former Directors of Forensics and 54 former Assistant Director of Forensics/Debate Coach/Graduate Assistants. Fourteen had coached CEDA, 7 NDT, 31 Lincoln-Douglas, and 26 National Parliamentary Debate. Some had coached more than one format of debate. Both American and National Forensic Associations were represented in the sample. Rank was dispersed with 6 associate professors, 36 assistant professors, 16 graduate assistants, and 2 adjunct instructors at time of coaching.

The first set of data followed the methodology of Jensen and Jensen (2004), reporting means, standard deviation, and percentages. All data in Study One and Two were analyzed using two-tail t tests, with a minimum 95% confidence level unless otherwise reported. Further, a Pearson's correlation analysis was performed on the nine attitudinal variables, and all results are reported with level of significance.

Program Demographics (see Appendix A)

To gain a better understanding of the kind and type of program respondents administered, several questions were asked to gather descriptive information about their programs. The average program had at least one-full time staff member (.70), while the remaining programs had two full-time staff members (.30) for a mean of 1.30. Less than a quarter of the programs had part-time staff (.22 mean) and even fewer enjoyed the help of graduate assistants (.17 mean). Slightly half (51.7%) of the respondents were in a tenure track position, while over one-third were not (38.3%). The mean for the squad size was 9.33, with 66% of the programs having had between 7 and 10 students. The respondents also represented a broad base of forensic events, with 75% participating in Individual Events (IEs) and 88% participating in debate. Finally, in reporting the number of weekends committed to tournament travel, the greatest number of weekends traveled was 8 ($n = 19$), 10 weekends ($n = 18$), and 12 weekends ($n = 13$).

Respondent Demographics (see Appendix A)

With regard to the amount of years respondents had participated in coaching forensics, the mean was 4.83 years with an *SD* of 2.55. Fully 50% of the respondents had left coaching after only 4 years, and between the 4- and 7-year points another 28.3% had left the activity. There was little diversity in duty titles among the respondents. Ninety percent reported their position as Assistant Director of Forensics, with 60% reporting the title of Assistant Professor; 26.7% were Graduate Assistants, and 10% were Associate Professors. The weekly duties and requirements for the respondents were primarily occupied in teaching (19.63 hours), while the remaining bulk of time was devoted to coaching (17.95 hours). Other commitments included research (9.02 hours) and administration (3.75 hours), with advising and service (2.1 hours) comprising the remainder of their time. The typical week during their tenure coaching forensics was 52.45 hours.[2]

Respondent Demographics—Personal Relationships

A majority of respondents self-reported as being in an exclusive non-platonic relationship (see Table 1). Sixty-one point seven percent were married, with an additional 17.2% being in either a committed or life-partner relationship. The remaining four categories (divorced, single, committed relationship, life-partner) comprised 11% or less for each category. Over 70% of the respondents reported involvement in a non-platonic relationship (1 = 41% and 2 = 30.5%), with a mean of 1.83 while professionally involved in forensics. Those results are reported in

Table 1

Personal Relationships for Non-Platonic Respondents		
Relationship	Number	Percent
Married	37	61.7
Divorced	9	15.0
Single	4	6.7
Committed Relationship	6	10.0
Life Partner	4	6.7

For a full breakdown and description of former coach and program demographics, see Appendix A. No significant differences between the data sets (former and current forensic educators) were noted other than length of time spent coaching, with the mean for former coaches at 4.83 years and current coaches at 16.34 years. There are also minor differences between groups in terms of current non-platonic relationships reported, with former coaches having a slightly higher mean for current marriages (61.7% compared to 56.8%), divorced (15% compared to 6.8%), and single (6.7% compared to 18%). In this comparison, former forensic educators reported a slightly higher rate of marriage, a divorce rate almost three times that of current coaches, but current coaches were almost three times more likely to be single.

Attitudinal Measures

Survey participants were asked to provide information on various attitudes about their former forensics career and the impact their participation in forensics had on their non-platonic relationships, including significant others and children. The data is provided in Table 2, with the range, means and SD reported for each item.

Table 2

Attitudinal Measures			
Survey Item	**Range**	**Mean**	**SD**
Negative impact on relationship	5	1.87	1.29
Negative impact upon children	6	4.88	2.00
Influence upon long-term planning	3	2.10	1.04
Relationship stronger w/o forensics	4	2.27	1.49
Choose between family or forensics	5	2.83	1.60
Incorporate family into forensics	5	5.37	1.44
Make forensics decisions based upon family	5	3.22	1.55
Forensics contributed to the end of a relationship	6	2.88	1.65
Forensics takes valuable time from relationships	4	2.48	1.21

$n = 60$

Jensen and Jensen's (2004) survey instrument was replicated with minor wording changes and some question omissions not relevant to the target population.[3] Since the target respondents were all former forensic educators, where appropriate, survey statements were modified to reflect a past relationship (e.g., "My forensic career negatively impacts my relationship with my children" was changed to "My forensic career negatively *impacted* my relationship with my children"). Participants reported their attitudes to nine statements by marking agreement (one) or disagreement (seven) on a Likert scale associated with each statement.

Table 3 reports Pearson's correlation analysis for each of the nine attitudinal measures. Seven of the nine attitudinal measures were found to be statistically significant at least the .05 level of significance, and individual levels are reported in the table. The two that were not found to be statistically significant are reported and discussed because of their possible impact on the coaches' decision process to exit coaching. Though not scientifically significant, the attitudes themselves still have the potential to be significant, and in an effort not to artificially exclude relevant descriptive data, those two attitudes are included for the reader's consideration; however, caution should be used in advancing generalized statements to the larger population. The two measures of attitudes were (1) influence on long-term family planning; and (2) negative impact on present relationships. Obviously, if they are no longer forensic educators, a correlation between past forensics involvement and present relationships should not be observed.[4]

Table 3

Attitude	1	2	3	4	5	6	7	8	9
1. Contributed to end of relationship	1.00	0.63	0.16	0.01	0.21	0.60	0.81	-0.60	0.00
2. Time from relationships	0.63	1.00	0.12	0.05	-0.04	0.43	0.65	-0.40	0.07
3. Negative impact on relationships	0.16	0.12	1.00	0.23	0.23	0.05	0.17	-0.20	0.03
4. Negative impact on child(ren)	0.01	0.05	0.23	1.00	-0.04	-0.06	0.10	-0.26	0.34
5. Influence long-term family plan	0.21	-0.04	0.23	-0.04	1.00	0.22	0.18	0.18	-0.13
6. Relation stronger w/o forensics	0.58	0.43	0.05	-0.06	0.23	1.00	0.45	-0.11	0.00
7. Choose family or forensics	0.81	0.65	0.17	0.10	0.18	0.45	1.00	-0.43	0.11
8. Incorp family into forensics	-0.60	-0.40	-0.19	-0.26	0.18	-0.11	-0.43	1.00	-0.06
9. Decisions based upon forensics	0.00	0.07	0.03	0.34	-0.13	0.00	0.11	-0.6	1.00

Intercorrelations Between Attitudes and Relationships of Former Coaches

$n = 60$

Each of the nine attitudes is explained:

"*My professional forensics experiences have contributed to the end of a meaningful relationship.*" The mean response was 2.88, indicating moderate agreement. Further, under a correlation analysis, this item was found to positively correlate with taking time from relationships ($r = .630, p < 0.000$), relationships were stronger without forensics ($r = .584, p < 0.000$), and choosing between family and forensics ($r = .811, p < 0.000$). Further, a negative correlation was observed with incorporating family into forensics ($r = -0.590, p < 0.000$).

"*My forensic career takes valuable time away from my personal relationships.*" The mean response was 2.48, indicating strong agreement. Additionally, a statistically significant positive correlation was observed with this item and contributing to the end of a meaningful relationship ($r = 0.630, p < 0.000$); relationships were stronger without forensics ($r = 0.432, p < .001$); and choosing family over forensics ($r = 0.646, p < 0.000$). Again a negative correlation was observed with incorporating family into forensics ($r = -0.404, p < .001$).

"*My forensics career has a negative impact on my present relationship.*" Respondents agreed somewhat strongly with this statement, with an observed mean of 1.87. A statistically significant correlation was not observed with this and other attitudinal measures.

"*My forensics career negatively impacts my relationship with my children.*" The mean response to this question was 4.88, indicating slight disagreement with the statement. A statistically significant positive correlation was observed between this statement and the making forensic decisions based upon family statement ($r = 0.336, p < 0.009$), and a negative correlation was noted between this statement and the incorporate family into forensics statement ($r = -0.262, p < 0.043$).

"*My forensics career has influenced my long-term family planning.*" Respondents agreed with this statement with a mean of 2.10. This item was not positively or negatively correlated to any other item.

There was an observed mean of 2.27 for "*My present relationship would be stronger if I were not active in forensics.*" There was a positive correlation between this item and the measures for contributing to the end of a relationship and taking valuable time from relationships as previously reported. Additionally, there was a statistically positive correlation to the measure for choosing family over forensics ($r = .445$, $p < .001$), which is reported next.

The seventh measure was "*I foresee having to eventually choose between remaining a forensic professional and maintaining a strong family.*" Respondents agreed, with a mean response of 2.83. As previously reported, there was a positive correlation with this measure and measures one, two, and six. There was a negative correlation with this measure and incorporating family into forensics ($r = -0.431, < p\, 0.001$).

"*Incorporating my family/personal relationship with my forensic career would ease any pressures created by my forensic responsibilities.*" The mean response was 5.37, indicating disagreement with the statement. There was a negative correlation between this measure and measures one, two, four, and seven, as previously reported.

The final measure, "*I make professional decisions based on my family/personal relationship,*" asked if family/personal relationships influenced respondents' professional decisions. Respondents slightly agreed with the statement, with a mean response of 3.22. This measure was positively correlated with measure four as previously reported.

Discussion—Study One

Generally, the results of this survey tend to support previous findings in the literature regarding typical forensics programs. Forensics programs are generally overseen by one full-time faculty or staff member who rarely enjoys the support of additional personnel. Forensics programs tend to be bi-modal, with approximately 9 students participating in both individual events and debate. Further, they compete in approximately 10 tournaments a year, not including national competitions.

In this data set of former forensic educators, the average coach was involved in forensics for just under 5 years, was not tenured, and spent a majority of his/her time in teaching, indicating that they were dual tasked between teaching and coaching. Of any given 4 coaches, three were in a committed relationship and had been involved in at least 1 non-platonic relationship. With one notable exception, all of the relational measures indicated that forensics had a negative impact on personal relationships. The reported mean for the item "contributed to the end of a meaningful relationship" was 2.88, with 1 representing agreement, 7 disagreement, and 4 neutral. More significantly, the response to the question of whether respondents believed that forensics had negatively impacting the relationship they had at the time they were coaching, the mean response was 1.87, indicating very strong agreement. The response that forensics did not have a negative impact on relationships with children was unexpected. Given that respondents were only in forensics for an average of 4.8 years, it is possible that children were not present in the family unit at the time of their active involvement. While the results of this study should not be interpreted as conclusive given the relatively small number of respondents ($n = 60$), it is clear that for this population participation in forensics negatively impacted personal/family relationships.

For those who left forensics, there were very strong correlations in seven of the nine attitudinal measures. While all of the measures with positive correlations were strong, the most significant correlation was associated with choosing family over forensics and forensics contributing to the end of a meaningful relationship (see results, measures one and seven). The second strongest correlation was choosing family over forensics and time away from relationships (measure two). The relative strength of these two correlations clearly demonstrates the dynamic tensions between forensics involvement and family/personal relationships. For this population, the Pushmi-Pullyu they faced was the choice between the continuing pressures of a career in forensics education or the meaningful pursuit of significant interpersonal relationships. This group chose to exit forensics.

The results reported in Study One clearly confirm H1: Former forensic educators will perceive that their forensic activities negatively impacted their familial relationships. These results are clearly in contrast with Jensen and Jensen's (2004) findings; thus, H2: There are significant differences in perceptions between former and current forensic educators with regard to the impact of forensics activities and familial relationships, is also supported. It is clear from the results that significant differences in attitude exist for those who are actively involved in forensics, as reported by Jensen and Jensen (2004), as opposed to those who have left forensics in this study data set. These two groups of people report very different lengths of tenure in professional forensics and, more significantly, in their levels of satisfaction. Even a cursory examination of the Pearson's correlation analysis for the groups clearly indicates a significant correlation in seven of the nine relational measures and the impact upon the forensics professional. While no one can say that forensics is the cause of these relational impacts, the data make it abundantly clear that participation in forensics is correlated with negative attitudes toward the ability to engage in and maintain meaningful relationships with others. Those who have left coaching have very different perceptions of the impact a professional forensics career had upon their interpersonal relationships.

Because of the stark differences in results between the two groups (current and former forensics educators), the data from both survey pools were merged and subjected to statistical analysis in an attempt to address RQ1: How will a heterogeneous sample perceive the challenge of balancing the duties of a career as a forensics educator and the commitments of marriage and family? By merging the two data sets, the inherent methodological weakness of a homogenous sample (only active coaches and/or only former coaches) should be mitigated and a clearer understanding of the relationship between relational stress and forensics should emerge from a heterogeneous sample.

Results—Study Two

First, the authors want to thank Jensen and Jensen. Full and open access to their original data set was granted. The Jensen and Jensen data set was merged with the data set represented in Study One, with a resulting sample size of $n = 105$. The nine attitudinal measures were tested using two tailed t tests with a 95% confidence level and Pearson's correlation analysis. Additionally, the measure of *years of coaching* was added to the correlational analysis because of the significant differences observed between data sets. Years of coaching is identified as measure 10. All of the measures were found to be statistically significant. Further, a Pearson's correlation analysis was performed on the nine attitudinal variables, and all results are reported with the level of significance.

The data are reported with the nine attitudinal measures following the order presented in Study One and are briefly referenced to aid the reader following Table 4.

Table 4

Summary of Binomial Regression Analysis for Predictors of Coaching Status			
Variable	B	SEB	-
Step 1			
Number of Years Coaching	0.50	0.12	1.64
Step 2			
Negative Impact upon Children	-0.83	0.30	0.44
Number of Years Coaching	0.50	0.15	1.65
Step 3			
Negative Impact upon Relationships	1.29	0.55	3.63
Negative Impact upon Children	-0.83	0.30	0.44
Number of Years Coaching	0.50	0.15	1.65

$n = 105$

Attitudinal Measures:

Measure 1—"Forensics contributed to the end of a meaningful relationship." The measure between the groups was found to be significant at the .05 level of confidence ($t(66.105) = 2.791$, $p = < .007$). The means for the two groups were 4.20 (slight disagreement) for those still participating and 2.88 (agreement) for those no longer coaching. Positive correlations were observed at the 0.01 level of significance with measures two ($r(105) = 0.371$, $p < 0.000$); three ($r(105), = 0.434$, $p < 0.000$); eight ($r(105) = 0.453$, $p < .000$); nine ($r(105) = 0.367$, $p < 0.000$); and ten ($r(105) = 0.375$, $p < 0.000$). A negative correlation was observed with this measure and question four ($r(105) = -260$, $p < 0.007$).

Measure 2—" valuable time away from my personal" At typical social science levels, the difference between the groups was not found to be significant using the t test ($t(74.146) = 1.348$, $p < 0.160$). The means for the two groups were 2.89 (agreement) for those still participating and 2.48 (agreement) for those no longer coaching. However, a statistically significant positive correlation was observed with this measure and items one ($r(105)=0.371$, $p < .000$); three ($r(105)=0.202$, $p < 0.039$); eight ($r(105) = 262$, $p < 0.007$); nine ($r(105) = 0.253$, $p < 009$); and ten ($r(105) = 0.252$, $p < 0.009$). A negative correlation was observed with measure four ($r(105)= -0.367$, $p < 0.000$).

Measure 3—"negative impact on present relationship." The difference between the groups was found to be significant at the .05 level of confidence ($t(103) = .199 p = < .000$). The means for the two groups were 4.13 (slight disagreement) for those still participating and 1.87 (strong agreement) for those no longer coaching. There were positive correlations between this measure and measure and items one ($r(105) = 0.434$, $p < .000$); two ($r(105) = 0.202$, $p < 0.039$); seven ($r(105) = 0.401$, $p < 0.000$); eight ($r(105) = 0.662$, $p < 0.007$); nine ($r(105)= 0.513$, $p < 0.000$); and ten ($r(105)=0.370$, $p < 0.000$). A negative correlation was observed with item four ($r(105)=-0.233$, $p < 0.017$).

Measure 4—"negatively impacts children." The between group difference was found to be statistically significant at the .05 level of significance ($t(103) = 4.293$, $p < .041$). The mean between groups is 2.02, indicating strong agreement for the proposition by those who are actively coaching. For those who were no longer coaching, the mean was 4.88, indicating some disagreement with the statement. A positive correlation was observed with item four ($r(105) = 0.202$, $p < 0.038$) and a negative correlation with item ten ($r(105)=-0.262$, $p < 0.007$).

Measure 5—"influence long term family" The between group mean for those still coaching was 3.60, indicating the slightest of agreement, and 2.10 for the former coaching group, indicating strong agreement. Also, the between groups difference was statistically significant at the .01 level ($t(53.368) = 3.869$, $p < .001$).

A positive correlation was observed with items two ($r(105)$ = 0.276, $p < 0.004$); three ($r(105)$ = 0.401; $p < 0.000$); eight ($r(105)$ = 320, $p < 0.001$); nine ($r(105)$ = 0.266, $p < 0.006$; and ten ($r(105)$ = 0.300, $p < 0.002$. No statistically significant negative correlations were observed.

Measure 6—*"stronger without forensics"* This measure also demonstrated statistically significant differences between groups ($t(65.518)$ = 4.467, $p < 0.000$). The mean for those still involved in coaching was 4.20 (almost neutral), while the mean for those not coaching was 2.27 (strong agreement). Positive correlations were noted with measures one ($r(105)$ = 0.453, $p < 0.000$), two ($r(105)$ = 0.262, $p < 0.007$), three ($r(105)$ = 0.662, $p < 0.000$), seven ($r(105)$ = 0.320, $p < 0.001$), nine ($r(105)$ = 0.628, $p < 0.000$) and ten ($r(105)$ = 0.244, $p < 0.012$). No negative correlations were observed.

Measure 7—*"family or forensics"* demonstrated a statistically significant difference between the groups ($t(67.054)$ = 3.588, $p < 0.001$). The mean for those currently in forensics was 4.44 (slightly agreement) and for those out of forensics the mean was 2.83 (agreement). Positive correlations were observed with the previously reported measure in one, two, three, five, and seven. Additionally, this item was positively correlated with item items ten ($r(105)$ = 0.210, $p < 0.032$) and negatively correlated with item four as previously reported.

Measure 8—*"incorporate family into forensics"* was also statistically significant between the two groups ($t(68.905)$ = -4.627, $p < 0.000$). The mean for those in forensics was 3.56 (slight agreement) and for those outside forensics the mean was 5.37 (disagreement). As reported above, this item was positively correlated with item six and negatively correlated with items one, two, three, eight, nine, and ten ($r(105)$ = -0.350, $p < 0.000$).

Measure 9—*"decision based upon family"* was not statistically significant ($t(74.764)$ = 1.107, $p < 0.272$). The mean for the two groups was 3.64 (in forensics) and 3.22 (out of forensics). This item was not positively or negatively correlated with any other item.

Measure 10—*"Years coaching"* has been reported in the findings of the previous nine attitudinal measures. There were positive correlations with items one, two, three, five, six, and seven. Negative correlations were observed with item four and eight.

Discussion—Study Two

In an attempt to examine RQ1—How will a heterogeneous sample perceive the challenge of balancing the duties of a career as a forensics educator and the commitments of marriage and family?—both data sets were merged to create a single, more heterogeneous respondent grouping (current and former forensic educators). This grouping should more adequately reflect a sampling of representatives from both ends of the forensic spectrum, i.e., those who have remained in coaching and those who chose to exit the profession. Hence, this grouping should give a more accurate picture of how forensic educators perceive the challenge of balancing forensics with family.

It is significant to note that from this normalized population, strong concerns continue to emerge, supporting the perceptions that forensics adversely affects familial relationships at all levels as reported in the literature. Further, as the years in coaching increased, so did negative perceptions and attitudes in every relational dimension within the study, with the exception of making coaching decisions based upon family issues. This would tend to indicate that forensic professionals, so long as they remain in the activity, maintain a professional commitment to their institutions, colleagues, and students. The final observation derived from the merged respondent population in Study Two—and possibly the most significant in contributing to the exodus of forensics professionals—is the continued perception that familial relationships would be stronger without the continued pressures of balancing them with a successful career in forensic education.

Conclusions

Before offering conclusions, some limitations in the current study should be acknowledged. First, some caution should be exercised when using the results of this study to make generalized characterizations about the larger population of both former and current forensics educators. Though the *n* is representative of a national pool of current and former forensics educators, who represent a variety of forensic competitive activities and organizations, a sample size of 105 is not sufficiently representative to risk broad-based conclusions without some degree of caution. Additionally, it should be recognized that both respondent pools may exhibit a degree of self-report attitudinal bias. That is, both groups may seek to justify their decisions. Former coaches may tend to overly blame family complications to justify their decision to exit coaching, while current coaches may underreport family complications in an attempt to justify their decision to remain in coaching. Though the merging of the respondent pools may mitigate this effect, again, caution should be used when making broader generalizations outside of the respondent pool of this study.

Second, though the Jensen and Jensen (2004) data set was comprised of a random sample, Study One relies on a sample of convenience: those former forensic educators known to the researchers and those referred to the researchers by former forensic educators. Though the merging of the two data sets in Study Two may mitigate this concern, a broader, random sample is called for in future research.

Third, the two data sets represent attitudes toward both forensics and relationships collected as a snapshot in time. Careers and relationships wax and wane over time. Neither study, therefore, takes into account the human tendency for attitudes to shift over time. To make insightful interpretations regarding attitudes over time longitudinal data should be collected.

Fourth, both studies collected one-sided perceptions. Equally important to a thorough analysis of how the pressures of forensics impact familial relationships are the forensic educators' wives, husbands, partners, and children. Future research should include attitudinal measures collected from these life participants who may see things in an entirely different light. This data should be collated and analyzed as dedicated pairs measured across a significant measure of time.

Fifth, in an attempt to most closely replicate the Jensen and Jensen (2004) study, neither survey asked the respondent to identify their sex or gender. Are the pressures faced by a father the same as those faced by a mother in forensics?

Do gays and lesbians face differing pressures than heterosexuals? Additionally, do different sexes or genders attempt to employ differing or similar coping strategies? What can one group learn from another? Finally, again in an attempt to most closely replicate the methodology of Jensen and Jensen (2004), some questions need a greater degree of clarity and applicability. For example, the question asking the respondent to identify the number of children currently in the home was difficult to replicate without the potential for confounding the variable's original intent. Since many of the former coaches had been out of forensics for quite some time, the number of children currently in the home no longer accurately reflected the familial unit that was present during their tenure as coaches. Many had been divorced, remarried, and had reconstructed familial units into blended families since their coaching tenure. Also, the relative ages of the children have the potential to greatly influence the degree of stress perceived by the participants when torn between the pressures of coaching and family commitments. Younger husbands, wives, and partners may feel greater perceptions of abandonment than older life participants. Young children may also feel a greater sense of abandonment than older children who have developed individual interests and activities. This may have created some decline in the richness of the descriptive data. Future research should be conducted using an updated survey instrument designed to capture current relevant data from dedicated familial units over an extended period of time.

Given these limitations in the study, some conclusions can be advanced. First, both of the original goals of the study have been met: (1) to validate previous findings within the literature that forensic educators feel frustration at what they see as a negative relationship between balancing coaching duties and family commitments; and (2) to provide quantitative validity to the literature through statistical rather than primarily anecdotal evidence. Though the study population reported in Jensen and Jensen was "generally neutral to the idea that forensics and family/personal relationships compete with one another" (2004, 12–13), when merged with the data set of former coaches in Study One, the group, *current and former forensic educators*, as a whole exhibited a dramatically negative perspective with regard to the outcomes of balancing forensics and family.

Second, this study has helped to clarify the relationship between increased personal and family pressure and non-standard work. Jensen and Jensen's (2004) study concludes that forensic educators dedicate an average of 75 hours per week toward their career. This study sets the number at 56 hours but does not include time spent traveling on weekends to attend competitive tournaments. There can be no argument that forensic educators work non-standard schedules, which include numerous weekends and holidays. The stresses to self and family are further exacerbated by working, for most, Monday through Friday juggling the teaching, research, and service commitments of a "regular" faculty member. All of the research cited reported a positive relationship between the number of weekends or holidays worked and the level of conflict between work and family life. Non-standard work duties have been found to be strongly associated with personal, marital, social, health, and organizational consequences. This study would seem to confirm Jensen's categorization of the director of forensics as an "at-risk population" (1998, 28).

One positive finding is that even though this study would seem to validate the previously reported "burn-out" rate for forensic educators at six years or less (Bartanen, 1996a; Gill, 1990), in this case a mean of 4.83 years, Jensen and Jensen's data set was comprised of coaches with a mean of 16.34 years of coaching experience. Since 74.8% were in a committed relationship (married, committed, or life partner) at the time of the survey, clearly, some forensic educators are "beating the burn-out odds." How did the forensic educators included in the Jensens' (2004) work avoid relational suicide while balancing successful careers in forensics? Obviously, those coaches who successfully balance forensics and family should be identified and studied. Further research should be conducted to identify and develop successful coping strategies for our at-risk population of forensic educators. Professional forensic organizations should take the lead in encouraging successful coaches to engage not only in a mentoring process but in the development and offering of educational, relational workshops and retreats for forensic families.

In conclusion, the greatest single asset of the forensic community is its people. To continue to ignore an at-risk population is something that is not only counterproductive to the goals and objectives of an educational experience rich in forensic experiences for future generations but something we continue to do at our own peril.

NOTES

1. This is slightly less than the figure reported by Gill (1990) and Bartanen (1996a) of an average of six years.

2. This figure (50.35 hours) is smaller than the figure reported by Jensen and Jensen of "almost 75 hours" (2004, 8). However, this discrepancy may be accounted for by survey error. As Jensen and Jensen (2004) note, "The number, in actuality, is probably higher because some individuals separated forensic travel time from coaching and administration; these results include reported travel time as part of the other category" (2004, 8).

3. Questions that could confound the reporting were omitted (e.g., How many children live at your home?). The number of children currently living at home could be significantly different than the number living at home during respondents' former coaching tenure.

4. Some researchers caution that participation in debate teaches and reinforces skills that are often in direct opposition to successful interpersonal skills necessary to maintain healthy relationships (Burnett and Olson, 1998). For example, Colbert (1994) and Infante et al. (1984) have argued that debaters often exhibit increased verbal aggression. Additionally, Hetlinger and Hildreth (1961) reported that debaters value friendships less and find it difficult to maintain relationships outside of forensics. Olson concludes, "As such, even the relationships forensics participants have, may not be healthy due to a constant and inherent world view that each position needs to be debated, and each controversy must have a winner" (2000, 8). Therefore, additional study may identify a relationship between past forensic participation and current relational conflict. The possible relationship between forensic participation and aberrant behavior is clearly beyond the scope of this study.

Appendix A

Program Demographics of Respondents				
Program Element	**Frequency**		**Percent**	
	Yes	No	Yes	No
Full-time staff	42	18	70.0	30.0
Part-time staff	47	13	78.3	21.7
Graduate assistants				
Zero	50		83.3	
One	10		16.7	
Two	6		10.0	
No other staff	60		100.0	
Tenure track positions				
Zero	23		38.3	
One	31		51.7	
Two	6		10.0	
Number of students traveling				
Five–Seven	11		18.3	
Eight–Ten	34		56.6	
Eleven–Fifteen	15		25.0	
Individual events participation	45	15	75.0	25.0
Debate participation	53	7	88.3	11.7
CEDA participation	14	46	23.3	76.7
NDT participation	7	53	11.7	88.3
LD participation	31	29	51.7	48.3
Number of weekends traveled				
Seven–Eight		20	33.3	
Nine–Ten		26	43.3	
Eleven–Twelve		14	23.4	

$n = 60$ for all groups

APPENDIX B

Respondent Demographics		
Survey item	**Frequency**	**Percent**
Years of coaching		
One–Two	14	23.3
Three–Four	16	26.6
Five–Six	17	28.3
Seven–Eight	7	11.7
Nine–Ten	4	6.7
Eleven–Twelve	2	3.4
Title		
Director of Forensics	6	10.0
Ass't Dir of Forensics	54	90.0
Rank		
Associate Professor	6	10.0
Assistant Professor	36	60.0
Graduate Assistant	16	26.7
Adjunct/Instructor	2	3.3

$n = 60$ for all groups

Intercorrelations Between Attitudes and Relationships of All Respondents

Attitude	1	2	3	4	5	6	7	8	9	10
1. Contributed to end of relationship	1.00	0.37	0.43	-0.14	0.18	0.45	0.37	-0.26	-0.01	0.36
2. Time from relationships	0.37	1.00	0.20	0.24	0.28	0.26	0.25	-0.37	-0.13	0.25
3. Negative impact on relationships	0.43	0.20	1.00	-0.04	0.40	0.66	0.53	-0.23	0.11	0.37
4. Negative impact of child(ren)	-0.14	0.02	-0.04	1.00	-0.02	-0.11	-0.04	0.20	0.12	-0.26
5. Influence long-term family plan	0.18	0.28	0.40	-0.02	1.00	0.32	0.27	-0.41	0.16	0.30
6. Relation stronger w/o forensics	0.45	0.26	0.66	-0.11	0.32	1.00	0.63	-0.21	0.16	0.24
7. Choose family or forensics	0.37	0.25	0.51	-0.04	0.27	0.63	1.00	-0.31	0.26	0.21
8. Incorp family into forensics	-0.26	-0.37	-0.23	0.20	-0.05	-0.21	-0.31	1.00	0.00	-0.35
9. Decisions based upon forensics	-0.01	0.13	0.11	0.12	0.16	0.16	0.26	0.00	1.00	0.06
10. Years coaching	0.36	0.25	0.37	-0.26	0.40	0.24	0.21	-0.35	0.06	1.00

$n = 105$

REFERENCES

Baba, V.V. and Jamal, M. (1991). Routinization of job context and job content to employees' quality of working life. *Journal of Organizational Behavior, 12,* 379–386.

Bartanen, K.M. (1996a). A preliminary assessment of the professional climate of forensic education, part I. *The Forensic of Pi Kappa Delta, 81,* 1–21.

—————. (1996b). A preliminary assessment of the professional climate of forensic education, part II. *The Forensic of Pi Kappa Delta, 82,* 1–16.

Bast, G.H. (1960). Ploeganarbeid in de industry. Arnhem: Contractgroepvoering Productiviteit Van Loghum Slaterus. (Cited in Health Consequences of Shiftwork, By D.L. Tasto, M.J. Colligan, E.W. Skjei, and S.J. Polly. SRI International Corporation Project URU-4426, March 1978.)

Blau, G., and Lunz, M. (1999). Testing the impact of shift schedules on organizational variables. *Journal of Organizational Behavior, 20,* 933–942.

Bohle, P. and Tilley, A.J. (1998). Early experience of shift work: influences on attitudes. *Journal of Occupational and Organizational Psychology, 71,* 61–79.

Burnett, A. and Olson, C.D. (1998). The dark side of debate: The downfall of interpersonal relationships. *Speaker & Gavel, 35,* 31–45.

Came, B. (1989). A difficult job to take home. *Maclean's,* January 9, 36–37.

Colbert, K. (1994). Replicating the effects of debate participation on argumentativeness and verbal aggression. *The Forensic of Pi Kappa Delta, 79:3,* 1–13.

Communication Technology. (1998). First published in *The Journal of Social Sciences,* December. Retrieved October 5, 2005, from www.cordis.lu/euroabstracts.

Cronn-Mills, D.D. (1999). Wandering by the Oasis of Wellness: Implications of Mentoring and Modeling Behaviors in Forensics. Paper presented at the Annual Convention of the Speech Communication Association, Chicago, IL.

Deaton G., Glen, R.J., Milsap, S., and Milsap, S. (1997). Forensic and Family: Attempting to Avoid the Collision. Paper presented at the Annual Meeting of the National Communication Association, Chicago, IL.

Dickmeyer, S. (2002). Give it to me straight, doc, how much longer can I coach: The length of the individual events season and its effect on the wellness of coaches. *National Forensic Journal, 20,* 57–61.

Drenth, P.J.D., Hoolwerf, G., and Thierry, H. (1976). Psychological aspects of shiftwork. In P. Warr (Ed.), *Personal Goals and Work Design* (pp. 209–233). London: Wiley.

Fenwick, R. and Tausig, M. (2001). Scheduling stress: Family and health outcomes of shift work and schedule control. *American Behavioral Scientist, 44,* 1179–1198.

Gill, M. (1990). Why forensic coaches quit: A replication and extension. *National Forensic Journal, 8,* 179–188.

Gilstrap, C.A. and Gilstrap, C.M. (2003). Managing emotions in forensics and family: A family dialogue about emotion labor and emotion work. *The Forensic of Pi Kappa Delta, 88,* 3–15.

Gleick, James. (1997). Push-Me Pull-You Internet management. First published in the *New York Times Magazine,* March 23, 1997. Retrieved on October 5, 2005, from www.around.com.

Hetlinger, D.F., and Hildreth, R.A. (1961). Personality characteristics of debaters. *Quarterly Journal of Speech, 47,* 398–401.

House, J.S. (1980). Occupational Stress and the Mental and Physical Health of Factory Workers. Research Report Series. Ann Arbor, MI: Institute for Social Research.

Infante, D.A., Trebring, J.D., Shepherd, P.E., and Seeds, D.E. (1984). The relationship of argumentativeness to verbal aggression. *The Southern Speech Communication Journal, 50,* 67–77.

Jamal, M. (2004). Burnout, stress and health of employees on non-standard work schedules: A study of Canadian workers. *Stress and Health, 20,* 113–119.

Jamal, M. and Baba, V.V. (1992). Shift-work and department type related to job stress, work attitudes and behavioral intentions: A study of nurses. *Journal of Organizational Behavior, 13,* 449–464.

———. (1997). Shift-work, burnout and well-being: A study of Canadian nurses. *International Journal of Stress Management, 4,* 197–204.

Jamal, M. and Jamal, S.M. (1982). Work and non-work experiences of employees on fixed and rotating shifts: An empirical assessment. *Journal of Vocational Behavior, 20,* 282–298.

Jensen, G.L. and Jensen, S. (2001, November). Assimilating Families and Forensics: Balancing Forensics Education and Family When Two Become One. Paper presented at the annual meeting of the National Communication Association, Atlanta, GA.

———. (2003, November). Pursuing Forensic Goals While Protecting Family Time: An Application of Brock's Commodity Theory. Paper presented at the annual meeting of the National Communication Association, Miami, FL.

Jensen, S. (1998). Preserving the Pedagogy: The director of forensics as an at-risk Professional. *Speech and Theatre Association of Missouri Journal*, 28, 28–41.

Jensen, S. and Jensen, G.L. (2004, November). The Contemporary Face of Forensics and Family: A Survey Analysis of the Relationship between Forensic Education, Participation, and Family Status. Paper presented at the annual meeting of the National Communication Association, Chicago, IL.

Jones, K. (1997, November). Forensics and Divorce: When Two Worlds Collapse. Paper presented at the annual meeting of the National Communication Association, Chicago, IL.

Kaplan, J. (1996). The most stressful Jobs. *Men's Health* (September), 128.

Krausz, M., Sagie, A., and Biderman, Y. (2000). Actual and preferred work schedules and scheduling control as determinants of job-related attitudes. *Journal of Vocational Behavior*, 61, 279–301.

Lauer, R. and Lauer, J. (1997). *Marriage & family: The quest for intimacy.* Chicago: Brown and Benchmark.

Littlefield, R.S. and Sellnow, T.L. (1992). Assessing competition & stress: The perceived effect of tournament atmosphere on students and coaches. *National Forensic Journal*, 10, 1–10.

Mann, F. and Hoffman, L. (1960). *Automation and the worker.* New York: Henry Holt.

Maurice, M. and Monteil, C. (1965). Vie quotidienne et horaires de travail: Enquete psychosociologique sur le travial en equips successives. Paris: Paris Institut des Sciences Sociales du Travail. (Cited in Health Consequences of Shift Work, by D.L. Tasto, M.J. Colligan, E.W. Skjei, and S.J. Polly. SRI International Corporation Project URU-4426, March 1978.)

McDonald, K.M. (2001). Demanding Expectations: Surviving and Thriving as a Collegiate Debate Coach. *Argument & Advocacy*, 38, 115–120.

McFarland, Steve. (2005). The Two Faces of Parental Involvement. The Internet Monk. Retrieved October 5, 2005, from www.theinternetmonk.com.

Newton's Third Law of Action/Reaction. Retrieved October 5, 2005, from www.physics.brown.edu.

Nissan's Pivo: The Cabin That Rotates 360 Degrees. (Sept. 30, 2005). Retrieved October 5, 2005, from News.com.com.

Nolte, P.J. (2005). Nolte Notes: A Push-Me Pull-You Market. Financial Sense On-Line: Uncommon News for the Wise Investor, August, 2005. Retrieved October 5, 2005, from www.financialsense.com.

Noran, A. (1995). Literature search on the wives of firefighters. *Employee Assistance Quarterly, 10,* 65–79.

Olson, C.D. (2000, October). Infusing Debate with Wellness: Starting Correctly. Paper presented at the 2000 International Debate Education Association Conference, Budapest, Hungary.

Presser, H.B. (1995). Job, family and gender: Determinants of nonstandard work schedules among employed Americans in 1991. *Demography, 32,* 4, 577–598.

Preston, C.T., Jr. (1995) Contributory factors to coach burnout and brain drain in forensics: Some suggestions for credibility and activity survival. *The Forensic of Pi Kappa Delta, 80,* 16–22.

Seigfried, T. (2002). Powers of the Fruit Fly in Flight. *The Why Files, Science Matters.* Retrieved October 5, 2005, from www.whyfiles.com.

Shamir, B. (1982). Work schedules and the perceived conflict between work and nonwork. Working Paper No. 3, the Hebrew University Bertelsmann Program, Jerusalem.

———. (1983). Some antecedents of work/non-work conflict. *Journal of Vocational Behavior, 23,* 98–111.

Sotile, W. (1997). Today's medical marriage. *Journal of the American Medical Association, 277,* 217–235..

Staines, G. and Pleck, J. (1984). Nonstandard work schedules and family life. *Journal of Applied Psychology, 69,* 3, 515–523.

Tanner, Alex. (2005). The Push-Me Pull-You Conundrum of Advertising in a PVR World. Retrieved October 5, 2005, from www.netimperative.com.

Venette, S.J. and Venette, P.A. (1997). Too much of a good thing: The director of forensics and wellness. *The Southern Journal of Forensics, 2,* 244–248.

Whitney, S.A. and Johnson, S.L. (1996, November). 'Til Finals Do Us Part: An Analysis of Committed Relationships among Forensic Educators. Paper presented at the annual meeting of the Speech Communication Association, San Diego, CA.

Williams, D.E. and Hughes, P.C. (2003). The Forensic Family: A call for research. *The Forensic of Pi Kappa Delta, 88,* 29–36.

Jack E. Rogers, Ph.D., is the director of forensics at the University of Central Missouri.

Arthur Rennels, Ph.D., is the director of debate at the University of Central Missouri.